DATE DUE

ANOREXIA AND BULIMIA

TO THE MEMORY OF MY FATHER,
M. ARTHUR GORDON,
WHO TAUGHT ME SO MUCH

AND FOR PATTI, ALEXA, AND CORINNE

ANOREXIA
AND
BULIMIA

Anatomy of a
Social Epidemic

Richard A. Gordon

Basil Blackwell

Library of Congress Cataloging in Publication Data
Gordon, Richard A. (Richard Allan), 1941–
Anorexia and bulimia: anatomy of a social epidemic / Richard A. Gordon.
p. cm.
ISBN 0–631–14851–5 ISBN 0–631–15928–2 (pbk.)
1. Anorexia – Social aspects. 2. Bulimia – Social aspects.
I. Title.
RC552.A5G67 1990
616.85'262 – dc20 89–38720 CIP

British Library Cataloguing in Publication Data
A CIP catalogue record for this book is available from
the British Library.

Typeset in 11 on 12½pt Ehrhardt
by Hope Services (Abingdon) Ltd
Printed in Great Britain by
T. J. Press Ltd., Padstow, Cornwall

CONTENTS

ACKNOWLEDGMENTS

Many individuals contributed to the writing of this book, directly and indirectly. Among earlier teachers, I would like to express my thanks to Stanley Diamond, who showed me that it was possible to discuss the intersections of culture and psychopathology in a meaningful way. Also, Melford Spiro encouraged me to pursue my interests in George Devereux's work, and his positive comments on a very early presentation of the ideas in this book were encouraging. I am particularly grateful to Leon Botstein, President of Bard College, who responded enthusiastically to my idea of writing a cultural interpretation of anorexia nervosa, helped me to gain the release time from my teaching duties that made it possible to conduct the early stages of the research, and encouraged me to seek a publisher for the work. Also at Bard, my friend and colleague, Dean Stuart Levine, provided support, encouragement, and good humor throughout the years that it took to complete this project. Finally, I would like to thank innumerable colleagues at Bard College for their interest in my work and collegial support; and in particular Frank Oja, my departmental colleague and chairman, who was willing to shoulder additional burdens in an already overtaxed psychology department so that I could find the time that this task demanded.

As I work in relative professional isolation, both as a teacher and a clinician, I found attendance in several national and international conferences on eating disorders to be an invaluable experience. Among those whose ideas particularly influenced me at these gatherings, both through their presentations and also informal personal discussions, I would like to mention David Garner, Craig Johnson, and Arthur Crisp. I would like to thank Patricia Warner, who invited me to attend a family meeting of Anorexia Bulimia Care, a self-help organization in the Boston area. Katherine Halmi gave me some suggestions for research in the earliest stages of the study. My thanks to William Davis, former President of the Center for the Study of Anorexia and Bulimia, for his interest in my work and invitation to contribute to a collection of papers on bulimia. I consider it my great misfortune never to have met Dr Hilde Bruch, whose groundbreaking work on anorexia nervosa, shining intelligence, and profound empathy for the struggles of anorexic patients were a great inspiration to me. I hope my respect for her work is evident in these pages.

I am deeply grateful to Jane Hryshko of the Bard College Library, who labored valiantly at securing an extensive amount of research material for this book through interlibrary loans and effectively put a vast library of literature at my fingertips. Also, a number of individuals helped me with translations of foreign language material, particularly Onno Reiners, Greg Eghigian, and Gennady Shkliarevsky. I am grateful to the many students who over the past few years have shared ideas with me about the social and cultural aspects of eating disorders.

I would also like to thank the many individuals at Basil Blackwell who worked with me at various stages of the preparation of this book. Specifically, I thank Christopher Kerr of the New York office, whose enthusiastic initial reaction to my initial proposal set the process in motion; Philip Carpenter, Editorial Director, who oversaw the project from start to finish and who sensitively understood the length of time needed to complete it; Martin Davidson, for his supportive review and commentary on earlier drafts of several chapters; Kim Didonato, who skillfully oversaw the project to its completion; Jan Chamier and Kate Chapman for their helpful guidance during the production stage; and Richard House for his meticulous copy-editing.

I wish to express my gratitude to my own clinical patients, whose personal struggles helped me to understand anorexia and bulimia in a way that no amount of reading could ever hope to do. Few of your stories appear on the following pages, but the insights that you gave me were a foundation for the overall understanding that I was able to achieve. Although you must remain anonymous, I am for ever grateful to you.

I would like to remember my parents-in-law, Goldie and Larry Hill, for whose profound interest in my work and personal devotion I will remain forever grateful. And finally, this book would have been inconceivable without the help and encouragement of my wife Patti, who for some years accepted and understood the intense absorption and inevitable distraction from family life that this task demanded. Without her loving support and understanding, I doubt that this work could have been completed.

I wish to acknowledge quotations from the following publications:

Beumont, P.J.V. Endocrine function in magersucht disorders. In Pirke, K.M. and Ploog, D. (eds) *The Psychobiology of Anorexia Nervosa*. New York: Springer-Verlag, 1984. Reprinted by permission of Springer-Verlag.

Bruch, H. Four decades of eating disorders. In Garner, D.M. and Garfinkel, P.E. (eds) *Handbook for the Psychotherapy of Anorexia Nervosa and Bulimia*. New York: Guilford Press, 1985. Reprinted by permission of Guilford Press.

Dresser, R. Feeding the hunger artists: legal issues in treating anorexia nervosa. *Wisconsin Law Review*, 2 (1984), 297–384. Reprinted by permission of the Wisconsin Law Review.

Harris, J. *Manhattan as a Second Language*. New York: Harper and Row, 1982. Reprinted by permission of Harper and Row.

Pope, H.G. and Hudson, J.H. *New Hope for Binge Eaters*. New York: Harper and Row, 1984. Reprinted by permission of Harper and Row.

Schwartz, H. *Never Satisfied: A Cultural History of Diets, Fantasies and Fat*. New York: Macmillan, 1986. Reprinted by permission of Macmillan, Inc.

PREFACE

My first encounter with the phenomenon of anorexia nervosa occurred in 1971, when, as an intern in clinical psychology at the Payne Whitney Psychiatric Clinic, I was asked to evaluate an anorexic patient – my very first psychiatric patient in this setting. My supervisor told me that I was very fortunate to have the opportunity to observe such a patient, as anorexia nervosa was a very rare condition and I was likely to encounter very few such patients in a lifetime of clinical practice. This particular young woman also had a secondary diagnosis of "bulimia" on her hospital form, a term which at the time was even more obscure than anorexia nervosa. The attending psychiatrist patiently explained to me the symptoms of bulimia, which he said sometimes occurred in anorexic patients. Undoubtedly, the notion that only 10 years later literally thousands of college students would be engaged in a compulsive cycle of overeating and self-induced vomiting would at that time have come as a great shock to any of us.

Following my early training, I heard little about the eating disorders for several years. As a professor in a small liberal arts college, I was aware of one or two of our students who developed anorexia nervosa in the 1970s. It was not until around 1980 or 1981, however, that I began to realize that eating disorders were proliferating. At that time, I had entered into the individual practice of clinical psychology, and encountered a female college student who presented the classic picture of what is now familiar to us as bulimia nervosa. She was deeply frightened about her weight, and had found herself caught in a compulsive cycle of overeating and vomiting ("making herself sick," as she said). Unlike patients with anorexia nervosa, she was of normal weight, perhaps slightly overweight. But in other respects, her obsessive calorie counting and preoccupation with food, as well as her overwhelming fear of losing control, seemed quite similar to the mind-set of anorexic patients. After my encounter with this bulimic patient, others soon followed. As I was hardly known at that point as a psychologist with a special interest in eating disorders, it was unlikely that these patients were suddenly appearing in large numbers because of a selective referral pattern.

In 1982, I attended my first conference on eating disorders, sponsored by the Center for the Study of Anorexia and Bulimia in New York City. I wondered (as I often have done when attending specialist conferences) whether this conference would attract much interest, and certainly anticipated a small audience – perhaps 50 or 100 professionals. To my own surprise, and to the apparent shock of Dr William Davis, the director of the Center for the Study of Anorexia and Bulimia and the conference organizer, several hundred health professionals appeared, filling an auditorium in one of New York's hotels. It immediately became apparent from the lectures at the conference, as well as from the remarks of the attendees, that my own sense of a sudden and dramatic increase in the prevalence of these conditions was no fluke.

This is a book about the social and cultural roots of the explosive increase in anorexic and bulimic conditions in our times. It is also a book about the larger questions of the relationships between culture and psychopathology, questions that have been of interest to me since my days as a graduate student in psychology. Increases in particular types of psychopathology signal the difficulties that certain vulnerable people have in coming to terms with the dilemmas of their culture and time. Psychological disorders require not only an understanding in term of individual factors, but also rquire an interpretation that is social and ultimately political. It is my hope that this work will make a contribution to the understanding of these larger relationships, over and above any light that it throws on the specific question of eating disorders.

Because of the overall focus in this book, I have not devoted a great deal of attention to questions of the practical treatment of eating disorders, except in so far as such considerations are relevant to their social and cultural context. There are now a number of good articles and books on the treatment of anorexia and bulimia, the most comprehensive of which is the *Handbook for the Treatment of Anorexia Nervosa and Bulimia*, edited by David Garner and Paul Garfinkel. Study of this impressive volume will afford the reader an idea of the enormous scope of new treatment approaches and ideas in this field. From my own standpoint, I will be happy if a reading of my book will deepen the awareness of the practicing clinician of the importance of the social and cultural background of eating disorders. I think it is not too pretentious to help that such awareness will implicitly affect one's approach to treatment and thinking about patients' problems; this has certainly been my experience.

A few words about terminology are in order. Technically, the precise nomenclature for the disorders that are the subject of this book are anorexia nervosa and bulimia nervosa. For the sake of readability, I sometimes refer simply to anorexia or bulimia. Strictly speaking, anorexia is a symptom (loss of appetite) that occurs in a number of psychiatric or medical conditions other than anorexia nervosa, especially depression. In this book, the term anorexia is always used as a shorthand for anorexia nervosa, unless otherwise specified. Similar considerations apply to the use of the term bulimia, which otherwise could have a number of meanings.

When it comes to referring to individuals with these problems, I have sometimes employed the terms "anorexics" or "bulimics" as a plural form. I wish it to be understood that in so doing, it is my least wish to imply a uniformity in these patients as individuals. It is true that the clinical symptoms of eating disorders are remarkably similar from one patient to the next; nevertheless, as individuals, they show an enormous diversity. As we have known since the "anti-psychiatry" critiques of the 1960s, there is an unfortunate de-individuating tendency in psychiatric terminology, which if misused can lead to pernicious consequences. My use of the terminology "anorexics" and "bulimics" is therefore strictly a matter of convenience. I profoundly hope that no one with these symptoms will be offended by it.

Finally, a word about the sensitive question of gender-linked pronouns. Throughout this book, I refer to anorexic or bulimic patients as "she." This is in large part a reflection of the overwhelming preponderance of female sufferers, a fact which is in and of itself of considerable sociocultural significance. Secondarily, I wish to avoid the awkwardness of such usages as the repetitive "he or she" or, worse, "he/she." However, I wish to make it clear at the outset that I am fully aware of the significant numbers of males with these problems, and once again sincerely hope that my use of the generic "she" will not leave them feeling discounted.

I

CULTURE AND
PSYCHOPATHOLOGY: THE NOTION
OF AN ETHNIC DISORDER

"The fact is that in all periods of history, mental disturbances of epidemiological significance or special fascination highlight a specific aspect of man's nature in conflict with 'the times' . . ."[1] In the waning years of the nineteenth century, medical doctors, neurologists, and psychiatrists in Western Europe and the United States were preoccupied with a mysterious "nervous disease" that occurred mainly in women, called hysteria.[2] Hysteria was a puzzling and elusive disorder which manifested itself through a variety of somatic symptoms: paralyses, sensory disturbances such as blindness, fainting spells, even seizures. It had been known of throughout recorded history, as early as ancient Egypt and later in Greece, but it had always lived a kind of shadowy existence.[3] But suddenly, in the second half of the nineteenth century, it seemed to burst onto the scene, into the forefront of medical controversy and public discussion. Although solid statistics are clearly lacking, available evidence does suggest that in fact the prevalence of hysteria during the nineteenth century actually increased, and that its increased visibility was not simply a consequence of the increased attention that was being paid to it.[4] By the late nineteenth century, according to one observer, the cities in Western Europe and the United States were "full of neurotics," and among these the female patients were mostly hysterics.

Hysteria, it turns out, was an exceedingly complex and baffling disease. The symptoms were apparently physical, and indeed they often began with real physical ailments; and yet unlike typical physical symptoms, they were remarkably transient and seemed to be linked to psychological factors and emotional distress. More and more, these latter factors were emphasized in clinical theory, a trend that culminated in the emergence of psychoanalysis itself.[5] But what is more, hysteria was very much a social illness, a highly patterned vehicle for the expression of female distress, one that involved a significant degree of role-playing and interpersonal manipulation. Indeed these latter factors led some to doubt the "reality" of "hysterical complaints," a position which still has its advocates today.[6] But in any case, the very character of hysterical symptoms was highly in keeping with the needs and style of the era in which they were prevalent, a period in which neurotic anxieties could still not be directly acknowledged and one in which the high drama of hysterical fainting and choking fits had credibility. Soon after the turn of the century, the prevalence of hysteria declined dramatically, and it seems clear that its eclipse was a function of the dramatic social transformations that accompanied the dawn of the twentieth century.

In the second half of the twentieth century, another obscure disorder, which had been known to a small number of medical specialists for at least 100 years but which had been totally unknown to the public, suddenly increased in prevalence and burst into public view. Anorexia nervosa, a puzzling and dangerous affliction in which a young person, typically an adolescent female, mercilessly starves herself, had been formally identified as a disease in both London and Paris during the 1870s.[7] Like hysteria, it also may have existed, although in guises that were not strictly medical, for centuries before; and also like hysteria, the characteristic behaviors may have at one point been described in terms of the language of the sacred and the spiritual.[8] In any case, by the early 1970s, anorexia nervosa had already been the subject of an extensive psychiatric literature stretching back to its modern discovery in the 1870s, and probably out of all proportion to the number of cases actually seen by practitioners.[9] It was described by one writer as a "curiousity and a rarity;" psychiatrists instructed residents that it would be unusual to see more than a small number of cases in the course of a lifetime. On the other hand, the spectacle of a young woman starving herself, sometimes to death, was enough to command intense practical and theoretical medical interest.

By the mid-1970s, though, anorexia nervosa suddenly became widely known to the American public, and by the next decade it was being described in psychiatric publications as well as the popular press in terms such as the "psychiatric disorder of the 80s." Anorexia was widely publicized, glamorized, and romanticized. Language such as "disorder of the 80s" suggests that diseases, and particularly psychiatric disorders, can easily become fashionable, and this was indeed the case for anorexia. Nevertheless, statistical studies as well as the experience of practitioners made it clear that anorexia nervosa had sharply increased in prevalence, both in its mild and more severe forms. Public awareness of anorexia reached a peak in the early 1980s with the widely publicized death through cardiac arrest of the popular singer Karen Carpenter, who had performed at the White House and was well known for her "girl-next-door" image; her death, which was associated with the abuse of the over-the-counter drug Ipecac, a potent emetic, thrust the shocking, self-destructive aspects of the illness starkly into public consciousness.

By the early 1980s, a related problem also suddenly came to public and professional attention – the eating disorder called bulimia, or bulimia nervosa. Bulimia, a pattern of binge-eating followed by purging (typically self-induced vomiting), had been known by psychiatrists specializing in the treatment of anorexia to occur in the advanced stages of anorexia nervosa; however, beginning in the mid-1970s, a large number of young women (typically college students) were described who were caught in a cycle of binging and purging, but without the drastic weight loss that was characteristic of anorexia.[10] Similar to anorexics, though, bulimics were known to idealize thinness and to be terrified of becoming fat. Bulimia first came to widespread public notoriety in the United States through a spate of articles in the popular press, including an article in the *New York Times* in 1981 describing a study that had documented a virtual epidemic of the disorder on a campus of the State University of New York.[11] Bulimia was little known prior to the 1970s, even among psychiatrists. Although the term had been used in the French literature ("la boulimie") as early as the eighteenth century to describe a pattern of overeating, it is likely that in its contemporary form it constitutes a new pattern, a variant or kin of anorexia nervosa. Probably the multiple names that have been proposed to characterize it (bulimarexia, binge-purge syndrome, dietary chaos syndrome, bulimia nervosa) represent uncertainty about the essential nature of the syndrome and its relationship to anorexia nervosa. However these issues are resolved, there is little question that the incidence of bulimia increased dramatically in the late 1970s and 1980s.

Anorexia and bulimia are termed eating disorders, and they do in fact involve abnormal patterns of eating. Nevertheless, the term eating disorder may be something of a misnomer: the most central feature of these disorders is the intense pursuit of thinness and a virtually morbid dread of becoming fat. In any case, undoubtedly in response to their rising incidence, professional interest in the eating disorders grew exponentially in the 1970s and 1980s, beginning with the publication of Hilde Bruch's book, *Eating Disorders*, in 1973.[12] Bruch, a German-born American psychiatrist, had been treating anorexic patients since the 1940s. Her book was published initially in some obscurity, and was only known to a psychiatric audience; it is only somewhat belatedly, with the enormous increase in the numbers of anorexic and bulimic patients, that it had been recognized as a classic work. In any case, during the 1970s and 1980s, the number of books and research publications on eating disorders has increased explosively. In 1982, a journal totally devoted to research on anorexia and bulimia, the *International Journal of Eating Disorders*, initiated publication; and since its inception, the number of articles appearing in it annually had grown rapidly. To give some idea of the proliferation of professional literature, a survey of the Medline index of medical literature indicated that the number of articles per year grew from 59 in 1972 to 161 in 1982. And since then, the date of the first volume of the *International Journal of Eating Disorders*, the number has risen rapidly.[13]

Given the increasing number of sufferers from anorexia or bulimia, the demand for treatment services, both on an inpatient and outpatient basis, has grown exponentially. Even as late as the end of the decade of the 1960s, only a tiny number of hospitals in the United States were known to have any experience or interest in the treatment of anorexic patients. By the mid-1980s, inpatient units devoted exclusively to the treatment of eating disorders, or at least having some specific accommodation for anorexic patients, had become commonplace. In 1984, a residential facility exclusively devoted to the treatment of eating disorders opened its doors in the Philadelphia area.[14] In addition, however, therapists working in the community found themselves besieged with patients seeking help. This was especially true at university counseling centers in the US and the UK, as eating disorders on college campuses really have become something of an epidemic.[15] Most psychotherapists, whatever their training, had little or no experience or understanding of eating disorders, and found themselves confronted with symptoms that were highly intractable to familiar counseling methods. Treatment techniques have developed in an atmosphere of ferment in the 1980s, in exciting and creative directions.[16]

The ascendancy of eating disorders has also given rise to an important social development, the proliferation of self-help organizations devoted to patient and family support as well as education. Typically founded by recovered patients or a family member, these lay organizations provided referrals, support groups for families and patients, and newsletters with recent information about treatment. Some of the largest and most influential of these are the American Anorexia Nervosa Association, based in Teaneck, New Jersey; the National Association of Anorexia Nervosa and Associated Disorders, in Highland Park, Illinois; The National Anorexic Aid Society, in Columbus, Ohio; Anorexia Nervosa and Related Eating Disorders, in Eugene, Oregon; and in England, Anorexic Aid, in High Wycombe, Bucks, and Anorexic Family Aid, in Norwich. Self-help support systems have become influential in their own right, and they reach large numbers of sufferers; and while the contemporary trend towards self-help extends far beyond the eating disorders, the very existence of these organizations for anorexia nervosa and bulimia suggests the extent to such disorders have become a pervasive social concern.

In this book I am interested in the contemporary increase in eating disorders as not only a clinical, but also a cultural, problem. Just as hysteria was a symptom of its times, one that expressed crises of identity in women in a form that was compatible with the cultural milieu of the late nineteenth century, so eating disorders have become a critical expression of dilemmas of female identity of our own time, in a period of very significant cultural transition for women. But eating disorders are not simply a modern version of hysteria; they stem from a very different set of issues to those that confronted women in the nineteenth century, and what is more they draw on a "vocabulary of discomfort" that is very much conditioned by the cultural milieu of the present.[17] In order to get a better handle on the problem, we need a framework to understand the interaction of culture, history, and psychopathology. For this purpose, I will utilize a set of concepts that have been in the literature for 30 years, but have been little utilized – the ideas of the psychoanalyst and anthropologist George Devereux. And in particular, I will utilize Devereux's specific ideas about how certain disorders become a core expression of the stresses and tensions of a particular culture or historical period – the notion of an "ethnic disorder."

Culture-Bound Syndromes:
The Notion of an Ethnic Disorder

The extensive writings of George Deverux on the complex relationship between culture and psychopathology have been little known to or assimilated by the psychiatric community, never mind a broader audience. And yet his work, which spanned five decades, was not only of enormous scope, but offered many seminal insights into the relationships between culture, the individual, and mental disorder – interdisciplinary problems that few have had the courage to tackle.[18] A key problem that fascinated Deverux was the relationship between the normal and the abnormal, and particularly the way in which certain psychological disorders express the core anxieties and unresolved problems of a culture. And central in his exploration of these relationships was the concept of an "ethnic disorder."

The notion of ethnic disorder was introduced by Devereux in one of his most important and provocative essays, published in 1955, and then elaborated in a later application of the concept to the cultural significance of schizophrenia.[19] In the initial essay, Devereux focused on what have been known as "exotic syndromes" or "folk illnesses" – patterns of psychopathology that had been discovered by ethnologists in non-Western societies and which did not seem to be like any of the known psychiatric disorders in the West. These so-called "culture-bound syndromes" included the likes of *Amok* (a disorder of homicidal violence that occurred mainly in Southeast Asia), *Latah* (a trance-like "fright-syndrome" that was found among women in the South Pacific), and *Koro* (a syndrome that involved a delusion in a man of a receding penis, especially prevalent in southern China).[20] But Devereux's interest extended beyond the exotic topic of folk illnesses and into the domain of Western psychopathology, as was evident in his application of the concept of ethnic disorder to schizophrenia and obsessive-compulsive disorders, as they are found in the West. Devereux was a student of Greek tragedy, of religion, and of physics; ultimately, he viewed psychopathology as a way to unravel the mysteries and paradoxes of culture itself.

By the term "ethnic," Devereux meant not the narrow sense of this term as in "ethnic group" or "subculture," but rather "of a culture" or "pertaining centrally to a culture." The term ethnic disorder is probably preferable to the more frequently employed "culture-bound syndrome," a term which implies that a disorder is unique to a particular society and carries the future implication of an exotic disorder in an unfamiliar (that is, non-Western) culture. In a sense, as some have pointed out, virtually all psychiatric disorders are culture-bound, to the extent that classification systems themselves are governed by cultural modes of thought. An ethnic disorder, on the other hand, is a pattern that, because of its own dynamics, has come to express crucial contradictions and core anxieties of a society.

In his essays on the subject, Deveurex enumerated a number of key criteria that qualify a particular syndrome as an ethnic disorder, which we can summarize as follows:

1 The disorder occurs frequently in the culture in question, particularly relative to other psychiatric disorders.
2 Because of the continuity of the symptoms and underlying dynamics with the normal elements of the culture, the disorder expresses itself in degrees of intensity, and in a spectrum of borderline, "subclinical" forms.
3 The disorder expresses core conflicts and psychological tensions that are pervasive in the culture, but are so acute in the person who develops symptoms that severe anxiety is generated and psychological defenses mobilized.
4 The disorder is a final common pathway for the expression of a wide variety of idiosyncratic personal problems and psychological distress; people who develop the disorder can range from mildly to severely disturbed.
5 The symptoms of the disorder are direct extensions and exaggerations of normal behaviors and attitudes within the culture, often including behaviors that are usually highly valued.
6 The disorder is a highly patterned and widely imitated model for the expression of distress; it is a template of deviance, a "pattern of misconduct," providing individuals with an acceptable means of being irrational, deviant, or crazy.
7 Finally, because the disorder draws upon valued behaviors, but on the other hand is an expression of deviance, it elicits highly ambivalent responses from others; awe and respect, perhaps, but also punitive and controlling reactions to deviance. The disorder gains notoriety in the culture; it generates its own "politics."

Some Examples

In order to illustrate the concept of an ethnic disorder, I will discuss a few non-Western and then Western examples.

Amok is a pattern of homicidal violence that occurs among men in Malaysia, Indonesia, and New Guinea.[21] It was considered to be rather common by early ethnological observers, and although it has declined considerably in the twentieth century with the inexorable transformations brought about by Westernization, a few cases are still reported.[22] The explosive madness of the *Amok* usually occurs in response to an insult or an accumulation of small stresses: following an initial period of withdrawal and brooding, the subject strikes out indiscriminately against strangers and kin, often killing a number of people during an episode, and then finally lapsing into exhaustion and amnesia. During the attack, the *Amok* would typically run through the streets and countryside – hence the phrase "running amok" – and it was typical for villages and towns to keep a lance-like weapon permanently in public places in the event of encountering an "*Amok* runner." The dynamics of *Amok* have been discussed in a recent analysis by John E. Carr. He suggests that the behavior is a response to a culture that demands a high degree of control over aggression and deference to authority.[23] What is more, Malaysian culture is characterized by a high degree of linguistic and cognitive ambiguity: behavioral expectations are highly explicit, and yet communication is shrouded in vagueness and abstraction.

Carr suggests that *Amok* can be thought of as an "escape hatch" or "loophole" for a man who experiences intolerable distress and has no other way of discharging enormous pent-up aggression that is acutely exacerbated following an insult. The term *Amok* itself is derived from the war cry of the ferocious Malaysian medieval warrior, a revered and heroic figure in the cultural mythology. The symbolism of *Amok* is a principal reason why this pattern is a template of deviance in this culture: it is actually patterned after behaviors that are highly esteemed in the cultural traditions. Of course, it goes without saying that the behavior is greatly feared and draws an equally violent or coercive societal response. Interestingly, *Amok* also has political implications, at least historically. Early observers noted that *Amok* was considered to be an instrument of social protest against rulers who had abused their authority. It was thought of, as Carr noted, as the "ultimate veto" that each man could use as a last resort against despotic control.[24]

Even today, it has been suggested that *Amok* is given tacit social approbation – much as "Jesse James has a certain following in the United States," as one observer put in. In fact, a recent Malaysian prime minister, prior to taking office, cautioned that if Malays were made to feel disenfranchised by Chinese and Indian citizens, they might retaliate by running amok.[25]

A second example is that of *Koro*, the "shrinking-penis syndrome," found typically in men primarily in coastal southern China and other areas of the Far East.[26] The symptom is typically a delusion that the penis is receding into the abdomen, and is accompanied by feelings of panic and anxiety about impending death. It has been suggested that the cultural origins of the symptom may have to do with sexual anxieties, particularly those that center around the masculine sense of potency, as well as archaic medical beliefs about the fatal consequences of genital retraction. The disorder is likely to occur in a neurotic individual who has suffered a blow to his self-esteem and confidence. *Koro* has some interesting parallels to anorexia, in that it involves a virtually delusional sense of a bodily transformation (in the case of anorexia, that of "becoming fat") that is triggered by a blow to self-esteem. It is also of interest that this predominantly male syndrome involves a fear of becoming "smaller," while the overwhelmingly female disorder, anorexia, is centered around a dread of becoming "larger." Incidentally, like many so-called culture-bound syndromes, *Koro* also occurs in modern Western patients, although rarely. Only in the Far East, however, where particular culturally patterned anxieties prevail, is it an ethnic disorder.

For a Western example, we can return to nineteenth-century hysteria, with which we began this chapter. Hysteria expressed the core cultural dilemmas and social contradictions experienced by nineteenth-century women, particularly those in the middle and upper classes.[27] These included the requirement to be exaggeratedly feminine and ornamentally sexual, while at the same time being expected to follow a morally repressive and hypocritical sexual code of behavior.[28] Also, though, while much sentimental value was placed on feminine frailty, women were expected to be a beacon of moral strength, and assume total responsibility for the home and child-rearing. The industrial revolution had served to make the middle-class woman peripheral and exclude her from public life: she was expected to accept her destiny as male helper, manager of domestic affairs, and the bearer and rearer of children. The hysterical women dramatized her powerlessness as well as her repressed sexuality through her symptoms, whose illness-like character gave her some power to passively control and manipulate her immediate situation. Hysterical symptoms exaggerated the stereotypes of femininity: they were dramatic, emotional, and conformed to the idea of female vulnerability and weaknesses. Hysteria was clearly a social pattern, a template, a model. The symptoms were commonly acquired through imitation, and they had a distinctly "contagious" character. They were a kind of exaggeration of a theatrical dramatic style that had become *au courant* in the urban cultures of Western Europe.[29] The fashionability of hysteria was reflected in the considerable notoreity the disorder attained. It was entertainment, an art form; in the 1920s, the surrealists celebrated the "fiftieth anniversary of hysteria." But it also involved politics, specifically sexual politics; it offered women an opportunity to protest indirectly against male dominance. Some recent interpretations have even suggested that hysteria was a kind of proto-feminist revolt.[30]

As a final example, Devereux suggested that schizophrenia is a prototype of a Western "ethnic psychosis." Despite typical assertions to the contrary, schizophrenia occurs rarely, if at all, in societies relatively uninfluenced by Western civilization.[31] It is increasingly difficult to think of schizophrenia as a culture-bound syndrome, given the mounting evidence of the importance of biological factors in its etiology. Nevertheless, particularly in the era of the 1960s, schizophrenia assumed a number of symbolic meanings that gave it (temporarily) the status of an ethnic disorder. For one thing, the experience of drug-induced psychosis, which was commonplace in the 1960s, led many to readily identify with the altered state of consciousness and the transcendental experiences of many schizophrenics. But furthermore, the schizophrenic was perceived as the ultimate victim of a society in which supposedly sane people (that is, political leaders) were behaving quite crazily, a world in which the boundaries of sanity and madness were blurred. Thus the schizophrenic became a culture hero, a trend which found its ultimate expression in works such as Laing's *The Politics of Experience*, which was not only a book about schizophrenia but which served as a cultural manifesto of the period.[32] The interesting aspect of all this is that the societal turmoil of the 1960s probably had little to do with the etiology of schizophrenia. But in a symbolic sense, schizophrenia had taken on the status of an ethnic disorder.

Eating Disorders as Ethnic Disorders

In this book, we will explore the sociocultural factors underlying the ascendancy of eating disorders in our own time, using the notion of an ethnic disorder as a framework. Like hysteria, anorexia nervosa expresses symptomatically the contradictions of female identity of the present, although the nature of the problems have changed considerably since the nineteenth century. Unlike the hysteric, the anorexic does not so much mimic a physical illness (although she may move into an illness role eventually), but manipulates her food intake and becomes obsessive about her body shape and weight. Anorexics and bulimics draw upon the common cultural vocabulary of their time, through latching onto the contemporary mania about dieting, thinness, and food control that have become endemic to the advanced industrial societies. They utilize these cultural preoccupations as defenses that enable them to escape from – and achieve some sense of control over – unmanageable personal distress, most of which revolves around issues of identity. Again similar to hysteria, anorexia and bulimia are socially patterned, the fashionable style of achieving specialness through deviance. And like hysteria, these disorders generate fascination and repugnance, simply because they are so closely tied to social contradictions experienced by all. Eating disorders are also ultimately political, since they are so closely connected with the issue of the control of the female body and the conformation to prevailing standards of beauty. Like hysteria, then, eating disorders partake in sexual politics, and they have also been taken up in the name of the feminist cause.

These are the themes that we will be exploring throughout this book. In the following chapter, we will look more closely at anorexia nervosa and bulimia as clinical disorders. In chapter 3, the incidence and prevalence of these disorders in different countries and social groups will be examined. Chapter 4 will focus on the issue of female identity, which I will argue is at the center of the psychological conflicts underlying the eating disorders. Chapters 5 and 6 will focus on the ideal of thinness and the closely related problem of obesity, respectively, both of which are crucial to understanding the increasing incidence of eating disorders. In chapter 7, the notion that eating disorders are spread throughout the culture by a kind of psychosocial contagion will be examined. Finally, chapter 8 will take up the issue of the "politics" of eating disorders, specifically the notion that these disorders represent a particular expression of powerlessness and that the response to these patients – as well as the cultural imagery surrounding their symptoms – is conditioned by a recognition of the peculiar combination of rebellion and conformity that they express.

2

EATING DISORDERS: ANOREXIA
NERVOSA AND BULIMIA

I do not remember that I did ever in all my practice see one that
was conversant with the living so much wasted . . .

Thomas Morton, *Phthisiologica*

Vomunt et edant, edunt et vomant
(They vomit to eat, and eat to vomit)

Seneca, *Ad Marcian*, xix

In the popular consciousness, anorexia nervosa is something relatively
new. Indeed, the disorder was unheard of by all but a few medical
specialists prior to the 1970s, when it suddenly burst into public view.
But in fact, as a clinical entity, the history of anorexia nervosa
probably extends back as far as three centuries.

In 1689, Thomas Morton, a religious nonconformist and English
physician, reported in a massive treatise on consumption two cases of
a "wasting" disease of nervous origins that should be considered as
the first clear medical description of anorexia nervosa. The chief
symptom described by Morton was "want of appetite" and weight loss
that were not accompanied by other typical symptoms of consumption
(for example, fever and coughing), and which was apparently
attributable to "sad and anxious cares." The first patient, one "Mr
Duke's daughter," Morton described as an 18-year old girl who
"pored over books" despite her evident emanciation and was
indifferent to the extreme cold of an abnormally severe winter. Like
modern patients, the girl refused offers of medication, and soon after
died following a fainting fit. The second patient was a 16-year old
boy, whose "wont of appetite" Morton directly attributed to "studying
too hard" as well as the "passions of his mind." However, the boy
followed Morton's advice to abandon his studies and pursue his

health in the country, upon which he "recovered his health in great measure."[1]

Anorexia nervosa was only rarely mentioned in scattered medical reports over the next two centuries, although there were a number of "fasting girls" who achieved considerable public notoreity in England and continental Europe and who may have represented a kind of quasi-religious precursor of the condition.[2] But it suddenly became the focus of intense medical attention and controversy in the latter half of the nineteenth century, when Sir William Gull in London and Charles Lasegue, a Parisian neurologist, simultaneously published papers in the early 1870s on a number of cases of a pattern of self-starvation that is now clearly recognizable as anorexia nervosa.[3] Gull, in fact, invented the term anorexia nervosa to distinguish the disorder, which he argued resulted from a "morbid mental state," from tuberculosis, whereas Lasegue, although clearly describing the same condition, clung to the tradition of subsuming all female neurotic disorders under the umbrella of "hysteria." These early writers noted what have become familiar hallmarks of anorexia. Gull, for example, marveled at the hyperactivity and excessive energy of his patients (all of whom were female), despite their starved condition; while Lasegue made keen observations about the anorexic's typical denial, her peculiar attitudes towards food, and her pathological family interactions. It is interesting to speculate whether Gull and Lasegue's simultaneous discoveries were responses to an actual sudden increase in the number of cases of the disorder, or whether they were redefining behaviors or symptoms that were already prevalent but had just gone unrecognized. This question bedevils virtually all discussions of psychiatric epidemiology, and is, in the absence of more solid data, essentially unanswerable. Nevertheless, it is at least plausible, on historical grounds, that there was in fact an actual increase in the prevalence of the condition at the time.

For the century following Gull and Lasegue's pioneering papers, anorexia nervosa was extensively written about, but little understood. In the early decades of the twentieth century, it was mistakenly viewed as an endocrine disease (Simmond's Disease), and for years through the 1920s, anorexic patients were treated with thyroid extracts. When it became clear during the 1930s that anorexia and Simmond's disease were different clinical entities, psychological explanations came into the fore, particularly in the form of psychoanalytic interpretations that argued for the disorder's sexual origins. Anorexics were seen as primarily defending themselves against fantasies of oral impregnation, or against promiscuous impulses.[4] While these views have little acceptance today, psychoanalytic writings rescued the understanding of anorexia from the dreary and unenlightening speculations of a purely medical somaticism. As long as the motivations and psychological development of the anorexic patient were ignored, little progress was bound to be made in comprehending the disorder. But the traditional psychoanalytic views, which had their heyday for about two or three decades, were themselves destined to lose their influence. The exclusive focus on sexual factors, as well as the interpretative and relatively passive approach to psychotherapy, proved ultimately of little value to these patients. A more encompassing framework was needed, one which took into account the particular needs and developmental peculiarities of anorexic patients. A watershed was the emergence of the work of Hilde Bruch, which paralleled the ascendancy of eating disorders in the contemporary period.

The publication of Bruch's groundbreaking book on eating disorders in 1973 signaled a major breakthrough in theory and practice, and interestingly, it coincided with the beginning of the sharp increase in the prevalence of anorexia nervosa and bulimia.[5] Bruch, who was originally trained in psychoanalysis, had worked for three decades with anorexic patients prior to the publication of her book, and had also made some important contributions to the study of obesity in children and adolescents.[6] *Eating Disorders* included a consideration of both anorexia nervosa and obesity, and Bruch argued that both of these revolved around issues of body image as well as certain characteristic problems in psychological development. At the time of writing of the present book, the notion of obesity as a psychological disorder remains a controversial one; nevertheless, Bruch argued forcefully for the intimate connections between disorders of body shape and weight, and in which the eating function had become the focus of psychological conflict.[7]

In *Eating Disorders*, Bruch argued that anorexia nervosa had to be understood in terms of the development of the total personality in the context of the family, rather than the narrow interpretation in terms of psychosexual development. Following up on the suggestions on some earlier writers, she proposed that there were really two types of anorexia nervosa, a primary and a secondary form. In the primary type, there were three distinguishing and central features that are always present:

1 a distorted body image, that consisted of the virtually delusional misperception of the body as fat;
2 an inability to identify internal feeling and need states, particularly hunger, but more generally the whole range of emotions; and
3 an all-pervasive sense of effectiveness, a feeling that one's actions, thoughts, and feelings do not actively originate within the self but rather are passive reflections of external expectations and demands.

This latter characteristic is very important, although not easy to formulate; it is a kind of lacuna at the core of the self, a sense of being "nothing," of not being an active agent in control of one's destiny. This deficient sense of self, which Bruch argued is grounded in the experiences of childhood, makes it understandable why anorexia so typically develops in adolescence, a period in which the development of a sense of autonomy, mastery, and competence is critical to achieving maturity and independence from one's parents.

The atypical form of anorexia nervosa, on the other hand, was seen by Bruch as a much more heterogeneous condition. Its central feature was severe weight loss due to psychogenic factors, but in which the pursuit of thinness and a pathological deficit in autonomy were not primary. Atypical anorexia nervosa involved in a more central way than the primary form psychological conflicts that centered around the eating function ("symbolic misinterpretations of the eating function," in Bruch's language) that could stem from a whole host of underlying personality difficulties, ranging from the neurotic to the psychotic. Bruch's distinction between primary and atypical anorexia has not been fully accepted or incorporated into contemporary diagnostic criteria, but in clinical practice the distinction is often real enough and of considerable importance from a treatment standpoint.

The most recent diagnostic definition of anorexia nervosa by the American Psychiatric Association, in its influential manual, the *DSM III-R*, clearly shows the impact of Bruch's thinking.[8] The *DSM III-R* stipulates the following as essential diagnostic criteria:

1 refusal to maintain body weight over minimum expected for age and height;
2 an intense fear of gaining weight or becoming fat;
3 a distorted body image (i.e. "feeling fat"); and
4 amenorrhea.

Not included in this list are Bruch's notions of a deficient sense of self and the inability to recognize internal states: these, however, are probably too vague for the DSM III, whose authors sought "operational definitions" of symptoms. The inclusion of amenorrhea, a nearly universal accompaniment of anorexia nervosa, was clearly intended to recognize the physical components of the condition. Amenorrhea is a typical consequence of severe weight loss, but in about 20 percent of cases it begins prior to the loss of significant amounts of weight. This, among other factors, has led some to argue that anorexia involves a primary physical disorder, particularly in the hypothalamic centers of the central nervous system that control feeding and hormonal function.[9] Whether such factors are primary or secondary is at present unresolved, but there is no question that once anorexia nervosa becomes established, its physical components represent a significant part of the clinical picture.

The vast majority of anorexics are female, although the disorder does occur in males at the rate of about 5 to 10 per cent of diagnosed cases.[10] Anorexia is mainly a disorder of adolescence, with peak ages of onset at 14 and 18.[11] Nevertheless, there are some cases that begin later, during the 20s and perhaps even the 30s, and recent reports suggest that the number of cases with post-adolescent onset have been increasing.[12] At the other end of the spectrum, reports in the 1980s suggest that the disorder is now emerging with greater frequency in younger, pre-adolescent individuals. Such developments may well be a function of such factors as the increase in dieting and weight preoccupation among various age-groups, but they may also be an artifact of the increased awareness of the disorder.

Overall, though, most contemporary observers agree that anorexia must be understood primarily as a disorder of adolescent development. It results from an inability to cope with the developmental demands of that period, particularly the need to develop a clearly defined personal identity and sense of personal competence. Anorexics typically grow up in families in which there is an extraordinary emphasis on achievement and external appearance. Underneath a façade of good behavior, they typically feel weak, unworthy, and obligated to live up to what they perceive as being relentless demands for perfection. The most characteristic time at which anorexia nervosa emerges is after puberty, when the requirements of adolescence confront the person with the need for independent decision-making, the challenges of sexual relationships, and the need to pursue self-chosen goals and activities. These developmental challenges typically exacerbate a profound inner sense of self-doubt and unworthiness.

Anorexia nervosa typically begins with a diet, which at the outset is virtually indistinguishable from similar efforts to lose weight by countless adolescents. However, given the anorexic's particular developmental vulnerabilities, dieting begins to yield a particularly powerful sense of control, for both internal and external reasons: internal, because it provides a sense of mastery and euphoria to a person who previously felt not only weak but depressed and empty; external, because in a culture that values thinness, the achievement of a thin body shape represents a triumph. The anorexic also derives secondary satisfactions from the manipulative power that her symptoms gives her within her family: in a situation in which she may have felt herself discounted, the refusal of food evokes a powerful response from others, an assertion of her presence that can no longer be ignored. In addition to these social and psychological reinforcements, there may well be physiological factors (perhaps resulting from the state of starvation) that "lock the anorexic in" to her emaciated and malnourished state.[13]

The Clinical Course of Anorexia

Once set in motion, anorexia nervosa has its own characteristic development as a disease, its own internal dynamic that may be to a considerable extent independent of the factors that gave rise to it. As dieting is transformed into fasting and finally into willful starvation, the anorexic typically withdraws from ordinary activities and relationships. She will typically intensify an already excessive exercise regime, and may for a time redouble her frenetic efforts at achievement. She becomes obsessed with thoughts of food, with details of dieting and calorie counting, and with the sight of her own image in the mirror. Early in the course of the illness, anorexics often experience a kind of euphoria, akin to the famous "fasting high" described by those who fast for health reasons or by religious mystics. These experiences are typically short-lived, however: the longer the period of abstention, the more a sense of depression is likely to supervene and become the dominant mood.

Once an anorexic patient has lost a significant amount of weight and the illness has progressed to a certain point, she will typically defend her low weight with all the resources she can muster. These include various strategies of deception and secrecy, for which anorexic patients are notorious. Ingenious methods of disposing of food, for example, or hiding shocking degrees of emaciation beneath loose clothing, or using devious means of inflating one's weight before a medical examination, are not uncommon. The anorexic not only deceives others, but to a considerable extent is able persuade herself that "all is well" or that she never has felt better. Probably no other disorder other than alcoholism is so invariably accompanied by denial. In fact, in many respects anorexia nervosa resembles an addictive disorder, in that it involves dependency on and obsessive preoccupation with an oral behavior (in this case, the negative one of food refusal) as well as pervasive denial and deception in order to maintain the "habit."[14]

By the time a person who has developed anorexia nervosa comes to the attention of clinical professionals, the disorder has in most cases progressed to a considerable degree. It is unfortunate, though understandable, that in the early stages of the illness, family members often cling to the hope that the change that has come over their offspring is a "passing phase." While in a certain number of cases this may in fact be true and the developing anorexic is able to extricate herself from a downward course, in most instances the family becomes entrapped in an escalating cycle of denial and unwitting collusion. The families of anorexics are particularly vulnerable to getting "caught" in such a cycle, in that they tend to be externally oriented and therefore particularly likely to deny the existence of "problems." In any case, by the time the anorexic reaches the point at which the disorder is clinically identified, she has already become entrapped in a complex web of psychological attitudes and physiological sequelae associated with prolonged starvation.[15] The latter are particularly dangerous from a medical standpoint, and typically prompt a focus on the physical aspects of the condition. An anorexic patient, for example, presents symptoms of cachexia (emaciation), such as pallor, weakness and muscle fatigue, growth of fine body hair (lanugo), and amenorrhea. She will typically show heart irregularities, such as brachycardia, along with the complex dysregulation associated with malnutrition. If weight loss has been extreme, a medical emergency has been created, resulting in hospitalization. Anorexia nervosa has a fatal outcome in between about 5 and 10 percent of diagnosed cases, a rate higher than that of any other psychiatric disorder.[16] It is hardly surprising, therefore, that the medical aspects of anorexia have been the subject of intense interest. There is no question that once the condition becomes established, anorexia nervosa involves complex and sometimes intractable physical derangements which in turn only serve to aggravate the patient's already distressed mental state. Nevertheless, the initial triggers for the disorder most likely lie in the developmental history of the subject, which is in turn embedded in a cultural context.

Despite the proliferation of treatment approaches in recent years, there is hardly agreement as to the optimal mode of intervention. In general, there is a consensus that both the physical and psychological aspects of the disorder must be addressed, through a combination of nutritional rehabilitation, weight restoration, and long-term psychotherapy. Beyond this very general prescription, though, opinions differ widely on how treatment should proceed. In general, the process of recovery tends to be a difficult one, in some cases involving multiple hospitalizations and a number of failed efforts at psychotherapy. Outcome studies indicate that approximately 75 percent of anorexic patients show some degree of improvement at long-term follow-up, if one restricts oneself to the criterion of weight restoration. However, the outcome is considerably less sanguine if one looks at such factors as body image, food preoccupation, and ongoing difficulties with social and sexual adjustment. A considerable number of former patients continue to struggle with these issues despite weight recovery.[17] Despite the increase in the prevalence of anorexia in recent years, the number of patients is still not large in absolute terms; but given the age and potential of the population which is afflicted, it represents a serious and often devastating affliction, with often tragic implications for the sufferer and her family.[18]

The Search for a Somatic Cause

Since the discovery of anorexia nervosa in the 1870s, considerable effort has been devoted to the identification of biological factors that may play a central role in its etiology. Such a quest for a somatic cause is understandable, given the gross physical complications of the disease. Also, because anorexics have until the relatively recent past typically been treated in medical hospitals, research into the cause of the disorder has frequently been conducted in a medical (i.e. somatic) framework. It might also be added that anorexics are notoriously difficult patients who often put up fierce resistances to treatment. The search for a "magic bullet" that would circumvent the vagaries and complexities of psychiatric intervention remains an alluring (although elusive) prospect.

Throughout the years, the anorexic's malnourished body has served as a virtual laboratory for the study of the effects of human starvation. Numerous investigations have revealed a host of physiological anomalies, including complex endocrine dysregulation, neurotransmitter deficiences, and abnormal feeding and digestive mechanisms.[19] More specifically anorexics have been shown, among other things, to evidence:

1 lowered oestrogen levels (lowered testosterone in males);
2 elevated growth-hormone levels;
3 reduced levels of neurotransmitters such as norepinephrine, serotonin, and dopamine;
4 anomalous carbohydrate metabolism;
5 abnormalities in temperature regulation; and
6 delayed gastric emptying.

A detailed review of these findings could easily fill an entire volume. But amid the welter of findings and increasingly sophisticated research methodologies, one crucial fact seems to stand out: that various physiological functions for the most part return to normal levels when weight and nutrition have been restored.[20] It is true, of course, that permanent impairments may remain in subjects after recovery (for example, menstrual and reproductive abnormalities, and, as has more recently been discovered, osteoperosis). But these must be considered to be consequences of the disease, not its causes.

Although the possibility remains that unknown physiological factors lead certain individuals to be vulnerable to anorexia nervosa, present understanding seems to suggest strongly that psychological and social factors are critical in precipitating the disorder. The point was argued strongly by P. J. V. Beumont, an Australian psychiatrist, who himself has conducted biological studies:

But does this knowledge [i.e. that derived from biological research – ed.] substantially increase our understanding of anorexia nervosa? I think not. The physical symptoms of anorexia nervosa are epiphenomena unrelated to the etiology of the illness. It is useful to know about them – but mainly to avoid unnecessary investigation of the patient . . . Of course, the presence of physical disorder does eventually affect the patient's behavior, and to some extent a vicious circle of illness is set up. But the many elaborate schemes of interacting variables that have been proposed . . . do not really *explain* the illness. Anorexia nervosa remains basically a neurotic disturbance, leading to deviations in behavior that bring about physical dysfunction. Its treatment, albeit unsatisfactory, is psychological.[21]

Such foreclosure of the issue at this point may be premature. But even if it could be demonstrated that physiological factors are involved in a primary way in the etiology of anorexia (and I do not rule out this possibility), one puzzling fact would still need to be explained: the dramatically increased incidence of the disease in Western societies. It would certainly seem that the most likely explanation for this phenomenon, which is the principal subject of this book, would lie in social and cultural factors.

Bulimic Anorexia

If an anorexic continues in a state of starvation for a long enough period of time, the pangs of hunger become intolerable and the rigid discipline of the starvation diet may be broken by a ravenous eating binge. For an anorexic, though, with her terrible fear of weight gain, nothing could be more disastrous than such an episode of gorging. The "crime" must be avenged by getting rid of the hated food, typically through self-induced vomiting, and less commonly through the consumption of frightening amounts of laxatives or redoubled efforts at starvation. Such episodes of bulimia (which means literally "ox-hunger") occur in between about 40 and 50 percent of anorexic patients, and their emergence is typically an ominous sign, making the disorder particularly recalcitrant to treatment.[22] Patients who develop bulimia have usually been ill longer, and it may be that bulimic urges are part of the body's normal compensatory response to prolonged starvation. The famous studies of experimental starvation in previously healthy males conducted in the 1940s showed that bulimic binges were common and persisted for months, even years after normal weight had been restored.[23] Bulimic anorexics, however, are also typically heavier before their illness than their abstinent cohorts, suggesting perhaps that the body's weight-regulating mechanisms may respond more violently to starvation than for a patient with a leaner frame. In addition, though, there is a further distinguishing feature of bulimic anorexics, and that is that they are typically more seriously psychologically disturbed than the "abstinent" or "restricting" anorexics.

Bulimic anorexics, for example, tend to have pervasive difficulty with impulse control, which manifests itself in alcohol or drug abuse, sexual promiscuity, or compulsive stealing.[24] Unlike the classic portraits of the typical anorexic family as highly controlled, fearful of conflict, and cultivating an image of perfection, the family histories of bulimics are replete with open conflict and turmoil. The bulimic's own relationships with others tend to be intensely dependent and emotionally "stormy." Bulimic anorexics are often openly self-destructive and prone to suicide attempts or gestures.[25] This entire pattern of impulsivity, emotional instability, explosive relationships, and self-destructive behavior is akin to what contemporary psychiatry refers to as a borderline personality disorder. Clearly not all bulimic anorexics are borderline personalities; but the bulimic symptoms are much more likely to emerge in these severely disturbed individuals when they develop anorexia.

Even more than anorexia, the bulimic cycle of binging and purging closely resembles an addictive form of behavior, and it sometimes been compared to alcohol abuse. Indeed, a significant proportion of bulimic anorexics have a history of problem drinking or drug abuse, which may continue concurrently with the eating disorder.[26] The concept of addiction seems especially applicable to bulimia, in that the behavior pattern becomes compulsive, secretive, and the person becomes ultimately dependent on it for solving life's problems. However, it is probably important to avoid the simplistic notion put forward by some that bulimia is an "addiction to food." While bulimics may early on use food binges as a way of relieving tension, it is ultimately the vomiting that becomes the "habit" to which bulimics become enslaved.[27] Perhaps it would be best to think of the entire pattern of binging, purging, and intermittent starvation for which the addiction concept is relevant. When superimposed on the anorexic pattern, which already involves denial and fierce resistance to external intervention, bulimia poses formidable treatment obstacles that can tax the capacities of the most skilled clinician and treatment staff.

Bulimia was occasionally mentioned in earlier accounts of anorexia nervosa, but it appears that in the late nineteenth and early twentieth centuries it was a much less prominent part of the clinical picture of anorexia than it is today.[28] Hilde Bruch, one of the few clinicians with continuous experience with eating disorders from the 1940s to the 1980s, herself observed that bulimia had become an ever more prominent part of the clinical presentation of patients in the later period.[29] Gerald Russell, an English psychiatrist, suggests that in fact the form of anorexia nervosa has changed in the second half of the twentieth century, with bulimia now a characteristic part of the clinical picture. Russell suggests that the change in anorexia is an example of the more general phenomenon of "pathoplasticity," that is, the malleability of a disease under the influence of historical factors or altered cultural conditions.[30] The ascendancy of bulimia in the contemporary clinical picture of anorexia has yet to be accounted for, but it is likely that a number of factors are involved, including the increasing availability of low-cost, calorie-rich food, tendencies towards desocialization and fragmentation in contemporary eating patterns, and the general emergence of a cultural "style" that includes greater impulsivity and addictive patterns of behavior.

Bulimia at Normal Weight (Bulimia Nervosa)

Bulimia has become increasingly prominent in anorexia nervosa, but the contemporary period has witnessed the rapid emergence of what appears to be a new pattern – that is, the syndrome of bulimia in a person who otherwise maintains weight in the normal range. Overeating and vomiting were known to the Romans (see the quotation from Seneca at the beginning of this chapter), but whether it represented the type of individual disorder that it does today as opposed to a social eating pattern that represented the excesses of a wealthy aristocracy is a matter of debate. Contemporary bulimics, like anorexics, are overwhelmingly female, obsessed with achieving thinness, and suffer from distortions of body image. Nevertheless, their weight does not drop to the dangerously low level that is characteristic of anorexia nervosa. "Normal-weight" bulimia (which may be a misnomer, since these patients' weights tend to fluctuate and they may be over- or underweight) first became known in the United States in the 1970s, and was dubbed "bulimarexia" by Boskind-Lodahl, who wrote the first contemporary paper on the syndrome.[31] Boskind-Lodahl described a number of college students who were high achievers but who suffered from extremely low self-esteem and were extraordinarily sensitive to male rejection. She subtitled her paper "A feminist interpretation of anorexia nervosa and bulimia," but it is clear, at least in retrospect, that she was discussing mainly bulimia. The term "bulimarexia," while suggestive of the link between the binge–purge syndrome and anorexia nervosa, was not widely adopted, and in fact was condemned by Bruch as a "semantic monstrosity." Bruch had been aware of a non-anorexic bulimic syndrome in her 1973 book, but she saw it as occurring in a formerly overweight person who shared the typical anorexic obsession with thinness. She adopted a phrase from an early twentieth-century writer, "un obese amaigri" (thin fat person), to characterize the pattern, but like the originator of the phrase, she agreed "mais il est toujours obese."

Significant numbers of patients with a normal-weight bulimic syndrome began to be noticed by clinicians in the late 1970s and early 80s. The syndrome was clearly appearing in the United Kingdom as well as the United States. In 1979, Dr. Gerald Russell, an English psychiatrist, published a now classic description of the syndrome, which he named "Bulimia Nervosa" to indicate its kinship and yet its difference from anorexia nervosa.[32] Bulimia quickly attained public notoriety with the publication of reports that binging and purging was occurring in epidemic proportions on college campuses in the United States.[33] Through the 1980s, bulimia rapidly came to supplant anorexia nervosa as the more common eating disorder.

Since its inception in 1982, the *International Journal of Eating Disorders* has witnessed a sharp increase in the number of publications on bulimic patients. Meanwhile, controversy has raged around the issue of how the bulimic syndrome should be diagnosed and defined, and particularly its relationship to anorexia nervosa. The confusion is indicated by the proliferation of names that have been proposed for the syndrome: the dietary chaos syndrome, bulimarexia, bulimia nervosa, or simply bulimia. In 1980, the American Psychiatric Association, in its influential diagnostic manual, the DSM-III, identified the disorder simply as bulimia, and the diagnostic criteria basically described a syndrome of binge-eating.[34] The 1987 revision, however, renamed the syndrome as "bulimia nervosa," and stipulated diagnostic criteria that brought the diagnosis more into line with anorexia nervosa.[35] Specifically the criteria for bulimia nervosa stipulate:

1 recurrent episodes of binge-eating;
2 frequent purging or severe food-restriction between episodes; and
3 persistent overconcern with body weight and shape

This definition seems more adequate than the earlier version, since it describes the characteristic abnormal eating pattern as well as the obsessive concern with shape and weight that are both typically found in these individuals.

Diagnostic definitions are of importance for the purposes of scientific clarity, but they do not really communicate how the symptoms of disordered eating are really experienced. For this, I quote the following graphic description of a bulimic episode:

It would start to build in the late morning. By noon I'd know I had to binge. I would go out . . . to the supermarket down the block, and buy a gallon, or maybe even two gallons of maple walnut ice cream and a couple of packages of fudge-brownie mix. . . . On the way home, the urge to binge would get stronger and stronger. I could hardly drive my car because I couldn't think about anything but food. There was a doughnut shop that I passed on the way home. Almost always I'd stop the car, buy a dozen doughnuts and start munching on them even before I was walking out the door. On the way home I invariably finished all twelve doughnuts . . . I'd hurry up to the apartment with the urge for more binging growing stronger by the minute. . . . I'd hastily mix up the brownie mix and get the brownies in the oven, usually managing to eat a fair amount of the mix myself as I was going along. Then, while they were still cooking, I ate the ice-cream. Only by constantly eating the ice-cream could I bear the delay until the brownies came out of the oven. Sometimes I'd finish the whole gallon even before the brownies were done, and I'd take the brownies out of the oven while they were still baking. At any rate, I'd start eating brownies, even though by this time I was feeling sick, intending to stop after two or three. Then it would be five or six. Pretty soon, I'd have put away about fifteen or twenty of the brownies, and then I'd be overcome with embarrassment. What if one of my roomates were to get home and see that I had eaten *twenty* brownies! The only way to disguise it, obviously, was to finish the other fifty-two brownies myself, wash the pan, and clean everything up. . . . Seventy-two brownies later, the depression hit. I'd go to the bathroom, stick my finger down my throat, and make myself throw up. I was so good at it that it was almost automatic – no effort necessary, just instant vomiting, over and over until there was nothing coming out of my stomach except clear pale-green fluid.[36]

A person can be entrapped in such a pattern for many years without getting help and without the problem being discovered by anyone. Since the bulimic maintains a more or less normal weight, the problem, unlike anorexia nervosa, may be secretly masked beneath a façade of normality.[37] Also unlike anorexia, which is often accompanied by unspoken feelings of pride, bulimic behavior is typically accompanied by feelings of profound shame and embarrassment. Bulimics also are typically extremely discomfited by feeling out of control, and it is this sense that often motivates them to disclose their problem and seek help. Even at this point, though, their feelings about getting help are typically ambivalent. They would like to reduce the sense of chaos created by the eating pattern, and yet fear that if they are treated that the freedom to binge and purge will be "taken away from them." The uncanny resemblance to the feelings described my many alcoholics is yet another parallel between bulimia and the addictive disorders.

Numerous studies, some of which will be reviewed in the following chapter, suggest that bulimia is probably between five and ten times as prevalent as anorexia nervosa.[38] Although bulimia often begins in the high-school years, the greatest prevalence of bulimia is most likely on college campuses, where the behavior has merged to some extent with socially prevalent practices of binge-eating and even of purging. One study showed that bulimic college students vary widely in their degree of psychiatric disturbance, from some showing barely detectable degrees of impairment while others manifested obvious clinical disturbance.[39] Apparently, there are some instances in which bulimia is no more than an unhealthy and risky technique of weight control. The number of such "pragmatic" bulimics is unknown. But probably for the majority, habitual binging and purging becomes a way of discharging severe degrees of psychological distress. Although bulimia is occurring in epidemic proportions among students, it is hardly limited to them. A number of older women, many of whom are overtly successful and well-functioning, are caught in a long-term pattern of binging, purging, and weight obsession, which they manage to keep carefully hidden for years. The prevalence of these bulimic adult women is at present unknown, but there is little question about their existence.[40]

Bulimia, like anorexia, is probably best understood as a developmental disorder, although it tends to emerge somewhat later than anorexia. The majority of bulimics first develop their symptoms between the ages of 16 and 20 – that is, in the late years in high school and the early years of college. While it is probably an oversimplification, it could be said that whereas for anorexia the principal developmental problem is the challenge of adolescence and the psychological issues that become organized around the maintenance of a post-pubertal weight, for bulimics the central developmental impasse is the psychological separation from the family and the entry into the adult world, and particularly the challenges that these pose to the sense of personal identity.[41] Hence, the disorder rarely emerges at puberty, but rather is more likely to begin in the late high school or early college years. Unlike anorexics, who tend to be phobic about sexuality and to avoid sexual encounters, bulimics tend to be sexually active and to be engaged in heterosexual relationships. Many have achieved a higher overall level of interpersonal maturity than anorexics, but nevertheless they tend to struggle with issues of independence and self-assertion.

The personalities of bulimics vary widely, and they are probably a more heterogeneous group than anorexics. However, there are some typical personality features that are encountered in a large number of cases. One of the most common personality types is what has been referred to as the "false-self," or "pseudo-independent" personality organization.[42] The false-self personality is typically on the surface a well-functioning and well-appearing (often physically attractive) young woman. Like the anorexic, she is typically an achiever in school and at work, and appears to be an independent and competent individual. Underneath the competent façade, however, she is troubled by profound feelings of neediness, dependency, and low self-esteem. This split in her identity typically resulted from a kind of childhood experience in which, because of the unavailability of parental figures due to illness, depression, or addiction, she was expected to develop a "pseudo-mature" adaptation which left little room for the expression of either dependency or rebellion. As a result, these needs remain split off and hidden from public view, and they are precisely what is expressed in bulimic gorging and purging: it is in fact only in the privacy of the kitchen or bathroom that she can only drop her façade of perfection and let herself go. The false-self type is an extremely common pattern in bulimia, but it is not the only one. Some bulimics are more severely psychologically disturbed borderline personalities, for whom the behavior serves to ward off a threatened sense of personal fragmentation and is virtually inter-changeable with a whole host of self-destructive symptoms, including alcoholism, self-mutilation, and sexual promiscuity. Still others are basically suffering from more typical adolescent conflicts.[43] For these latter, the bulimia tends to be a more transient and superficial symptom, and therefore more easily dislodged from a therapeutic standpoint. The point is that bulimia is a final common pathway through which a variety of developmental problems can be expressed. However, all bulimics share a common central obsession with weight and body shape.

Like anorexia, bulimia can easily become a chronic pattern, and the longer the person maintains it the more difficult it is to dislodge. Bulimia, like anorexia, may also become "locked in" by physiological factors once it has become habitual. The chronic pattern of binge-eating and purging may vastly upset the normal equilibrium of hunger and satiety mechanisms; and this dysregulation may make the intensity of both eating binges and vomiting episodes more pro-nounced.[44] In addition, both binge-eating and vomiting may have powerful effects as immediate reinforcers – that is, in relieving states of emotional distress and tension. These "addictive" consequences of the components of the bulimic cycle may be based on physiological as well as psychological mechanisms. The point is here that like anorexia, once the binging and purging pattern has become established, it may be sustained autonomously by factors other than those that initially gave rise to it: and adequate treatment typically should take these factors into account.

A number of approaches to the treatment of bulimia have been proposed, but it is not firmly established yet which treatments are especially effective. Individual psychotherapy, structured along psychodynamic or interpersonal lines, is important, although it will probably be ineffective without some direct attention to the symptomatic behavior. A promising approach to the treatment of bulimia is the "cognitive-behavioral" method, which combines the "normalization" of eating and nutrition along with discussing and challenging a bulimic's ideas about weight and body shape.[45] There are also interesting programs of direct behavioral intervention, which may be useful for more intractable cases; in these, the bulimic is given tools to help her deliberately restrain her eating or purging behavior.[46] Bulimics tend to respond more favorably than anorexics to group interventions, which may have something to do with the generally greater responsiveness of bulimics to social influence and support.

In addition, during the 1980s a further treatment approach has emerged, one based on the idea that bulimia is mediated by biological depression. Considerable excitement was generated by the reports of Pope and Hudson that a certain number of normal-weight bulimics respond favorably to antidepressant medications, such as the tricyclic antidepressants and the MAO inhibitors. These dramatic findings led Pope and Hudson to argue that bulimia is grounded in an endogenous depression or "primary affective disorder."[47] These arguments were buttressed by findings of an elevated history of depressive disorders in the first-degree relatives of bulimics, as well as increased frequencies of related disorders in their families, such as alcoholism or anxiety disorders. While a certain percentage of bulimics (but not all) appear to be helped by antidepressant medications, the hypothesis that bulimia is an expression of a primary affective disorder has been sharply questioned by many and is probably an oversimplification.[48] Bulimia ultimately needs to be understood in terms of the interaction of developmental factors with the complexities of weight regulation, the pursuit of thinness, and the use of food and purging as methods for the regulation of emotional tension. The fact that some bulimics respond well to antidepressant medications is an important one, but a satisfactory explanation for the effect has yet to emerge. Perhaps some bulimics do have a coincident predisposition to depression, and therefore its alleviation may also lead to an improvement of their bulimic symptoms. Another possibility, though, is that the "antidepressant" drugs have their effect on bulimics not so much through the alteration of mood but by interrupting the cycle of binging and purging through the improved regulation of satiety mechanisms.[49]

The Psychobiology of Weight Regulation

Contemporary developments in research on the mechanisms of weight regulation may have considerable bearing on our understanding of the etiology of eating disorders. Based on well-established findings such as the tendency of humans and animals to maintain a stable weight over time, despite significant fluctuations in caloric intake, set-point theory posits that a system of physiological feedback within the brain acts so as to maintain or "defend" weight at a particular level or within a certain range. For a particular individual, the set-point is determined by a complex set of interacting factors, such as genetic makeup, individual weight and metabolic function, and the ongoing level of energy expenditure. Set-point mechanisms operate analagously to a thermostat, so that significant deviations in weight from the set-point (either increases or decreases) will be compensated by biological reactions that work to offset the change. Dieting, for example, triggers a slowing of metabolic rate, which then makes the utilization of food intake more efficient. This type of process may account for the tendency of anorexic patients to regain weight during a refeeding program much more rapidly than one would expect based on the amount of calories that they have consumed. Set-point also offers a conceptual explanation of the notorious difficulty that most obese individuals experience in maintaining weight loss over the long-term after a period of dieting. Some modification of the set-point is possible, for example, through changes in energy expenditure brought about by exercise, or under the influence of stress or certain drugs. For any individual, however, there are limits to its alterability, beyond which more drastic physiological complications may occur. These notions may have important implications for the eating disorders, in which the effort to maintain a low body weight is pursued relentlessly and by drastic measures.

Set-point theory is not without its critics, and there are clearly a number of problems with it from a scientific standpoint. However, the study of the psychobiological mechanisms of weight regulation may be crucial to an integrated framework for understanding the eating disorders. For example, it could readily account for the eating binges that follow periods of semistarvation by bulimic anorexics or bulimia nervosa patients. It might also clarify why many obese individuals who undertake radical dieting may develop a syndrome virtually indistinguishable from bulimia nervosa. More generally, the study of the pathology of weight regulation could throw light on the interactions of cultural, psychological and biological factors in the development of anorexia or bulimia. By demanding uniformly that individuals maintain unrealistically low body weights, cultural standards could provoke certain psychologically vulnerable individuals (i.e., those with low self-esteem or who are especially susceptible to external pressures) to violate their own biological limits, thereby giving rise to the destructive psychosomatic spirals known as anorexia and bulimia nervosa.

Shape, Weight, and Personal Identity

Eating disorders are obviously complex clinical conditions, and a full understanding of them must take into account psychological, developmental, and biological factors. What unites anorexia nervosa and bulimia, however, is that they are both disorders of development that revolve around the core issues of shape and body weight, and in which the person, most typically a female, obsessively focuses on the achievement of thinness in order to solve problems of personal identity. For the anorexic, this is typically a problem that first emerges at or shortly after puberty, when the body develops its adult shape and functions and the person first confronts the typical developmental challenges of adolescence. For the normal-weight bulimic, the developmental problems are a bit more advanced, and they typically involve issues of achieving a balance between relationships and a sense of separateness, issues that typically become critical at the separation from the family and confronting the challenges of achievement and relationships of young adulthood. For both, however, the core symptom is the same – that is, an obsession with food, weight, and body shape that becomes a defensive substitute for dealing with the conflicts associated with the achievement of an identity. The term eating disorders is something of a misnomer, therefore, although eating is definitely involved in the symtoms. The essence of anorexia and bulimia, as A. H. Crisp has suggested, is "dysmorphophobia," an anxious avoidance of the challenges of life through a focus on body shape and weight.

In this book, we will examine why these particular symptoms have become the most characteristic disorders of female adolescent development in our own time. Before doing so, though, it will be worthwhile to look at what is known about the prevalence and cultural distribution and eating disorders, a question that will be the subject of the next chapter.

3

THE SOCIAL DIMENSIONS OF AN EPIDEMIC

In order to lay the groundwork for a sociocultural understanding of eating disorders, we need first to establish some of the basic social and demographic facts about their rapid increase. In this chapter, therefore, we will devote ourselves to questions of epidemiology: the prevalence rates of eating disorders, their distributions according to gender, social class, and ethnic and national groups, and the data that points to an increasing incidence. While there are many gaps in our knowledge about these issues, enough information has been gathered in the relatively short period of time in which eating disorders have become problematic to make some definitive statements. We will conclude this chapter with a wider view of eating disorders in the contemporary social scene, and particularly the increased professional interest in eating disorders, the prominence of eating disorders on college campuses, and the emergence of self-help organizations as a grass-roots response to what has become a significant social problem.

Female Prevalence

If there is any one fact that would evoke nearly universal agreement, it is that the overwhelming number of people who develop eating disorders are female. This association between being anorexic and being female extends back not only to the nineteenth-century history of anorexia (all of Gull and Lasegue's patients were female, for example) but to the pre-history of the disorder – the "holy anorexics" of the Middle Ages and the fasting girls of the eighteenth and nineteenth centuries. Contemporary studies tell us with almost near uniformity that the ratio of female to male anorexics (and bulimics) is at least 9 to 1, and some suggest that it is even higher than this.[1] This overwhelming preponderance of female patients confers on the eating disorders the distinction of having the most lopsided sex ratio of any disorder known to psychiatry, even exceeding that of other strongly gender-linked conditions such as agoraphobia.[2] The extremely skewed sexual incidence of anorexia nervosa and bulimia is widely acknowledged, and yet its implications for an understanding of the sudden increase of these conditions have not yet been fully drawn. It will play a central role in the sociocultural interpretation developed in this book.

Along with the high female prevalence, it is also very important to note that male ànorexics and bulimics do exist, and in clinical presentation they closely resemble female patients (with the obvious exception of symptoms such as amenorrhea).[3] Some observers have argued that male anorexics are more psychologically disturbed than their female counterparts and that their clinical presentation is "atypical." This perception, however, may be partly in the mind of the observer, as male patients are by definition manifesting uncharacteristic sex-role behavior. It is also of interest that there has been some informal speculation recently that male anorexia may be on the increase, a trend that has been linked with an increasing preoccupation among males with weight and body image. While the latter trend is undeniably real, it is not at all clear that males would be led to the same types of obsessions with thinness comparable to those in females who develop anorexia. For one thing, the emphasis on thinness for males is less demanding than that for females: in fact, males also tend to be drawn to the opposite emphasis, of developing more imposing frames. In addition, however, as will become clear in the next chapter, it takes a particular psychological situation, one that is much more likely to arise in females, to drive certain individuals to abuse dieting and food in the way that anorexic or bulimic patients do. There is no question that male anorexics are a neglected group of patients. Some feel stigmatized for having a "female" disorder and the resulting sense of shame can make them reluctant to seek help. One such patient, seen by myself, had seen the family doctor, who remarked to his mother that "this problem is only something that happens to girls." The extent of male anorexia, as has been suggested by some, may well be underreported. Nevertheless, there is no systematic evidence for an actual increase in male anorexia; in fact, the studies that have been done suggest that the proportion of females has become if anything even larger.[4]

The Rising Incidence of Anorexia Nervosa

Lewis Hill, in a paper on epidemiology, commented that prior to 1970 anorexia nervosa was considered to be a "curiousity and a rarity."[5] In fact, an American publisher resisted the idea of an English translation of a 1963 book by the Italian psychiatrist, Maria Selvini Palazolli, on the grounds that "it dealt with a rare disease of interest to too few specialists." The book, which was first published in translation in England, is now widely recognized as one of the classic works on anorexia.[6]

At a symposium held in Germany in the mid-1960s, a number of commentators suggested that anorexia had been on the increase since the Second World War, in particular in Germany and Japan.[7] However, the first *formal* documentation of an increase did not appear until 1970, as part of an elegant monograph on the subject by a Swedish psychiatrist, Sten Theander.[8] Theander surveyed the archives of all departments, medical as well as psychiatric, of the two major university hospitals in an area of southern Sweden over the period 1930 to 1960. From these records, he unearthed 11 cases of anorexia nervosa in the first decade of the study (1933–39), 25 in the second (1940–9), and 58 in the last (1950–9). Thus, there was a virtually fivefold increase in incidence over the three decades. Theander cautioned that the apparent increase might be misleading, in that improved detection of cases and greater awareness of the disorder could be important factors contributing to it. In addition, he noted a larger number of patients from the lower social classes in the later period, which he attributed to the greater accessibility of medical care by the less affluent. It is of course also possible that the disorder was beginning to "spread" throughout the socioeconomic spectrum, a phenomenon that seems to have been in evidence in more recent studies.

A number of surveys conducted in the 1970s and 1980s have confirmed the impression of a rising incidence. One study found, for example, a sharp increase in the number of treated cases in three different locales in the United States and United Kingdom over the decade of the 1960s.[9] From the first to the second half of the decade, the number of cases increased from 9 to 15 in Monroe County, New York (the Rochester area), from 0 to 8 in the Camberwell district of London, and from 10 to 20 in Northeast Scotland. A later study of the Monroe County area showed that the trend continued into the mid-1970s, with the number of cases doubling. Also, almost all of the new cases in the 1970s were females.[10] Continuing increases in hospital admissions for anorexia in the late 1970s and early 1980s were reported for Aberdeen (Scotland).[11]

It could be argued, though, that the increased number of diagnosed cases of anorexia nervosa could be a result of an increased professional awareness of the disorder, as opposed to a real increase in incidence. This is an issue that is very difficult to resolve, and bedevils virtually all discussions of changes in epidemiology. There are, however, a number of counterarguments. For one thing, the symptoms of anorexia have been well known to physicians for much longer than they have been familiar to the public. What is more, the clinical picture of anorexia, involving as it does severe weight loss and characteristic attitudes, is not a vague set of symptoms that is easily confused with other conditions; to the contrary, anorexia nervosa is one of the most readily diagnosable psychiatric disorders. What is more, it could just as easily be argued that the number of cases that show up in medical statistics *underestimate* rather than overestimate the increase in prevalence. This is because surveys such as those we have described only count treated cases, which tend to be the most severe. There is good reason to think that the number of "borderline" cases, most of which never come to the attention of clinicians, is much greater than the number of formally diagnosed and treated ones.

It seems clear, then, that the number of treated cases of anorexia has actually increased, at least in the US and the UK. But what about other countries? One investigation conducted in the canton of Zurich, Switzerland revealed a quadrupling in the number of hospitalized cases by decade from the 1950s through the 1970s.[12] In Prague, Czechoslovakia, the number of cases hospitalized for anorexia increased fivefold between 1974 and 1983.[13] In Japan, a survey of a large number of medical facilities all over the country showed that the number of patients in treatment for anorexia nervosa doubled between 1976 and 1981. Even from 1980 to 1981 alone, the total number of patients in treatment jumped from 1,080 to 1,312.[14] While formal epidemiological studies have not been done, an expanding literature and informal observations suggest an increasing prevalence in France,[15] Germany,[16] Italy,[17] and Belgium.[18] The Eastern European countries are also not exempt from an increase in eating disorders, as is evidenced from a number of research reports from countries such as Poland, Czechoslovakia, and Yugoslavia.[19] Interestingly, also, one gets the impression of an increasing prevalence in the Soviet Union, as large series of patients have been reported on there, with the volume of published literature increasing in the late 1970s and early 1980s.[20]

It seems reasonable to conclude, therefore, that anorexia nervosa has generally increased throughout the United States, Western Europe, and Japan, and possibly (although perhaps to a lesser degree) in Eastern Euopre and the Soviet Union. Given the relatively lower prevalence in the non-Western world (see below), it would seem that the increase in eating disorders is largely a phenomenon of the Western industrialized societies, or nations such as Japan that have been heavily influenced by Western values. The issue is not so much a geographic one, as it is a cultural one. For example, anorexia nervosa shows a substantial prevalence among the Caucasian population in South Africa,[21] and among the upper socioeconomic classes in Santiago, Chile.[22] In the absence of more complete data, on the other hand, it is impossible to say at this point whether the increase in some Western nations has been higher than in others. It is apparent, for example, that the problem of anorexia nervosa has received considerable attention in France. It is possible, though, that its prevalence may not be as extensive as, say, in the United States. France is known as a "culinary culture," in which the pleasurable and esthetic aspects of eating are strongly emphasized: such a cultivation of the culinary arts might make disorders that involve food avoidance less likely.[23] In the absence of more specific epidemiological studies, though, it is impossible to say much about the possible impact of such differential cultural attitudes on prevalence rates.

By way of contrast, though, it appears that anorexia nervosa is virtually unheard of in the non-Western world. Shridhar Sharma, for example, a noted Indian epidemiologist, reports a very low prevalence of the disorder in India. The *Indian Journal of Psychiatry*, which has published since the 1930s, has yet to publish a single article or report on anorexia nervosa.[24] Similarly Dr Burton Bradley, a psychiatrist who has spent decades studying psychiatric disorders in New Guinea, reports never having seen a case of anorexia or bulimia there.[25] L. Bryce Boyer, an anthropologist with extensive experience with the Alaskan Eskimo, indicates that anorexia is non-existent among this population.[26] Even in those areas undergoing rapid industrialization, such as Malaysia, where anorexia is occasionally diagnosed, the relatively low incidence of the disorder, with cases apparently occurring only in the affluent Chinese population, has apparently remained stable.[27]

Why has the rising incidence of anorexia nervosa been a phenomenon specific to the Western, industrialized societies? A first and oft-cited reason is that of food supply and nutrition. It seems obvious that disorders of self-starvation are unlikely to occur in societies with limited food supply, particularly where famine is a real threat. The notion of anorexia nervosa developing among the starving millions of Ethiopia is virtually ludicrous. And yet this commonly made observation is probably not sufficient to account for the pattern. Fasting, for example, is an essential part of the religious tradition of Hinduism and is widely practiced in India; yet, it does not seem to translate into anorexia nervosa, which has been frequently likened psychologically to the stance of religious asceticism.[28] The thesis of this book is that much more is involved in the genesis of eating disorders than the simple fact of food abundance – specifically, a whole host of factors more typically associated with Western industrialization, including:

1 a changing female role, in which women find themselves struggling to strike a balance between new ideals of achievement and traditional female role expectations;
2 a preoccupation with appearance and body image that is associated with rise of mass fashion and consumerism; and
3 a culturally pervasive preoccupation with weight control and obesity, which seems particularly characteristic of the industrial societies.

It is this complex of cultural factors which provides the fertile cultural soil for the appearance of eating disorders.

How Common is Anorexia Nervosa?

Although the incidence of anorexia nervosa has clearly increased, it could be argued that it is still not a common disorder, particularly in its severe form. This is particularly the case if one looks at the incidence rates from the case register studies described earlier. For example, Theander estimated that the prevalence of anorexia in Sweden in the 1960s (when the number of cases had increased substantially) was only 0.45 cases per 100,000 population.[29] The surveys conducted in Monroe County, New York, the Camberwell district of London, and Northeast Scotland that were referred to earlier in this chapter indicate a prevalence on average of about one case per 100,000 population.[30] These figures hardly give the impression of an epidemic disorder.

However, figures based on the total population convey a misleading impression about the real prevalence. Anorexia, for example, rarely occurs in males, and it is typically not seen in children or females over the age of 30; and yet the rates for the general population include all of these groups. A more realistic idea of the prevalence would be obtained from looking at the "population at risk," that is females in their teens and early twenties. Among girls in English secondary schools, for example, the prevalence of anorexia falls between ½ and 1 percent (about 1 out of every 100) and comparable rates have been estimated for American college students.[31] These rates may again not seem high, but a more concrete estimate of the number of cases puts the matter into perspective. For example, the number of young women with clinical anorexia in England, using these prevalence rates, turns out to be about 10,000; whereas in the United States the total number would be around 120,000.[32] When we take into account the severity and potentially long-term effects of the disorder, and also the fact that it afflicts a segment of the population that is generally free of major health problems, then the problem indeed appears to be a significant and alarming one.

But there is another way in which surveys of medical cases underestimate the true prevalence of anorexia. Such studies count only treated cases of the disorder, a strategy that, while manageable from a research standpoint, fails to take into account untreated cases but also includes only the most severely afflicted. This probably results in significantly underestimating the true prevalence. A more meaningful method would be to look at an unselected sample of the population at risk and inquire into the prevalence of eating-disorder symptoms. This task was undertaken by Ingvar Nylander, a Swedish psychiatrist, who surveyed a large population of high-school students in Stockholm in the early 1970s about their dieting habits, body-image attitudes, and physical symptoms. Nylander found that over 50 percent of the girls had at some time "felt fat" and had undertaken rigorous dieting in order to counteract these feelings. Fully 10 percent of the 1,241 female students had experienced at least three symptoms of anorexia nervosa, such as chilliness, constipation, fatigue, amenorrhea, anxiety, and depression. Nylander concluded that "most cases of anorexia nervosa are incipient and/or mild and never come to medical attention but are spontaneously cured with increasing maturity." Her findings suggest that the symptoms of anorexia nervosa exist along a continuum of severity and that diagnosed cases represent the tip of the iceberg of a much larger number of subclinical disorders.[33]

The notion that eating disorders exist along a spectrum of severity and that many experience borderline forms of these conditions has also been confirmed in studies of college students in the United States and the United Kingdom, which consistently show that at least 5 percent of female students evidence a combination of pervasive concern with body image, feelings of fatness, stringent dieting, binge-eating, and purging behaviors.[34] The spectrum notion is not without its problems. It is probably true that a clinically significant disorder (meaning one requiring treatment) does not exist unless the symptoms have reached a certain level of severity and are associated with an underlying personality or emotional disorder. Nevertheless, the fact the symptoms of the eating disorders are experienced by a much larger number of individuals than those who become patients suggests that a spectrum concept does have some validity. And of course, the reason for a spectrum of borderline conditions is that the symptoms of anorexia are continuous with pervasive cultural pre-occupations among women with dieting, body image, and food control. The existence of a spectrum of anorexia disorders merging imperceptibly with the normal is one major justification for thinking of eating disorders as ethnic disorders.

Religion, Ethnicity, and Assimilation

Despite some earlier speculations that anorexia nervosa was more prevalent in the United States among Jewish or Catholic families, there are as yet no clearly established associations between particular religious backgrounds and the development of eating disorders.[35] Clinical experience suggests, however, that anorexics frequently come from religious backgrounds characterized by strict, puritanical attitudes, particularly towards female sexuality. A. H. Crisp, an English psychiatrist, suggests that one source of cultural stress that may be contributing to the increase in the incidence of anorexia nervosa is the clash between such a prohibitive religious background and the far more fluid and destructured contemporary mores regarding sexuality. Crisp cited one case of an Arab girl who felt forced to "choose" between the "liberated" morality of the con-temporary culture and the highly restrictive prohibitions of her own village Islamic tradition.[36] Such severely conflicting value choices are typical of the major identity crises that can precipitate anorexia, and provide a context for understanding the negation of the bodily self that is so central to the disorder.

No one has as of yet unearthed clear associations between the incidence of anorexia and particular ethnic groups, say, within the United States, at least within the Caucasian population. However, until recently, anorexia was exceedingly rare among blacks and uncommon in the American Hispanic population.[37] In the 1980s, though, the number of black patients in both America and in the UK begun to increase.[38] Presumably, a major reason for the earlier absence of anorexia among blacks had to do with differences in ideal body image. A study of teenagers in California in the 1960s, for example, indicated that black females had much less concern with dieting and the achievement of thinness than their white counterparts.[39] Most likely, the recent increase in anorexia and related disorders in black women represents the growing assimilation to the ideals and values of the dominant (Caucasian) culture, and not only those of body-image but also middle-class values of upward mobility and achievement. This was evident in a 1985 report of three female anorexics of Afro-Caribbean extraction, who were the first patients from this ethnic group to be seen at the eating-disorders clinic at Maudsley Hospital in London. While the families themselves were all working-class and did not appear to be upwardly mobile, in all three cases the patient was the one child among many who aspired to rise above the family's economic status. Two were outstanding students, and one developed her anorexia in typical fashion while studying for A-level exams.[40]

The impact of assimilation to Caucasian, middle-class culture, and the resulting increased vulnerability to eating disorders, is also evident in the first report of a case of anorexia in a Black African to appear in the literature.[41] The patient, from Zimbabwe, was throughout her childhood and adolescence an excellent student, always achieving the highest honors. When she later became a university student in England, she became depressed and lost interest in her studies, and was distressed by being surrounded by other female students who continued to excel and achieve. She felt particularly pressurized by the intense demands of an authoritarian, rigid, and demanding father. Her anorexia was triggered by a first sexual experience at the age of 20, following a period of turmoil regarding her studies.

It seems inevitable that when non-Western groups are rapidly exposed to Western culture, with its emphases on individuality, achievement, and consumerism, the vulnerability to disorders such as anorexia nervosa is likely to increase. Two studies provide some strongly suggestive evidence, both of which employed the Eating Attitudes Test, a scale that assesses attitudes towards eating, body shape, and dieting similar to those found in anorexic patients. In the first of these, a group of Egyptian students who had come to study in London was compared with college students at the University of Cairo. Not only did the Egyptian students in England have much higher scores than their counterparts who studied in their native land, but a further interview indicated that about 10 percent had diagnosable symptoms of bulimia.[42] In the second study, the eating attitudes of groups of white, mixed-race, and black students in private schools in Zimbabwe were assessed. All three groups showed a significant percentage of subjects who were preoccupied with thinness and manifested other "anorexic" attitudes, but they were most prevalent among the white subjects, intermediate among the mixed-race subjects, and least in evidence among the blacks. The author of this study cited the traditional emphasis of black Zimbabwean culture on fatness as an explanation of the relatively lower scores of the black subjects, but it was evident too that these attitudes were in the process of changing.[45]

Bulimia: An Epidemic Increase

If anorexia nervosa, once a rare disorder, has increased in prevalence to the point where it is considered not uncommon, the sudden ascendancy of bulimic syndromes since the mid-1970s seems nothing short of spectacular. The first epidemiological survey of bulimic symptoms, carried out at the State University of New York at Purchase in 1981, revealed that fully 13 percent of a group of summer-school registrants (87 percent of whom were female) met all the DSM-III criteria for bulimia – that is, they reported a history of binge-eating, followed by attempts at food restriction or vomiting.[44] This widely publicized finding was followed by a survey conducted in a shopping mall in suburban Boston, in which female shoppers were asked at random to complete a questionnaire geared towards eating and dieting practices. Of the 300 who returned the survey, 10 percent reported a history of bulimia, and almost 5 percent were actively bulimic at the time of the study. All of these were in their teens and twenties.[45] These findings, which were repeated in a number of different studies on college campuses, paralleled a sharp increase in the number of normal-weight bulimics seeking clinical help in the early 1980s in the United States.[46] Overall, these surveys suggested a prevalence of bulimia for the at-risk population of between 10 and 20 percent – clearly, a figure that in the words of one researcher suggested a "public health problem of alarming proportions."[47]

Impressive as these results appear, these surveys were not without their problems. For example, they all used questionnaires, which tend to be unreliable, and some of the questions (such as "Have you ever engaged in binge-eating?") could easily be interpreted differently by different individuals. Secondly, the criteria that identified a given respondent as bulimic were rather loose. For example, a subject who reported any history of binge-eating, coupled with dieting or occasional vomiting, would qualify as bulimic. These loose criteria for bulimia were actually those put forth by the American Psychiatric Association in 1980, and they have been the subject of considerable controversy.[48] A more stringent definition of bulimia would require that a subject engage in frequent binging and purging, and even better, that the subject be preoccupied with shape and body weight. The loose criteria for bulimia would tend to inflate the estimates of prevalence, which was probably the case for most of the surveys carried out in the early 1980s.

One study that attempted to correct for this problem, a survey of first-year students at the University of Minnesota in 1980, compared the rates of bulimia using loose criteria (any history of binging and purging) and the more stringent definition.[49] Using "loose" criteria, the prevalence turned out to be around 8 percent, a figure comparable to the other college surveys; however, when it was stipulated that a subject would qualify as bulimic only if she binged and purged on a weekly basis, the percentage dropped to 1 percent. In order to see whether the prevalence of bulimia was increasing, the same researchers carried out an identical survey of first-year students three years later.[50] Using the same stringent criteria, and adding the stipulation that the a bulimic subject should have an intense fear of becoming fat, they found that the percentage of students who were bulimic had jumped to 3 per cent. The figure of 2 or 3 percent probably represents a conservative estimate of the prevalence of bulimia among college students; but even using this estimate, one can extrapolate that between 1 and 2 million young women in the United States have a clinically significant problem with bulimia. Other studies have indicated that bulimia has also become a significant problem for high-school students, at least in the United States. One survey, conducted by Craig Johnson and his colleagues at a suburban high school in the Chicago area, indicated a prevalence of bulimia of around 4 percent, a figure comparable to the estimates for college students.[51]

The survey of University of Minnesota students is actually the only controlled study that demonstrates an increase in bulimia in a similar population over a short period of time. Unlike anorexia nervosa, we have virtually no information at all on the prevalence of bulimia in the 1960s or earlier. On the one hand, it is probably the case that some teenagers and young adults occasionally used vomiting as a means of weight control, particularly among weight-conscious groups such as dance students. On the other hand, a retrospective survey of women who had been college students in the 1950s and early 1960s indicates that such behavior was actually quite unusual.[52] The situation contrasts sharply with the present, in which virtually every college student knows at least one other who is bulimic. The full-blown syndrome of bulimia nervosa – binging and purging in a normal-weight subject who experiences body-image distortion and dreads fatness – is probably a uniquely contemporary phenomenon. It began to manifest itself in the 1970s, concurrent with the increase in anorexia nervosa, and was undoubtedly associated with the same set of factors that were associated with the increase in anorexia – namely, an increasing obsession with thinness and appearance and the pervasive confusion associated with a changing female role. Why the particular syndrome of bulimia at normal weight, as distinct from anorexia nervosa, became so prevalent is a question that is at present unanswered. But at the time of writing of this book, bulimia has become *au courant*, a final common pathway through which a variety of personality and emotional disturbances is expressed. Problems such as depression, which now often express themselves in the form of bulimia, undoubtedly existed two or three decades ago, but expressed themselves quite differently. Binging and purging, which has become an almost acceptable behavior on college campuses, has become a convenient "hook" on which to "hang" a variety of psychological problems. And as I pointed out in the first chapter, this is one of the central characteristics of an ethnic disorder.

Bulimia has been described as a "hidden" epidemic, in that only a relatively small number of sufferers come to the attention of clinical authorities, and, unlike anorexia nervosa, the symptom can be masked by an apparent normality. Bulimic behavior, particularly purging, is typically subjectively felt to be shameful, and only when a sufferer feels totally out of control will they seek some sort of professional help. Thus, most of the bulimics identified in the foregoing studies had never received treatment for their disorder. Aggressive attempts at identifying symptoms, on the other hand, typically reveal substantial numbers of symptomatic individuals, as has been the case for a survey of a general family medical practice at the University of Iowa,[53] a family-planning clinic in Oxford,[54] and a group of psychiatric inpatients in Scotland.[55] In the latter study, 10 percent of a randomly selected group of psychiatric patients were revealed to have a previously undetected, clinically significant eating disorder.

Like anorexia nervosa, the incidence of bulimia has increased throughout the Western world, and has been described not only in North America, but in England,[56] France,[57] Germany,[58] and Japan.[59] As is the case for anorexia nervosa, we lack the data to make precise national comparisons in prevalence. Nevertheless, it is this author's impression, which is not firmly grounded in data, that the prevalence of bulimia is higher in the United States than it is in other countries, although the formal data that corroborate this are only available from the UK. If this is in fact the case, then the question immediately comes to mind as to why. Perhaps, for example, the high prevalence in the United States relates to a long-standing cultural tradition of overeating, which reaches back to the early nineteenth century.[60] Perhaps, also, it may have something to do with the high prevalence of morbid obesity in the United States, a fact that may be intimately connected with bulimia. And finally, it may be that the desocialization of contemporary eating patterns – fast food, the decline of family and group eating, the rise of "snacking" or "grazing" eating styles – has gone further in the United States than elsewhere. Additional cross-cultural data could illuminate these issues.

The Question of Social Class

Anorexia nervosa was traditionally thought of as a disorder of the affluent – a "rich girl's" syndrome. Bruch, for example, reported in her 1973 book that a disproportionate number of patients came from families of the super-rich: almost all others were from middle-class homes, and the few that were from working-class families were driven by the ethic of achievement and upward mobility.[61] Similar findings were reported by Theander in Sweden, who also found that the fathers of anorexics tended to be involved in professions that made them the "guardians of traditional values:" judges, headmasters, and wealthy industrialists.[62] In an English series, 77 percent of the patients were from the upper social classes, and 23 from the middle class. The fathers' professions included doctors, teachers, barristers, artists, businessmen, architects, stockbrokers, and accountants.[63] One might argue that these findings reflect the fact that only the affluent can afford psychiatric care, or to seek out professionals with strong reputations. But a study in Norway found that when anorexic patients treated at various centers were compared with patients with five other types of "psychosomatic disorder" – including asthma, colitis, and stomach ulcers – only the anorexic patients were overrepresented in the upper socioeconomic levels.[64]

During the 1970s, though, as the incidence of anorexia increased, the social-class distribution became less skewed, with an increasing number of patients coming from the middle and lower-middle classes.[65] The lowest social classes, though, continued to spawn few anorexics. The association of anorexia with middle- or upper-class status has often been explained, somewhat facilely, by invoking such factors as plentiful food and material abundance – as if, somehow, this would explain why a person would relentlessly starve themselves. What is much more likely is that the skewed class distribution represents the conflicting impact of middle-class values on females, particularly in those families who simultaneously place a great emphasis on achievement but also convey ambivalent messages about female independence (see chapter 4).

Such factors probably also partly explain why eating disorders have become most prolific on college campuses, where these collisions in value systems are most acutely felt. In the United States, eating disorders have become one of the most distressing health problems in the universities, particularly in the most competitive settings. By the mid-1980s, many college campuses had begun to institute counseling or support programs for students with eating disorders, and yet the consensus seems to be that the problem is still far from being adequately addressed. Attention to the problem seems to have been somewhat attenuated by the AIDS epidemic, which is understandable in terms of the deadly implications of the latter disease. It has also become known that eating disorders, particularly bulimic syndromes, have become relatively common among women at the most prestigious professional schools, particularly at medical schools.[66]

Clinical experience suggests that there is a substantial prevalence of bulimic disorders among career women, particularly those in high-status occupations or competitive professional settings.[67] As yet, there is no systematic documentation of the prevalence of eating disorders among professional women, but the existence of the problem is hardly in doubt. Career women, particularly those in formerly male-dominated professions, are under particularly intense pressure to maintain a façade of perfection and competence. In a way, these external demands play right into the false-self psychology of bulimia, which typically involves a split between a façade of normalcy, independence, and super-performance and an underlying sense of deprivation, dependency, and neediness. Professional women, para-doxically, are among the most intensely weight conscious, and therefore they are particularly prone to equate thinness with competitiveness and achievement. Bulimia among such individuals is a contemporary "stress syndrome," parallel in many ways to closet alcoholism or substance abuse. These bulimics are typically highly competent and comfortable when involved with their work: their symptoms manifest themselves at home at night, reflecting "disturbed patterns of solitude."[68]

It should not be thought, though, the bulimia is a symptom restricted to the high-achieving high-school student, to the distressed collegian, or to the professional or managerial woman. Bulimia is a symptom that cuts more along social-class lines than anorexia, and has become a more ubiquitous expression for a whole host of psychological problems. It can, in one and the same individual, be one of a battery of addictive or self-destructive symptoms, which is frequently "picked up" by a woman who is already alcoholic, sexually compulsive, or drawn to self-destructive relationships. With these other symptomatic behaviors, it is sometimes interchangeable, waxing and waning along with the intensification of the others. As one clinician has pointed out, bulimia, as compared with anorexia, is more "easily learned." But once acquired, it does tend to take on, so to speak, a life of its own.

Eating Disorders in Societal Perspective

When this writer undertook a clinical internship at the end of the 1960s at a well-known medical-psychiatric center in New York City, my first patient was a young woman who carried a diagnosis of anorexia nervosa. I was told by my supervising psychologist that I was very fortunate to have the opportunity to work with such a patient, as anorexia nervosa was a very uncommon condition and the hospital at which I was training happened to be one of the few centers which had a tradition of treating the disorder. He suggested that it would be to my benefit to learn as much as possible from my work with this patient, as it was unlikely, particularly if I eventually worked in an outpatient setting, that I would ever encounter more than a few (if any) such cases again.

It is interesting to contrast the supervisor's observations, which were probably an accurate reflection of the times, with the status of eating disorders in the late 1980s – less than 20 years later. In the United States, virtually every major psychiatric teaching hospital treats and houses some patients with anorexia or bulimia. Inpatient units specifically designed for the treatment of eating disorders have multiplied, and yet experience suggests that the need for services far outstrips the supply, particularly for those without financial resources or insurance coverage. Parallel developments have occurred in outpatient settings. Psychotherapists with special interests in the treatment of eating disorders have multiplied, as is evident from a casual perusal of the telephone listings for psychotherapists in any major American city. In contrast to the situation in the 1960s, it would be rare indeed for a contemporary psychotherapist, particularly one who sees adolescents or young adults, not to have encountered at least some patients with anorexia or bulimia. Some have commented, perhaps with justifiable skepticism, that eating disorders have become a growth industry for the helping professions. Indeed, the quality of professional services, as well as the experience of those presenting themselves as experts, varies enormously; and unfortunately, as in most areas of psychotherapy, the public has little to go on in evaluating the quality of services. One fact is certain, however; the tremendous increase in professional services and interest is obviously a response to a vastly increased demand.

The one environment in which eating disorders are most in evidence is the college campus. College students are not only at the age and stage of development of greatest risk for the development of eating disorders, but a number of features of the social milieu of contemporary college life make it a virtual breeding ground of anorexic and bulimic symptoms, particularly for those who are already vulnerable.[69] These include a fluid and unstructured environment, social and academic competition, a concern with appearance and physical attractiveness, a destructured eating environment in which food binging and weight gain are commonplace, and the contradictory pressures regarding achievement and sexuality that are specifically felt by contemporary female collegians. That eating disorders represent a major social and health problem on college campuses is now widely recognized.[70] A survey conducted in the late 1980s revealed that at least 290 colleges in the United States incorporated specific services within their counseling programs for students with eating disorders. Of these, 19 had developed specific comprehensive programs for the treatment of eating disorders alone, including individual and group psychotherapy, nutritional counseling, medical evaluation, and self-help, support groups usually conducted by a student who had recovered from an eating disorder. The author of this survey concluded that even on the campuses of small colleges, the level of awareness of eating disorders was quite high.[71] This situation contrasts dramatically with that as recently as the 1960s, in which the presence of eating disorders was virtually non-existent.

The emergence of lay organizations devoted to providing support to patients and families and information to the community at large is a phenomenon deserving of attention in its own right. These organizations, several of which were mentioned in the first chapter of this book, are commonly started by a recovered patient or family member in concert with interested professionals. They typically serve multiple functions, from the sponsorship of support groups to political advocacy and community education. The oldest such organization in the United States, the National Association of Anorexia Nervosa and Associated Disorders, based in Highland Park, Illinois, provides written guidelines to those who wish to start support groups. It currently sponsors over 400 support groups in the United States alone, and has also helped to form groups in countries as diverse as West Germany, Ghana, and Saudi Arabia.[72] Similarly, the American Anorexia Nervosa Association in Teaneck, New Jersey, sponsors about 20 chapters throughout the Eastern seabord, and publishes an informative newsletter. Another group, the National Anorexic Aid Society in Colombus, Ohio, conducts an excellent annual conference on the treatment of eating disorders, which draws a large audience from all over the United States. The phenomenon of lay organizations and support groups is a grass-roots movement that reflects the pervasiveness of the problems of anorexia and bulimia.

From a wider vantage point, the rise in eating disorders can be seen as one instance of a more general spectrum of problems that revolve around the regulation of "appetite", that have become prolific in the advanced industrial societies.[73] This symptomatological style, which has been identified (probably inadequately) with such terms as "addictive" or "compulsive," perhaps represents a general pattern of difficulties in self-regulation experienced in societies characterized by an increasing degree of social fragmentation, by consumerism, and by the management and manipulation of desire. The proliferation of self-help groups that struggle to come to terms with problems of drinking, spending, sexuality, and eating represents an effort to come to grips with a social milieu in which people experience an increasing loss of control. Aside from the specific problems of female identity, shape, and body weight that the eating disorders represent, they must also be situated in this broader cultural context.

4

A Changing Female Identity

> My own observations suggest that the changing status of (and expectations) for women plays a role [in the increase in anorexia nervosa]. Girls whose early upbringing has prepared them to become "clinging-vine" wives suddenly are expected at adolescence to prove themselves as women of achievement. This seems to create severe personal self-doubt and basic uncertainty. In their submissive way, they "choose" the fashionable dictum to be slim as a way of proving themselves of deserving respect.[1]

The overwhelming majority of people who develop problems with anorexia and bulimia – regardless of nationality or social class – are female. This simple fact, which is acknowledged by virtually all researchers and clinicians, no matter what their particular theoretical persuasion, is of critical importance in a sociocultural understanding of why these problems have become an epidemic in recent times. And despite its virtually universal acknowledgment, its theoretical significance has yet to be fully appreciated.

At the outset, it is important to acknowledge the possibility that such a lopsided sex ratio may have something to do with biological differences between the sexes. There are a number of possibilities that suggest themselves. For one thing, laboratory studies show that female animals are more able to withstand starvation (that is, they survive longer) than males.[2] Such differential tolerance may have evolutionary significance. In times of food scarcity, the female's ability to tolerate starvation may have particular adaptive value in light of the female role in species propagation. This of course does not account for anorexia nervosa, which occurs under conditions of relative affluence, but it makes it more understandable why females are more likely to draw upon self-starvation as a means of coping with stress. A second possible link has to do with the generally higher ratio of fat to lean tissue in females relative to males, a fact that also can be interpreted from the standpoint of evolution. Again, in periods of famine or food scarcity, it would have been advantageous to females to have reserve stores of fat tissue in order to sustain pregnancy and lactation.[3] In human cultures that emphasize the importance of thinness in women, females may experience more stress in efforts at dieting, given their greater biological propensity towards adiposity. A third possibility has to do with the relative complexity of female pubertal development, from the standpoint of hormonal functions and the intricacy of related brain mechanisms. Such differential complexity may make the pubertal process more susceptible to disruption under stress, as in anorexia nervosa.[4] And finally, it is possible that females are more vulnerable to endogenous depression, which may have some bearing on the proposed linkage of some cases of bulimia to depression.[5]

Despite the possible role of biological factors in predisposing women to developing eating disorders, it seems virtually impossible to account for the specific psychological features of these conditions without taking into account social and cultural influences. For example, anorexic patients have an enormous drive to be thin and an equally intense fear of becoming fat. It is difficult to understand the centrality of these concerns without taking into account the social and cultural pressures on women to achieve thinness, as well as the specific stigma, peculiar to Western societies, attached to fat women. As we shall see in the following two chapters, these pressures have increased significantly throughout the twentieth century, and the particular meanings that they have for women are centrally involved in understanding the eating-disorders epidemic. But in addition, there are more subtle features of the psychology of eating disorders that demand an interpretation in social terms. These revolve around the nearly universal concerns of eating-disordered patients with issues of autonomy, self-esteem, achievement, and control. And this spectrum of psychological issues can be broadly understood as relating to the larger problem of the development of psychosocial identity.

The concept of identity is a difficult one, but it is critical in understanding the central problems confronted by women with eating disorders. It has received its most elaborate formulation in the writings of Erik Erikson.[6] Erikson suggests that the notion of identity relates to the individual's experience of self-cohesion, or, as he puts it, the sense of continuity and sameness in time. The development of a cohesive or "viable" identity depends on many individual and social factors, but among the most important is the individual's ability to "synthesize" or bring together the divergent and conflicting aspects of his or her social experience." The development of identity is a dynamic process, which unfolds throughout a person's life, and is influenced by a host of factors – historical and sociological conditions, the particularities of family experiences, biological predispositions, and the accidents of development. However, the most critical period for the formation of an identity is during adolescence, the period in which the individual must put together the foundations of the self laid down in childhood experience with the new demands and challenges posed by the personal and social experiences of that period. The process of identity formation is particularly susceptible to disruption by radical changes in social roles or cultural expectations. This is one reason why individuals suddenly exposed to a radically different culture – say, in a situation of migration – seem particularly vulnerable to psychological problems.[7] But it also suggests that even within the same culture, a particular group which is exposed to dramatic changes in cultural expectations – say, through a sudden change in social role – will also be highly susceptible to epidemic symptoms of identity confusion.[8]

In this chapter, I wish to apply this latter notion to an understanding of the epidemic increase in eating disorders. More specifically, I want to develop the notion that eating disorders are the extreme expression of radically altered social expectations on women that have emerged on a mass scale since about mid-century, but particularly since the 1960s. Over a relatively short period of time, young women have encountered a new set of pressures, demanding an orientation towards achievement, competitiveness, and independence, a set of values that conflict sharply with traditional Western definitions of the female role. In a period of increased opportunities but also intensified pressures, many have found it difficult to synthesize a "viable" or "workable" identity, and suffer inwardly from a sense of fragmentation, confusion, and self-doubt.[9] What I am proposing here is that the central psychological problems experienced by patients with eating disorders, that center on issues of self-esteem, autonomy, and achievement, are a magnified reflection of much more pervasive conflicts in the wider culture about the female role. The young woman with an eating disorder therefore is the unwitting carrier of pervasive cultural crisis.

From the standpoint of the theoretical framework of this book, the person who develops an ethnic disorder, as Devereux suggested, suffers from psychological conflicts that are pervasive in the culture, but are experienced by the patient in a particularly acute form. The resulting anxiety, depression, or confusion are sufficiently severe for the person to develop symptoms, which serve as defenses against underlying psychological distress. The situation for anorexia is parallel to that of hysteria in the late nineteenth century, which also was an expression of confusion and contradictory prescriptions in the female role.[10] The nature of the conflicts experienced by hysterical patients, however, was quite different, and had to do with the specific historical situation of women at that time. They revolved around issues of strict sexual repression, as well as blanket restrictions on female education and participation in public life. Nevertheless, the current epidemic of eating disorders is very much parallel to the wave of conversion hysteria that seemed to sweep over Europe and America in the nineteenth century. Both are expressions, appropriate to their own times, of the dilemmas of female identity, in a cultural climate in which the female role is ambiguously defined and still limited by institutionalized male control.

Female Identity in Anorexia Nervosa

So central are issues of female identity in anorexia nervosa that it is difficult to see why more has not been made of this issue in previous formulations. Most cultural interpretations of anorexia have stressed the fashion of female slenderness, which is undoubtedly of central importance in understanding the eating disorders.[11] But few have addressed the more complex issue of *why* the emphasis on thinness is so important to contemporary women, and particularly to those who develop eating disorders. More detailed study of the psychological conflicts that lead certain women to develop anorexia lead centrally to the underlying issues of identity and self-worth that lead the single-minded pursuit of thinness to be "chosen" as the principal symptom.

A central feature of anorexic patients emphasized by Hilde Bruch is that these are girls or women who grow up with a profound sense of ineffectiveness, a sense of deficiency in their ability to influence their environment and determine their own fate.[12] This lacuna in the sense of the self is a consequence of growing up in a family which places intense emphasis on achievement and performance, but simultaneously deprives the child of opportunities for self-initiated behavior or for the development of her own unique possibilities. When such a child becomes an adolescent, therefore, she is not well equipped to cope with the typical developmental demands of that period, which require a greater degree of independent functioning and autonomous choice. The events that typically trigger the onset of anorexic dieting are typically just those experiences that challenge the adolescent's sense of independence and power: the first heterosexual relationship, the loss of a friendship, an illness or death of a valued family member, or moving away from home.[13] For those whose sense of autonomy is deficient, these "normal" developmental stresses precipitate a crisis in self-confidence. Dieting and weight loss, which not only bring about positive comments from others but also give the individual an experience of power that she has never before known, become quickly reinforced and then entrenched as a source of pride and perhaps even superiority.

This description of the typical developmental course of anorexia nervosa is now widely accepted, and is well borne out by clinical experience. What is usually not stated is the extent to which the characteristic experiences and problems of anorexic patients mirror and magnify common problems of female identity, problems that are typically encountered in especially acute form during adolescence. For the intense sense of ineffectiveness and exclusive focus on external expectations is the extreme version of a common developmental pattern among girls in Western societies. Studies of normal female development, which have a certain degree of cross-cultural consistency, show that despite changes in public ideology about sex roles, girls are still socialized to be pleasers and are given far less encouragement than boys to develop self-initiated and autonomous behaviors.[14] Bruch's suggestion that the mothers of anorexic patients fail to respond to their daughter's self-initiated activities and signals actually reflects a more general pattern, established by developmental research, of providing girls with significantly less "response-contingent stimulation" than is typically given to boys.[15] The orientation towards pleasing others and the intense sensitivity and responsiveness to external demands is of course consistent with girls' socialization to be nurturers, a pattern which persists, despite the changes brought about by feminism. Jean Baker Miller, in her pioneering book about female identity, suggests that women's self-worth is still determined by the requirement to help and assist others, a project that requires the subordination of one's own needs to the needs and expectations of another.[16] Such a formulation is directly applicable to the core experiences of those who develop anorexia nervosa, although the latter is an extreme version of the norm.

One consequence of these patterns of socialization is that by the time a girl reaches adolescence, she is often affected by feelings of powerlessness and dependency, feelings that make it very difficult to break away from the family and establish her own life. This is especially true for anorexic patients, and it provides a direct explanation of why the disorder typically erupts in adolescence. The experiences that typically trigger anorexic dieting, experiences of loss or separation (real or anticipated), are those that present particular challenges to autonomous functioning. To the pre-anorexic teenager, whose self-esteem is highly vulnerable and sense of autonomy very fragile, such experiences can come as a crushing blow. Going on a diet, and ultimately a starvation diet, becomes a way of achieving a sense of power and independence for a person who has been painfully confronted with his or her own powerlessness. In a culture that values dieting and thinness, such a "solution" seems readily understandable in terms of the positive social response that it typically arouses (at least initially). But also, radical dieting is also powerfully reinforcing for a person whose sense of power and self-control has been so compromised.

For anorexics, another factor typically comes into play, one that is at once familial and social: the intense pressure to achieve. The families of anorexics typically place an enormous value on achievement and performance. Although they are not necessarily "affluent," virtually all are driven by middle-class values of upward mobility, performance, and the work ethic.[17] Many have a history of economic insecurity and have advanced significantly beyond the economic status of their parents. There is often a sense of anxiety in these families about maintaining their hard-won economic and social status, a concern that falls particularly heavily on the shoulders of the daughter who becomes anorexic. In addition, some studies show that in many of the families of anorexics, there has been a history of male failure or inadequacy, something that may only become apparent if one looks at the grandparent generation.[18] In any case, there is often a mythical notion in these families that women must be strong in order to compensate for perceived male inadequacies. These anxieties are not explicitly articulated, but the young woman who develops anorexia often feels them very acutely.

It is extremely important to understand that because of their external focus and pleasing orientation, anorexics feel that their achievements in school or in athletics are a performance *for others*, not a proof to themselves of their own worthiness. In fact, one of the paradoxes of anorexia nervosa is how worthless these young women feel, despite what is often a high degree of success from an external standpoint. This is again not a unique experience, but one that is very characteristic for contemporary women. Jean Baker Miller suggests that women often get caught in a cycle of pleasing and depletion, of "doing good and feeling bad."[19] This is the consequence of an identity that is based on pleasing and supporting others, rather than behaving according to one's own needs and self-chosen goals. The entire complex of externally oriented achievement and pleasing behavior has been idealized in popular culture in the imagery of the "superwoman," the woman who "has it all" and pleases a largely masculine audience with her feminine charm and worldly accomplishments. This modernized version of the traditional notion of the "good girl" has been widely and justifiably attacked by feminists as a perversion of the ideals of female equality. Because of their own developmental experiences, anorexics seem particularly vulnerable to internalizing this distorted ideology. As Bruch pointed out, many anorexics experience the ideology of liberation as one more external demand for perfection that they feel compelled to live up to: "growing girls can experience this liberation as a demand and feel that they *have* to do something outstanding . . . Many of my patients have expressed the feeling . . . that there were too many choices and they had been afraid of not choosing correctly."[20]

While not always explicit, anorexics sometimes openly articulate their experiences in terms of confusions about gender role and female identity. Many grow up with a secret though powerful fantasy about being a boy – a "tall, long-legged prince," as one patient put it – a dream which, as Bruch suggests, it typically shattered by the experience of puberty.[21] In some cases this fantasy may represent a wish to be the male child that the father either never had or was disappointed with, but in others it may be a yearning for the power that boys are perceived to have and the anorexic feels so acutely that she lacks. For some anorexics, the slenderness and loss of curves that result from dieting represent a triumphant transformation of the female figure into that of preadolescent boy. Casky, in an interesting treatment of these issues, suggests that the anorexic seeks an identification with an ideal of asensual intellectuality, the mythical image of the *puer*, an image projected onto her father, whose own frequent orientation towards and emphasis on intellectual achievement has had a powerful impact on his anorexic daughter.[22] Some anorexics are quite explicit about their resentment of suffering the social disadvantages of being female. One of Bruch's patients, Fawn, commented that "it wasn't fair as a little girl. There wasn't any way of winning. You were wrong before you started."[23] And in a wry comment on her feelings about being out of step with new standards of female assertiveness, another patient, Annette, suggested that "it would have been worse [if I had been a boy – ed.], because I would have the same ghastly peace-minded temperament and that is unacceptable in boys. At least in girls it used to be acceptable, but now it is a culturally unacceptable way of behavior. But I continue to behave like that."[24] Annette, in fact, felt that her accomplishments in school were strangely alien to her, as if they were really those of a man – and the purpose of which had been to please her father.

This desire to escape womanhood and to achieve a certain type of masculine ideal – one of intellectuality and spiritual purity – can be understood on one level in terms of familial dynamics. Many anorexics feel particularly bound by their father's expectations, and seek to disengage themselves from their own bodily feelings of femaleness – an effort that is frequently reinforced by a disturbance in their emotional connection to their mothers. However, equally important is the wider social context of these feelings. In an age in which women are thrust into a situation in which they must prove their worth through work and intellectual accomplishment, many women feel that they must prove themselves the equal of men, and for some this may mean disengaging oneself from their own femaleness, which has undergone a cultural devaluation. Anorexics carry out this purge of femaleness in a particularly radical and concrete fashion. The cultural ideal of female thinness, to which anorexics aspire to the extreme, may itself have something to do with the aspirations of women to equal power with men, an idea that will be explored further in the next chapter.

Of particular interest is the much-discussed relationship of anorexic patients with their mothers. The mother–daughter bond in these families tends to be unusually intense, and it is often a consequence of the mother's powerful identification with her daughter as a compensation for a disappointment in her relationship with her husband – a disappointment which typically is unarticulated in the service of preserving "family harmony." The mothers of anorexics have been too frequently blamed in the past for their daughter's illness, partly as a result of long psychiatric (particularly psychoanalytic) tradition of "mother-bashing." While it is true that the mother's intense closeness and control often blocks the daughter's efforts to achieve autonomy, the social context of the mother's situation is typically not taken into account. The mothers of anorexics are, as Bruch suggested, typically talented women who sacrificed their own ambitions and careers in the service of their families. Many gave up their careers when their first child was born.[25] In effect, these were the social expectations of women from an earlier, "pre-liberated" generation. Their resulting depression and clinging to their daughters can therefore be understood not only as an individual flaw, but rather as a product of their own social circumstances and experience. What makes the whole situation particularly explosive is that in the environment of the 1970s and 1980s, adolescent girls are everywhere surrounded by an ideology of independence, an ideology that can often induce its own feelings of guilt and inadequacy for not being able to "break away." This poses a particularly painful dilemma for the girl who becomes anorexic, who tends to feel a poignant sense of responsibility for her mother's well-being.

While it is not always the central issue, sexuality frequently plays an important role in the development of anorexia nervosa. The issue of sexuality was probably overemphasized in earlier psychoanalytic formulations about anorexia, in which the resistance to food was seen invariably to represent a symbolic fear of oral impregnation.[26] However, for a number of anorexics, unwanted or problematic sexual experiences trigger the crisis in self-confidence that precipitates severely restrictive dieting. In some instances, the first sexual experience, while voluntary, is experienced as "disgusting" or "painful," and further lowers an already vulnerable sense of self-esteem.[27] In a certain number of cases, the experience is a more drastic instance of sexual assault or abuse. In one of the most accessible autobiographies of anorexia, Aimee Liu opens her story with an account of a preadolescent rape by two boys that took place during a holiday family visit. While Liu does not explicitly tie this experience to the development of her anorexia a few years later, it is clear that this experience of violation and bodily vulnerability is implicated in her efforts to rid her body of its emerging signs of femaleness.[28] Liu's experience is not an isolated one, as clinical experience suggests an extraordinarily high rate of sexual abuse among women with eating disorders, a phenomenon whose significance is just beginning to be appreciated.

Theoretically, the role of sexuality in the development of anorexia nervosa has been emphasized by the English psychiatrist Arthur H. Crisp.[29] Crisp underscores the important links between female pubertal development and the development of body fat. It has been well established that the emergence of the menstrual cycle is critically connected to the development of a certain amount of body fat (the so-called "critical fat threshold").[30] In addition, experientially and socially, the development of secondary sexual characteristics, in the form of curves, is also dependent on the development of a certain degree of fatness. Thus, biologically, experientially, and socially, fatness in females is critically connected with the emergence of sexuality in adolescence. The widespread preoccupation of female teenagers with curbing bodily shape and appetite is critically connected with the self-regulation of sexual desires, in an environment in which traditional middle-class sexual morality has unravelled. Anorexia, which Crisp suggests commonly emerges from a family background of puritanical sexual morality and anxiety about unrestrained female sexuality, represents among other things a fearful regression to a prepubertal state, in which the presence of disturbing sexual feelings has been effectively banished.

From a cultural standpoint, sexuality is an important component of the wider transformation of female identity. The general relaxation of sexual constraints that took shape in the 1960s probably have had a more powerful impact on females than on males, for whom adolescent sexual activity was formerly tolerated and perhaps even acceptable. Studies of adolescent sexual behavior in the late 1970s and early 1980s, while still few, indicate that female adolescents have in general become more active sexually and at an earlier age, and in fact differ little in their sexual experience from males.[31] Meanwhile, the cultural climate regarding sexuality has changed radically in the direction of permissiveness – and exploitation – since the 1960s. The commercial exploitation of the new atmosphere of sexual openness, including soap-opera titillations, sexualized preadolescent fashion models, and pornography, has not been pretty. In this atmosphere, it is not surprising that some vulnerable adolescent females have developed a symptom – anorexia – that represents a radical avoidance and withdrawal from the implications of sexuality. It is of considerable interest that during the same period in which eating disorders have increased, teenage pregnancy has become a problem of growing concern in Western societies, particularly in the USA. As Brumberg has suggested, both anorexia nervosa and teenage pregnancy may represent two sides of the same coin, the problem of control of female sexuality in an environment in which traditional constraints and standards have crumbled.[32] And these two apparently opposite responses to the dilemma of sexual control may be tied in turn to differences in socioeconomic status, with teen pregnancy representing a hyperaffirmation of sexuality by a deprived adolescent who has no other route to a sense of power, while anorexia represents its negation in the service of newly reinforced cultural ideals of female achievement.

imia: The Façade of Perfection and the Secret Self

e dynamics of bulimia, too, seem inextricably bound up with sex-
ıᴄⅈe issues. An early attempt to understand bulimics from this
standpoint was a 1976 paper by Boskind-Lodahl, which attempted an
explicitly feminist interpretation of both anorexia nervosa and
bulimia.[33] Her analysis was based on her observations on a large
number of bulimic college students whom she had seen at the Cornell
University student health center. One of her aims in writing the paper
was a critique of the earlier psychoanalytic formulations, which
suggested that all women with eating disorders are symbolically
"rejecting femininity" or "refusing womanhood." In contrast, Boskind-
Lodahl asserted that precisely the opposite is true. Rather than
rejecting the female role, bulimics (or bulimarexics, as she called
them) excessively conform to feminine sterotypes. She described her
subjects as excessively pleasing, unassertive, and particularly sensitive
to criticism or rejection by men. Their striving for thinness and
preoccupation with their appearance represents an exaggeration,
rather than a rejection, of a cultural female norm. While Boskind-
Lodahl's descriptions of bulimics ring true to clinical experience, her
critique of the traditional psychoanalytic formulations was somewhat
misplaced, since these interpretations were about anorexia nervosa,
not the bulimic syndrome. With respect to anorexia, the notion of the
"rejection of femininity" has much greater applicability.

It is my experience, as well as that of others, that most bulimics
have experienced some form of significant emotional deprivation in
their early life.[34] For some, an illness in a parent, or a problem with
depression or alcoholism, leads to the temporary (or chronic) absence
or unavailability of a parental figure. In other cases, the parents are in
open conflict (much more commonly than is the case in anorexia),
sometimes eventuating in a separation or divorce.[35] In many
instances, the chronic preoccupation of the parents with external or
interpersonal problems results in the child's emotional needs being
ignored. Whatever the cause, the child typically early on turns to food
as a means of solace, of filling the void left by parental inattentiveness
or implicit abandonment. On the surface, however, she typically
cultivates a positive façade, an appearance that she "can manage."
Underneath, though, she feels needy, childlike, and dependent,
feelings of which she is deeply ashamed. Under no circumstances
does she permit herself to reveal her primitive feelings of abandonment,

sadness, and rage. These are discharged in episodes of binging and purging.

When compared with anorexics, bulimics typically maintain a strong conscious identification with the traditional female sex role. Unlike anorexics, a significant number of whom are sexually avoidant and inexperienced, most bulimics have a history of active sexual involvement and are oriented to pleasing males. Bulimics tend to have had an intensely ambivalent relationship with their fathers. Often, the father has been admired as a role model, and has set high standards of intellectual or professional achievement for his daughter.[36] Typically, though, the father has been extraordinarily critical, and in some instances overtly abusive; in any case, he continues to be for the bulimic a figure of mystery and fascination. She remains enormously sensitive to male criticism and rejection, and her relationships with men are often turbulent as a result. Nevertheless, for the bulimic the father is a powerful identification figure. In contrast with anorexics, who typically are deeply enmeshed with their mothers, bulimics typically attempt to distance themselves from their mothers, whom they typically perceive as weak and powerless. As Wooley and Wooley point out, in a period of changing sex-roles in which women increasingly identify with ideals of mobility and power, bulimics reject what they see as their mother's traditionalism and ineffectuality; it is their father's power that they admire and idealize.[37] For bulimics, these attitudes are intimately connected with their ideas about thinness and fatness: thinness is associated with masculine power, fatness with feminine weakness.

Like anorexics, bulimics are unable to work out a satisfactory solution to the problem of identity. They are caught in the dilemma of how to integrate ambition and a need to be powerful with an identity based on pleasing, compliance, and unassertiveness. Their resolution of the problem of identity is a deep split within the self, which entails a façade of perfection, pleasing, and competence, on the one hand, and a secret self that both expresses and binds "messy" feelings of neediness, rage, and helplessness. Thinness is for them the ideal which brings together the conflicting strands of a new female identity, one which is on the one hand powerful, competent, and in control, but on the other is nurturing, submissive, and pleasing to men. Bulimics tend to be extraordinarily vulnerable to external influences, and given their intense concern with their appearance, fashion models and media figures typically have a powerful impact on the standards that they feel they must live up to.

As I suggested earlier, bulimia is a common stress symptom among college-age or working woman, a self-destructive method of working out feelings of loneliness, anxiety, depression, or other discomfiting emotions. The contemporary college campus is an environment in which many of the new contradictory pressures confronting females seem to converge.[38] Intense academic pressures, a fluid and unstructured eating environment, the challenges of sexual relationships in an environment in which the possibility of sexual exploitation is increasingly a matter of concern, all contribute to a situation that can be overwhelming for those who are vulnerable. Of particular significance for many women who develop bulimia is their relationships with men. Many contemporary female college students (as well as males) find heterosexual relationships difficult, for a number of interrelated reasons.[39] One of the most important of these is male anxiety in response to female ambition and academic or professional competitiveness. Bulimics are particularly vulnerable to these reactions, given their intense needs to be accepted as feminine and their inordinate need to please men. As a result, they will be more likely than most to suppress their own individual needs and ambitions in the service of maintaining acceptance. Associated feelings of anger and resentment tend to be taken out on the self in the form of binging and purging episodes. In my experience, bulimic women are especially sensitive to the subtle (and not-so-subtle) "put-downs" of females by men, particularly in situations associated with competitiveness or assertion. The relatively high prevalence of bulimia in environments that are bastions of male power – such as medical schools, or the higher levels of the corporate world – is probably understandable in terms of the ambiguities confronting women in these situations.[40] The maintenance of thinness, as well as a façade of perfection, competence, and control, serves to establish an external adaptation to the demands of an environment in which one must compete and not show the softer, more vulnerable side of one's femininity. Secret rituals with food become the only avenue of expression of these carefully hidden needs and feelings.

Cultural Confusion about the Female Role

It has been the main point of this chapter to argue that the transition to a new female identity has left many young women vulnerable to developing eating disorders. The shifts in contemporary Western societies to a new emphasis on female achievement and performance represents a sharp reversal from previous role definitions that emphasized compliance, deference, and unassertiveness. A new sexual ethos, in the direction of greater permissiveness and a loosening of traditional controls, has brought new problems along with it, including an increased vulnerability to exploitation and anxieties among those from conservative or traditional backgrounds. It is not my intention to argue that these changes in and of themselves are bad; this is not a conservative polemic for returning women to the kitchen, the nursery, or the 'MRS' degree. It is just that in a period of such radical cultural transition, some young women are vulnerable to becoming caught in the uncertainties and ambiguities of a drastically altered set of expectations. Most female college students, even those who are not having difficulties with food or weight control, will quietly assert that they themselves feel vulnerable to the same problems experienced in acute form by those who develop eating disorders.

I would like the conclude this chapter with mention of two additional problems that make the attainment of female identity in the present environment difficult. The first is that the definition of the new ideal social role (and psychological identity) for women is far from clear. Most contemporary women feel that along with the increased expectations for achievement and performance, the pressure to be traditionally feminine – in the sense of being attractive, pleasing, and unassertive – is as powerful as ever before. It is the multiplicity of role demands, many of which seem to conflict with one another, which makes the contemporary situation for women so difficult. Popular culture has mythologized the notion of the women who "has it all" (that is, who performs all of these roles) in the imagery of the "superwoman."[41] The superwoman is both competent, achieving, and ambitious, and yet pleasingly feminine, sexual, and nurturing. In one popular book promoting this imagery of perfection, it is clear that in addition to fulfilling the multiple demands of modern womanhood, the superwoman devotes considerable attention to her appearance, and is meticulous in the area of weight control – she is, above all else perhaps, thin.[42] Research by Catherine Steiner-Adair in a private population in New York State showed that those girls who strongly identified with the ideology of the superwoman were the very ones who showed symptoms of eating disorders, while those who criticized or rejected the stereotype were relatively free of these problems.[43] Similar conclusions were drawn by a group of researchers at Yale, who found that college students with disordered eating aspired to fulfill both stereotypical male and stereotypical female ideals, while at the same time attributing enormous importance to their physical appearance.[44] Conflicts between new cultural ideals and traditional identifications were evident in a German study, in which a group of bulimic women were shown to have relatively large discrepancies between their sex-role attitudes, which were relatively progressive, and their actual behavior, which tended to be more traditional. For example, a bulimic woman might agree with an "attitude" statement such as "In a partnership, both partners should have equal rights," but also might simultaneously endorse a "behavioral" item such as "If I like someone, I give in in cases of disagreement, even if I know I am right."[45]

A second issue is that of persisting devaluation of femininity, despite (perhaps because of?) the gains resulting from feminism and the women's movement. These cultural biases take on a number of forms. One is that despite lip-service to the contrary, female intelligence is still not respected, or alternatively perceived as threatening to male power and dominance. Female college students are often acutely aware of this in the classroom, particularly in the hostile or dismissive reactions of male peers (and sometimes professors) to their efforts to express their opinions. In the corporation, women have experienced the phenomenon of tokenism, whereby even though they have been able to acquire a position, but have had difficulty in advancing to higher levels of management or power.[46] Thus, either female intellect and ambition are discounted, or they are perceived as too aggressive and unfeminine. This problem reinforces the dilemmas of anorexics, who have difficulty in reconciling their own intellectual aspirations with their own female-ness.[47] Their own solution to the dilemma – diminishing the female characteristics of the body – can be seen on one level as an internalization of cultural mysogyny.

The other side of this issue is that contemporary industrial cultures also devalue the traditional female role, that of nurturance. The world outside the family places low value on nurturing activities. Consider the professions in which nurturing is a primary activity – nursing, teaching, child care. These are not high-status occupations in contemporary society, and they are low on the ladder of remuneration. Ambitious women experience particular conflicts along these lines, as it becomes very difficult to balance the demands of a career in the extra-familial world and simultaneously to raise children. Some women have also responded to this cultural devaluation of nurturance by identifying with traditional male values of power, toughness, and control – but often only by repressing their own nurturing side. A suppression of the nurturing side of the self is a central problem for anorexic and bulimic women, who are most obviously unable to nurture (i.e. nourish) themselves.[48]

Males with Eating Disorders: A Neglected Population?

In this chapter, I have argued that women who develop eating disorders are caught in the conflicting expectations and pressures of a period characterized by a dramatic change in the female role. But what about male anorexics and bulimics? Where do they fit into the picture?

Some have asserted that the number of male anorexics (and particularly bulimics) may also have been increasing. There is, however, very little documentation for this.[49] Most of the evidence that we do have on this question suggests that the increase in eating disorders is particularly prominent among women, with the number of male anorexics remaining relatively constant.[50] If this is in fact the case, it would be consistent with the notion presented in this chapter that the psychological issues in the eating disorders are largely those that affect females, not males.

Interestingly, a significant percentage of those male anorexics who have been studied tend to have explicit conflicts in their *sexual* identity (as opposed to the conflicts in social gender role that we have described for females with eating disorders) – that is, many have explicit homosexual conflicts.[51] In addition, there is some evidence to suggest a relatively higher prevalence of male anorexia and bulimia in the gay community than among heterosexual males.[52] This latter could be attributable to a presumably greater preoccupation among gay males, particularly those who play the "female" role, with their physical appearance.[53] It is possible that if males in general become more preoccupied with appearance and thinness, as does seem to be happening to some extent, they too may experience an increase in eating disorders.[54] To me, however, such a development seems unlikely, since it is the broader issue of identity as well as those of appearance that seem to give rise to the eating disorders. And the types of issues that are involved – conflicts about achievement and autonomy, feelings of external determination and low self-esteem – seem peculiarly characteristic of the contemporary female experience.

5

THE THIN BODY

Sudden mutation of the body (after leaving the sanatorium): changing (or appearing to change) from slender to plump. Ever since, struggle to return it to its essential slenderness (part of the intellectual's mythology: to become thin is the naive act of the will to intelligence.)

"But I never looked like that!" How do you know? What is the "you" you might or might not look like? Where do you find it – by which morphological or expressive calibration? Where is your authentic body? You are the only one who can never see yourself except as an image; you never see your eyes unless they are dulled by the gaze they rest upon the mirror or the lens (I am interested in seeing my eyes only when they look at you): even and especially for your own body, you are condemned to the repertoire of its images.[1]

In German, the term for anorexia nervosa is *Pubertätsmagersucht* – "mania for leanness," or to use a more contemporary metaphor, "thinness addiction." The German term is actually a much better characterization of contemporary anorexic patients than *anorexia nervosa*, which implies a "nervous loss of appetite." Many anorexics, in fact, report ravenous hunger and intense suffering from starvation, although for most, such admissions will only occur after significant weight restoration.[2] Anorexics fear that admitting to hunger will result in enforced weight gain, a prospect which induces terror. What is more, the experience of starvation can enhance feelings of martyrdom, as well as a sense of absolute control. Contemporary anorexics, though, tend to be most invested in their external appearance, which they prefer to be skeletal. Many spend hours inspecting their image in the mirror for signs of the hated moral flaw – fat. "My legs are fat," said one patient plaintively, staring at her inflated skeletal thighs as they pressed into her chair. Gerald Russell, an English psychiatrist, has speculated that contemporary anorexic patients are more preoccupied with body shape than their nineteenth-century counter-parts.[3] This may well be the case, as references to thinness are largely missing in nineteenth-century case reports. But, then again, female patients may have been highly reluctant to tell most physicians about feelings about body weight, so closely tied as they are to issues of sexuality and therefore an indelicate subject for a physician–patient dialogue still governed by conventions of nineteenth-century prudery.[4] Even now, some patients hide their pride in their thinness until late in therapy, clinging to it like a treasured secret, fearful that a confession will lead to the ultimate catastrophe – enforced feeding.

In general, though, contemporary patients are more vocal about their feelings about body shape. Surely one of the most intriguing puzzles of anorexia nervosa is the typical symptom of distorted body image, the perception that one is fat, an illusion that paradoxically tends to increase with worsening emaciation.[5] Anorexics (and bulimics of normal weight), when asked to adjust a televised image of themselves to accurately represent their size, or when asked to view their bodies in distorted mirrors, will typically choose a width much larger than their emaciated frames.[6] One patient reported having fleeting success in perceiving her thinness accurately, but then felt victimized by a "pumping mechanism" that made her "balloon up" as she stood before a mirror.[7] What is the significance of this bizarre distortion? Is it a delusional misperception, one that must be corrected before recovery can occur?[8] Is it the product of the deranged thinking of a starved and metabolically disregulated organism? Some have suggested that the overestimation of body size is a phenomenon analogous to the famous "phantom limb," when an amputated body part is felt to be still present (the limb in this case corresponding to the sense of the body's mass before weight loss).[9] Most likely, overestimation of body size is a "cognitive" rather than a perceptual phenomenon.[10] Anorexics will typically admit to their emaciation when confronted with its reality in a mirror, on videotape, or when urged to "break through" their denial.[11] In fact, body-image overestimation is now pervasive in a culture obsessed with thinness and dieting. A number of studies have had difficulty in distinguishing anorexics from "normals" in the degree of overestimation of body size.[12]

Anorexics experience their thinness as a sense of purity, of control, of distinctiveness. The angular shape, the shocking sight of bones, creates a sharp boundary between themselves and the world, insulating them from dreaded intrusions. Through her shape, the anorexic makes a powerful statement of rejection of gender expectations, in effect, "I have sharp contours, I am not soft, I do not merge with you. I have nothing to give you."[13] Some are quite explicit about the relationship of thinness to the rejection of femininity, like one patient who said "and I want to stay slender because I look more like a man. I push myself to do as much as any man can do. It's difficult to be with a woman who is strong and efficient, and I can't admit that I am not as strong as she is. It's easy to admit this to a man."[14] The famous patient, Ellen West, felt torn between an ethereal student with whom she was infatuated and the man whom she was destined to marry. She experienced her dichotomous feelings about masculine and feminine identifications in terms of the extreme polarities of her body image: "I mean my life's ideal, to be thin, continued to occupy me more than all else. I shall really become a wife only when I have given up my life's ideal." The anorexic body has been likened to the pencil-thin sculptures of Giacommetti, with their strange isolation, their paradoxically heightened self-definition through their minimal consumption of space, their impression of distance, their intrinsic visualizability from afar.[15] One patient offered a dramatic statement about her existential aloneness, comparing her feeling of herself with the Statue of Liberty, the "lady of the harbor . . . like the statue, untouched and untouchable, on a little island in the gray ocean, with no relationship to anybody and anything."[16]

The Increasing Cultural Emphasis on Thinness

Much evidence has accumulated now for an increasingly demanding thin-body ideal in the Western nations, particularly the United States, but also in Western Europe and probably throughout the industrialized world. The idealization of thinness and the emphasis on weight control have been a part of Western culture since the early twentieth century, but it is only since the Second World War, and particularly since the 1960s, that dieting and thinness attained the status of a mass cultural obsession.[17] The chief bearers of the burden of the contemporary demand for thinness are women, a fact attributable to the central role of physical appearance and sexual attractiveness in women's self-esteem and social success.[18] Given the centrality of shape and weight concerns among contemporary patients with eating disorders, and given the overwhelming predominance of women in the patient population, it seems clear that the contemporary concerns with thinness must play an important role in their increased incidence.

The best-known study documenting an increasingly stringent thinness ideal was one of an important series of investigations by David Garner and Paul Garfinkel, and their colleagues. The authors studied two standards of female attractiveness, the winners of the Miss America pageant and the Playboy "Playmate of the Month", over a 20-year period, beginning in 1960.[19] In each case, the model became not only progressively lower in weight over the period, but also less curvaceous (as measured by the width of the hips relative to the waist). The development of this "tubular" appearance was mirrored in the world of fashion, where slender, almost boyish models, such as Jean "The Shrimp" Shrimpton and Twiggy took the fashion scene by storm in the 1960s. Meanwhile, Garner and his colleagues also documented that while the standards of thinness were becoming ever more stringent, actuarial data indicate that the weight of the average American woman had become steadily *heavier* over the same period. Taken together, these data point to a fundamental contradiction: as weight standards became more stringent, actual body weight in the population was steadily increasing. Surely, this contradiction between cultural ideal and biological reality must play a role in the increase in eating disorders.

An interesting aspect of this widely quoted study is the particular figures that were chosen to reflect cultural standards: the winners of the best-known (and now most notorious, in some circles) beauty pageant, and the "centerfold" of the most widely read "skin" magazine. Both of these represent body types that are idealized by a largely male audience. But is the female concern with thinness nothing more than a response to the male expectation for a certain type of body? Or are there other factors involved? A related question is, do men and women's standards for (female) thinness differ? Certainly the models of high fashion, particularly those that fill the pages of *Vogue* and *Elle*, appear to be thinner and less curvaceous than the sex symbols studied by Garner, even in the face of the decreasing weight and increasing thinness of the latter.

An interesting investigation of these issues was undertaken by two researchers from the University of Pennsylvania.[20] The authors asked both male and female college students to view a series of sketches of male and female figures of varying size (they were all the same height) and to make the following rankings:

1 the figure that looked most like their own;
2 the figure they would most like to look like;
3 the figure they thought would be most attractive to the opposite
  sex; and
4 the opposite sex figure that they found most attractive.

The authors also asked students to estimate what percentage of the students at the university was heavier than they were. In general, female students, in contrast with males, tended to overestimate their current weight. Furthermore, the figure that they selected as representing their current weight was consistently heavier than the one they selected as their ideal as well as the one they thought would be most attractive to men. Particularly interesting is the fact that *women's ideal figure was smaller than the one that they thought would be most attractive to men.* Apparently, then, women's weight concerns are driven by more than the effort to please men, although the latter motive is clearly important. Perhaps even more intriguing is the fact that women's estimates of the figure that would be most attractive to men were smaller than the figure that the male students actually preferred. These patterns of female preference stand in sharp contrast to those for the male students, who showed no discrepancies on the average between their perceived weights, the ideal weights, and the weights that they thought would be sexually attractive. In only one respect did the males resemble the females, and that was their misperception of the weight that would be most attractive to the opposite sex. But they miscalculated in the opposite direction than the females, choosing a *heavier* figure than the one females selected as their ideal for a man. Apparently, then, both sexes misjudge the standards of attractiveness of the opposite sex; but the overall level of body-image dissatisfaction in female students is much higher than it is in males.

Popular surveys indicate that contemporary women are consumed with an obsession about their body weight. For example, a survey of 33,000 women, of varying age and employment levels, by *Glamour* magazine in the early 1980s revealed that 75 percent felt that they were too fat, even though according to conservative weight tables only 25 percent were actually overweight.[21] The particular body parts that were the targets of the greatest dissatisfaction were the thighs, hips, and stomach. Most of the respondents also reported being constantly preoccupied with their weight, with a typical comment being "there isn't a day that goes by when I don't think about it." When asked what of the following would make them happiest – "losing weight," "hearing from an old friend," "a date with a woman you admire," or "success at work," 42 percent indicated losing weight, while 21 percent indicated dating and 22 percent indicated work success.

The concern about weight and shape seems to have had the greatest impact on female adolescents. This has been true at least since the 1960s, when a survey of over 1,000 high-school students in Berkeley, California revealed that 56 percent of 12th grade girls considered themselves to be overweight, whereas objective measurements revealed only 25 percent to be moderately or extremely overweight.[22] In contrast, most boys in the sample felt that they were underweight and therefore wanted to put on pounds. Feelings of being overweight were far more prevalent among white girls than blacks, perhaps due to ethnic differences in body image, as well as the lower socioeconomic status of the black girls. Similar concerns were voiced in a study of Swedish adolescents by Ingvar Nylander in the early 1970s.[23] Of the 1,241 female students surveyed, over half had "felt fat" at least some of the time, and dieting was highly prevalent, particularly among the older adolescents. In addition, nearly 10 percent of the study sample reported at least three clinical symptoms of anorexia nervosa, the most common of which were fatigue, increased interest in food, depression, chilliness, constipation, anxiety, and amenorrhea. Further analysis of an American sample indicated that feelings of fatness among adolescent females are most pronounced in teenagers from middle- and upper-income families, and at that time at least, the desire to lose weight emerged and intensified in step with the growth spurt of puberty.[24] Recently, in the late 1980s, the concern with weight and feelings of fatness have been seen to be increasingly prominent among much younger children, even as early as age 7. Such findings deeply concern workers in the eating-disorders field, and reports of a growing number of pre-adolescent patients with anorexia nervosa and delayed pubertal development have appeared in the late 1980s.[25]

The Relationship between the Idealization of Thinness and Eating Disorders: The Case of the Ballet

While standard for thinness and ideal body shape have undergone dramatic change and increasing numbers of women have become obsessed with their weight, is there any direct evidence that this preoccupation has led to a higher incidence of eating disorders? This was the question that led David Garner and Paul Garfinkel to undertake a study of young women who were studying at professional-caliber ballet schools in Canada.[26] In the ballet, there are particularly intense pressures to attain a thin body shape, a requirement that is attributable to contemporary aesthetic standards of the art form. The ballet dancer is expected to trace out a sharp, moving contour in space. For this purpose, slight body bulges are seen as a drastic impairment. Commenting on the ideal shape for ballerinas, Agnes de Mille wrote

Very few dancers develop the bodies of mature women; they keep lean in the hips and flat-breasted, a phenomenon remarked on by all costume designers. It is also the fact that the greatest performers, the women best capable of producing sensuous satisfactions, are in their bodies the least sensual. In effect they have sacrificed all organs of personal fulfillment and maintain and cherish only the means for public satisfaction, the system of bones and sinew for levitation and propulsion.[27]

Gelsey Kirkland, who in her painful autobiography reported developing anorexia and bulimia during an emotionally stressful period as the premiere ballerina of the New York City Ballet, reported that following a "watermelon feast," the revered George Balanchine tapped on her sternum and rib cage and commented "must see the bones." His recommendation: "eat nothing." Kirkland describes the ballet as being governed by a "concentration camp aesthetic."[28] It seems that ballet training provides a virtual "natural experiment" for the study of the pressure for thinness.

In their study, Garner and Garfinkel compared a large group of aspiring ballerinas to a group of college students on their scores on the Eating Attitudes Test, a screening device that has been used widely in the assessment of anorexic and bulimic symptoms. Of 131 ballet students, over 30 percent obtained scores on the Eating Attitudes Test comparable to those obtained by anorexic patients, whereas only 12 percent of the college students scored in this range. Interviews with the high scorers revealed that 12 out of the 131 (6.5 percent) of the ballet students met complete diagnostic criteria for anorexia nervosa, even though none of these was undergoing treatment or had been recognized by school authorities as suffering from an eating disorder. In contrast, none of the high-scoring college students could be diagnosed as anorexic on interview; apparently their high scores reflected only a preoccupation with weight, not the full-blown clinical symptoms of an eating disorder. Furthermore, almost all of the ballet dancers had developed their anorexic symptoms after commencing their training, suggesting that the training itself with its associated thinness may have been the chief factor that triggered the eating disorder. Similar high rates of anorexic symptoms were found for a group of modeling students – that is, 7 percent of those tested met the criteria for anorexia nervosa, although half of these had developed anorexia prior to their training. As Garfinkel and Garner point out, these percentages reflect the fact that in an environment in which thinness *per se* is a premium for success, the rate of anorexia nervosa is about ten times greater than that which is found in a comparable age-group of females in the general population.

Garner and Garfinkel were also interested in the specific role of high performance-expectations in the development of anorexia. Could it be that the pressures of the extraordinarily competitive environment of the professional ballet school was what was triggering anorexic symptoms in so many students, rather than the specific expectations for thinness? Accordingly, they compared the ballet students with a group of students of comparable age who were studying at a professional-caliber music conservatory, which presumably presents comparably intense competitive challenges in students, but without an emphasis on body shape. The conservatory students scored much lower on the Eating Attitudes Test than the dance students, and in fact they were indistinguishable from the comparison group of college students. Thus, the specific pressure for weight control, and not just performance demands and competition in general, is a critical factor in the development of anorexia nervosa. As one final refinement, the students in the national ballet school were compared with students in college dance departments, who presumably were under less competitive pressure but were necessarily concerned with weight control. The ballet students still had much higher scores. In other words, it is the *combination* of stringent requirements for thinness with the highly competitive environment of the ballet school that significantly elevates the risk for the development of eating disorders.

The vulnerability of ballet dancers to eating disorders was the subject of a book by L. M. Vincent, a psychiatrist and former dancer.[29] Vincent depicts the ballet school and dance company as virtual hothouses of competition and performance pressure. He criticizes ballet teachers for setting dangerously low weight-standards for young students, many of whom are still physically maturing, and documents widespread starvation dieting, food faddism, and vomiting and laxative abuse among aspiring ballerinas. In the subculture of the ballet school, these "anorexic" behaviors gain a degree of social acceptability, as is evident from the following comment of one student: "You should have seen this place on Sunday nights [weigh-ins were on Monday] . . . Nobody would eat anything past twelve noon, and the whole second floor bathroom [of the women's residence] would smell so bad that you couldn't use it."[30] One 18-year old student, who experimented unsuccessfully with various techniques to induce vomiting (including bizarre concoctions of spices and ipecac) "settled" finally on the use of laxative and diurectics in order to control her weight.[31] Students tend to be extraordinarily competitive and resentful about each other's disordered eating behaviors: "A modern dancer in her mid-twenties who vomits three to four times per week recalls being 'jealous as hell' over the vomiting of her best friend and roommate before embarking on the method herself, which she has now maintained for over seven years."[32] Menstrual irregularities, along with diminished sexual interest, are not uncommon. Vincent points out that the athletic demands of the ballet are as rigorous of those of any sport, but in no other athletic activity is the *appearance* of the body so crucial to success and acceptance.

More recent studies have systematically documented the widespread presence of disordered eating in professional ballet companies.[33] In a major investigation that included approximately one-quarter of the female ballet dancers in North America and Western Europe, fully 15 percent of the Americans and 23 percent of the Europeans queried reported having had anorexia nervosa, while 19 percent of the Americans and 29 percent of the Europeans reported having had bulimia. This is obviously a shockingly high percentage, considerably higher than the rate found by Garfinkel and Garner in their study of ballet students. Interestingly, though, there were no cases of either anorexia or bulimia among black dancers, whose numbers were 11 of the total sample of 66. The black dancers in general indicated a higher degree of body-image satisfaction, suggesting perhaps that ethnic group differences in body image may continue to be an influence even given the rigorous standards of weight control in dance companies. The anorexic dancers were mostly from the more competitive, national dance companies, a finding which may be attributable to the higher competition pressures of these settings (although the national companies also had more rigorous weight standards and required more daily exercise).

All of this research indicates clearly that an increased demand for thinness, particularly in a competitive setting, greatly increases the likelihood that some individuals will develop eating disorders. It is interesting to think about these pressures in the light of gender. It has often been suggested, for example, that when men are under comparable pressures for weight control, for example as is the case among wrestlers and racing jockeys, that they too will be vulnerable to developing eating disorders. Certainly, anecdotal clinical evidence suggests that this is so. Male adolescents, for example, sometimes develop anorexia when struggling to "make weight" for competitive wrestling. However, in one of the few systematic studies of such a population, a group of racing jockeys in the Newmarket and Epsom areas of England, the prevalence of eating disorders was not found to be high.[34] Perhaps the particular emphasis in the dance on the external shape of the body, along with the ethic of perfectionism and competition, makes dancers particularly vulnerable. It is also likely that, given the socialization pressures that we described in the last chapter, females will be more vulnerable to the development of eating disorders even in these high-risk environments, owing to the fact that certain of them are particularly susceptible to external demands and competition pressures.

Why Thinness?

Let us recapitulate the argument so far. It seems clear that an increasingly thin body-ideal, one that is moving in the opposite direction to the realities of average body weight, has been on the ascendant from the 1960s through the 1980s. Women, particularly younger women who must compete in the sexual, academic, and occupational realms, have come under increasing pressure to lose weight and mold their bodies to an increasingly procrustean and narrow external standard. The contemporary emphasis on body shape also has to be understood in the wider context of a society that places an increasing emphasis on externals, on appearance, on image.[35] Given the "natural experiment" of the ballet, which suggests that eating disorders proliferate in an intensely competitive environment that places stringent demands on body shape, then the proliferation of eating disorders in the wider cultural milieu of the 1970s and 1980s becomes readily comprehensible.

This argument essentially restates, if in somewhat reformulated terms, previous sociocultural interpretation of eating disorders.[36] There is, however, a problem that underlies the argument, an issue that has given little previous attention, and that is the question of *why* thinness in particular, and not some other body shape, has become the dominant body ideal, so intensely sought after, for women in our time. In previous writings, the emphasis on thinness has been treated as if it were a totally arbitrary standard, a "given," that could just as well be some other body shape.[37] But it is unlikely that such a highly valued cultural ideal, one that is felt to be of such central importance and drives many into self-destructive patterns of behavior, is arbitrary. From here, therefore, we will turn to a discussion of the historical and cultural forces which have given rise to the present value placed on thinness, a discussion that will considerably deepen our understanding of why disorders that specifically revolve around body image and thinness have become ethnic disorders at this particular time and in this particular place.

The Century of Svelte

Human cultures have placed value on a variety of body shapes. A comprehensive history of the preferred morphology of the body has yet to be written. Nevertheless, a certain amount of cross-cultural and historical evidence can begin to illuminate the origin and meanings of contemporary thinness.

Cross-cultural studies indicate that for the majority of human societies, fatness has been valued over thinness, particularly in females.[38] A common explanation for this preference is one that invokes economic determinism; in societies where resources and wealth are limited, the large body is admired because it is symbolic of wealth and plentiful supplies (particularly food). This interpretation, while probably having some validity, is also undoubtedly simplistic. For example, thinness was also desirable during Europe's Little Ice Age in the late Gothic period, as well as among the Gurage of Ethiopia, who were troubled by collective anxieties about scarcity.[39] Preferred body weight, most likely, is a complex social construction, not a simple result of economic factors. For women, in particular, one of these factors is of particular importance – the value placed on reproduction.[40] This connection is nowhere more dramatically evident than in the African institutions of the "fattening ceremony" and "fattening sheds," which at one time were pervasive throughout Eastern and Central Africa.[41] At a certain point after puberty (usually between the ages of 15 and 18), girls were intentionally overfed and then their ample bodies displayed in a ceremony that celebrated their reproductive potential and economic status. The fattening ceremonies have generally disappeared, although one writer reports observing their continued existence recently in rural Eastern Nigeria.[42] Apparently, older African women can still recall the experience of the fattening ceremony in their childhoods, but their daughters, particularly if they are university students in urban Africa, have now come under the influence of the diametrically opposite modern ideals of thinness.[43] It is important to realize, though, that the symbolic association of fatness with fertility may be a cultural intuition of a biological reality – that is, the close connection between female adiposity and reproductive capacity.[44]

In Western Europe and the United States, despite previous intimations of what was to come in the nineteenth-century fetish with the corset and ante-bellum "Steel-engraving Lady," the ideal of female thinness did not really take hold until the twentieth century, which has been dubbed by Bennett and Gurin, in their excellent book on dieting, the "century of Svelte."[45] By the end of the nineteenth century, it seems that the symbolism of thinness was strongly linked with the idea of class. In his *Theory of the Leisure Class*, for example, in which he published his famous theory of conspicuous consumption, Veblen wrote about the wives of the wealthy: "There are certain elements of feminine beauty . . . which come in under this head . . . The ideal requires delicate and diminutive hands and feet and a slender waist. . . . It results that at this cultural stage women take thought to alter their persons, so as to conform more nearly to the requirements of the instructed taste of the time."[46] By the first decade of the twentieth century, the fashion models of Paris had already adopted the standard of extreme thinness. As early as 1908, the *Vogue* correspondent in Paris wrote that "the fashionable figure is growing straighter and straighter, less bust, less hips, more waist, and a wonderfully long, slender, suppleness about the limbs . . . the petticoat is obsolete, prehistoric. How slim, how graceful, how elegant women look!"[47] Obesity was coming under harsh criticism, and the burden of weight control fell particularly heavily on the shoulders of women, as evidenced in the following confession in a 1907 magazine article: "The gown was neither more nor less than anticipated. But I . . . the fault was on me . . . I was more! Gasping, I hooked it together. The gown was hopeless, and I . . . I am fat."[48]

It was not until the 1920s, however, that the tubular, thin body became adopted by the mass of upwardly mobile and aspiring women. In America, the symbolism of thinness was condensed in the imagery of the flapper, whose flamboyant style, mobility, shortened skirts, and liberated sexuality shocked those who held to the lingering traditions of nineteenth-century female delicacy and heralded the democratization of new ideals of female economic and sexual independence. Bennett and Gurin suggest that the credo of the flapper was distinctly anti-maternal: "I am my own sexual boss; I am in control of myself; I am not a motherly, housewifely person."[49] The flapper's boyish, androgynous body was clearly the forerunner of the tubular look that was once again to emerge in the 1960s, and it was disseminated by powerful forces that were to play an even stronger role in the contemporary period. These included the new media of communication (in the 1920s, the movies), an emerging consumerism, which in turn was fueled by the democratization of fashion and clothing styles.[50] In the hands of the institutions of the consumer economy, though, what was originally an image of liberation and self-determination was quickly transformed into a more sophisticated instrument of external control.

The flapper, along with the entire exuberant culture of the 1920s, vanished into the abyss of the depression and then the consuming preoccupations of the Second World War. In the post-war period of domestic retrenchment and suburbanization, a new emphasis on the hourglass figure, and particularly on the large-breasted female, took hold, particularly among males. In the period of Marilyn Monroe and Jayne Mansfield, the preoccupation with weight control, particularly among women, never really disappeared, but it seemed to be dampened somewhat by a period in which a number of economic, political, and international threats fueled a greater attention to pragmatic concerns. But even as early as the late 1940s, "new-wave" models were arriving in New York and appearing on the pages of *Vogue*, models who were secretly rumored to "eat nothing."[51]

The return and subsequent entrenchment of thinness in the 1960s, heralded by the sanctification of Twiggy, brought with it some new features and emphases – an extreme androgyny, almost boyish and prepubertal, a trend towards the use of younger and younger models (the huge billboard of Brooks Shields that towered over Times Square was one of the fashion symbols of the era of the 1970s), and an increased flaunting of a sexuality that carried Nabakovian overtones. The consumer culture that emerged in the 1970s (the infamous "me" decade) was obsessed with youth, haunted by the spectre of aging, and all too ready to exploit and absorb images of a free sexuality that only a decade earlier had been the symbol of the political rebellion of a "counterculture." Concretely, the emphasis on youth was driven by the enormous expansion of fashion markets for teenagers, who in the 1980s increasingly constituted a significant proportion of the consumers at American shopping malls. Meanwhile, despite the glamorization of free sexual expression and authentic selfhood ("Zena is you," one advertisement proclaimed), many women still experienced getting into a pair of designer jeans as no more liberating than the bone-crushing corsets of the nineteenth century:

> We burned 'em in the sixties,
> girdles, she said walking
> into Bloomingdale's, grabbing
> a pair of cigarette-legged
> tight denim jeans off the rack.
> Hoisting them up to her hips,
> how do ya get em on, she said.
> have surgery, take steam baths,
> slimnastic classes'n Dr. Nazi's
> diet clinic fatshots for a month.
> These aren't jeans for going
> to lunch in, she said trying
> to do the snap, these
> aren't even jeans for eating an hour
> before ya put em on, just
> for standin up in without
> your hands in the pockets,
> there's not even room
> in here for my underpants.[52]

By the mid-1980s, there were also some signs of a new look, one which however hardly denies the importance of thinness. Fashion writers exuberantly announced that "curves are back," a trend that essentially seems to signify a movement back to a preference for larger breasts (a signal of the increasing acceptability of having children?).[53] Meanwhile, the requirement for overall slenderness remains, particularly in the hips and the waist, resulting in a body type that in some instances may even result in greater distortion. Reports are that a number of models in New York City have turned to cosmetic surgery to produce the necessary modifications. A second trend, one which began in the early 1980s along with the fitness boom, has been the emphasis on muscle building and strength. Even here, though, the trend is coupled with the requirement for slenderness, as is evident in the relentless stream of articles on weight control in one of the most popular American magazines on the subject (appropriately entitled *Shape*). Where these new trends will ultimately lead is uncertain, but in an age of extraordinary confusion about female identity and the ever pressing need of the fashion industry to promote new images, it seems likely that the natural spectrum of female body sizes and shapes will remain unacceptable.

The Marketing of Body-Image Distortion

The role of commercial interests and the media in promoting contemporary body ideals cannot be underestimated. In the environment of the consumer-oriented, post-industrial societies, electronic and photographic images have a potent and far-ranging influence. Given the impact and pervasiveness of this imagery, it is not surprising that disorders of body image, in which people have difficulty in seeing themselves accurately, have become rampant.

The distortions that are characteristic of anorexia or bulimia are sometimes literally and concretely evident in fashion advertising. Aside from the general glamorization of thinness, some advertisements literally present female models in which the calf is larger than the thigh.[54] Such distortions in the natural proportions of the body pass virtually unnoticed and are accepted as the norm. Some high fashion models appear to be literally anorexic (as indeed some may be), although the popularity of the emaciated figure may have waned somewhat since the 1960s and 1970s. It is generally conceded that while such figures may not be sexually attractive, they have the virtue (for the fashion industry) of "looking good in clothes." To achieve a certain kind of "look" has become a paramount virtue of contemporary fashion, regardless of the consequences for health of consumers.[55]

The overvaluation of thinness is also exploited to promote products other than those related to body adornment. In one advertisement that appeared a number of times in the *New York Times* Sunday Magazine, a full-page spread depicted an impeccably lean and shapely young woman in a leotard thrusting a barbell over her head, and was accompanied by the caption "She has more fat on her than our salami." The comparison of the female body with a piece of meat is buttressed (in small print) by appropriate statistics comparing the percentage of body fat on the average woman to that on the average salami. In an even more outlandish example, Hershey promoted a new slender milk-chocolate bar with the Dutchess of Windsor's famous (and now notorious) dictum, "You can never be too rich or too thin." This clever promotion unwittingly intensifies the contradiction so acutely felt by anorexic or bulimic patients between the desire for calorie-rich food and the equally intense desire for thinness. This last advertisement was the target of a campaign against advertising conducive to eating disorders by the Illinois-based National Association for Anorexia Nervosa and Related Disorders, a campaign that resulted in its withdrawal by the company.[56]

While it is exceedingly difficult to measure precisely the impact of the media, there is little question that many anorexic and bulimic patients feel directly affected by the relentless assault of commercial imagery promoting thinness. In a particularly grotesque example of such intrusiveness, a certain weight-loss product (a liquid diet) was promoted via computerized mass mailings to teenagers. In the margin of the promotional text, "personalized" comments were "handwritten" (actually by machine), such as "Annette, it really works, try it." Several teenage girls in an eating-disorders support group felt that the advertisement was in fact personally directed to them by someone who "knew" that they were "too fat." One mother commented, perhaps not inaccurately, that the impact of the mailing was tantamount to a "psychological assault."[57]

There is little question that the commercial exploitation of insecurities regarding body image has had an impact on the rise of eating disorders. An effort to counter these influences has therefore been directly incorporated into some therapeutic methodologies. Thus, for example, at an appropriate point in treatment, David Garner may ask his patients to develop an "atrocity file", in which toxic images of thinness from the media are accumulated by the patient in a scrapbook. Through discussion with the therapist of the unrealistic standards promoted by the commercial culture, the patient can potentially develop a more realistic body concept and an awareness of the distorted standards that she has internalized.[58] Such direct incorporation of cultural forces into therapeutic discourse has become increasingly common in the treatment of eating disorders. It suggests that therapy has not only a healing role, but one that is also implicitly political.

A Symbol of the New Female Identity

Fashion and media are not totally autonomous cultural institutions; they both create *and* reflect dominant cultural values and concerns. It would be unlikely, therefore, that the fashion and media conglomerates could successfully promote images of women of Rubensian proportions in the present social environment. Thinness sells because it amplifies emotions and values that are already latent within the populace.

A recent series of investigations by Brett Silverstein and his colleagues from the City University of New York serves to illuminate the connection between thinness and the dilemmas of female identity.[59] Silverstein hit upon a method for systematically measuring the extent to which thinness was idealized in any particular period. By sampling photographs of models from *Vogue* and *Ladies Home Journal* within a given year, in which the models wore either bathing suits or underwear, the ratio of the bust to waist width could give an accurate measure of the extent to which the preferred body ideal was "tubular," non-curvaceous. On sampling photographs from the beginning of the twentieth century to the early 1980s, Silverstein found that this ratio plumeted during the period of the 1920s and then in the late 1960s and 1970s. So far, these results only systematically document a trend with which we are already familiar. What is of greater interest is the fact that the measure of leanness was strongly correlated with an increase in the number of women graduating from college, as well as the number of women in professional and managerial positions. Thus, the greater the number of women aspiring to male privilege and status, the greater the number involved in intellectual and vocational competition with men, the more women aspire to a tubular, androgynous ideal and may be willing to virtually starve themselves to achieve this result. This is not only a phenemenon of the present, but may also have been characteristic of the 1920s, as Silverstein found a number of previously overlooked references in the popular press of that decade to epidemics of self-starvation among female students in the United States.

In further studies of contemporary college students, Silverstein found that the aspiration to thinness, as well as disordered eating, were specifically related to ambiguities regarding sex-roles (and female achievement in particular) within the family.[60] For example, the more a student remembered her father as doubting her intellectual competence, the more she tended to aspire to a slender body ideal. Furthermore, female students who engaged in binge-eating as well as purging more frequently recalled that (1) their parents believed that women's place was within the home, (2) their mothers were dissatisfied with their own careers, (3) the father had a disparaging view of the mother's intelligence, and (4) the father compared his daughter's intelligence unfavorably with a male sibling. Thus, for women with disordered eating, negative biases about female intellectual competence, already pervasive in the wider culture, are specifically amplified by familial attitudes, and particularly so by the negative judgements of the father.

Silverstein's research thus further illuminates the relationship between disordered eating, changing sex roles, and attitudes toward female achievement. In historical periods in which women have felt under pressure to prove their intellectual ability and competence, the slender body ideal has been dominant. And the reason for this is that under the persistent influence of gender bias and negative stereotypes, female curvaceousness is associated with a lack of intelligence and competence (i.e., the "dumb blonde"). But in addition, as we have seen, the roundness of the body, particularly any implications of fatness, also are closely linked with notions of fertility and reproductive capacity. Thus, the aspiration to be lean and non-curvaceous also is mostly an effort to escape the patriarchal judgement (a judgement that is internalized) that "women's reproductive function defines her character, position and value." Ultimately it also represents, through the language of body shape, an emulation of the male, an effort at mimesis, one which unfortunately has self-destructive consequences and fails to solve the real issue of powerlessness.

Ethnic Disorders Revisited

We are now in a position to synthesize the arguments that have been raised in the last two chapters and to further elaborate the notion of eating disorders as ethnic disorders. In the recent period of history, women have been undergoing a vast change in their social role, and on a psychological level, their own identities. The increasing involvement of young women in higher education and male-dominated professions has left many struggling to synthesize contradictory ideas of independence versus dependence, individual achievement versus the nurturance of others. Those who are particularly vulnerable to these conflicts internalize the prevailing ideology of body shape as an obsessive solution to the problem of identity, as a means of reducing the distress attendant upon feelings of weakness and internal conflict. Women who develop eating disorders draw upon a "solution" to the problem of identity by drawing upon a cultural symbolism of body shape that itself contains the latent, contradictory meanings of female identity. For thinness, as one group of authors suggested, is a highly potent symbol, a synthesis of the "divergent axes of nurturance and assertion."[61] Thinness is both "female" (the current ideal of sexual attractiveness) and "male" (the non-curvaceous, mobile, and active body). Like the Sinhalese phenomenon of "matted hair," which not only grows but is culturally recognized as a subject takes on the status of the "sacred" or "possessed," thinness is a symbol whose meaning is both social and personal.[62] A variety of individual experiences, conflicts, and pathologies may be expressed as anorexia or bulimia; but they all partake in this common cultural meaning.

Women with eating disorders therefore draw upon a cultural idea that has become the norm as a "defense" against particularly intense psychological, developmental conflicts (which are themselves culturally constituted). Eating disorders are ethnic disorders precisely because they magnify a culturally typical solution to a problem that is much more pervasive in the culture at large. The difference is more a quantitative than a qualitative one. The weight obsessions from which many "normal" women suffer are no more productive (and no more or less explicable) than those of the anorexic or bulimic patient, for whom they become all-consuming. Fortunately, in the usual case, their physical consequences are not so drastic as to lead them down the pathway of disease.

openly that they would rather perish of starvation than exceed their "magic number" on the scale (usually less than 100 lbs, and typically "89" or "99") by so much as a pound – a figure that in their minds arouses as much anxiety as any primitive taboo. The fear of fatness is the motivating force behind the food rituals, the fad diets, and the punishing exercise regimes so typical of anorexia nervosa. For anorexics, vegetarianism, new-age diets, and most recently the avoidance of cholesterol, are not so much followed in the pursuit of health (although health ideologies may be conveniently invoked as a rationale) as they are by the dread of weight gain.[3] Meat is an object of particular avoidance, since animal fat is, in the mind of the anorexic, immediately and magically transformed into body fat.[4]

A number of anorexics begin their weight-reducing regimes in response to teasing or critical comments about adolescent overweight, or at least what is judged to be so. Even if the pre-anorexic is not heavy by objective standards (which she often is not), there is a concern with overweight, and sometimes a history of frank obesity, in the anorexic's family. In one case a 13-year old girl began dieting after an athletic coach suggested that she might be too heavy to continue to be on a gymnastics team. The girl's father, himself almost frighteningly lean and highly weight-conscious, had himself suffered from a history of obesity in adolescence. In response to merciless teasing, he undertook a radical diet when in college through which he lost over 80 pounds over the course of a summer, a dieting success that had become a part of the family's mythology and when brought up in conversation was surrounded by considerable joking. In undertaking self-starvation herself, the daughter was emulating and replicating her father's triumph, but she was also throwing it in his face as a way of rebelling against his own demands for perfection (this applied particularly to his expectations for athletic prowess, but also his own hatred of fat).

In the families of anorexics, a "morally bracing tone," as one writer put it, surrounds the topics of obesity, dieting, and physical fitness.[5] Many of these families subscribe to a highly puritanical ethic of work and self-control; fat is a symbol of sloth, of slovenliness, of self-indulgence. Ultimately, also, fat stands for the "sins of the flesh," namely sexuality – never a comfortable topic in the families of anorexics, who tend to be phobic about sensual matters.[6] Anorexics themselves internalize this contemporary version of the Protestant ethic. As one patient put it "if you are thin they don't think that you are rich and that your life is too easy. Being fat is like the kings in the

6

THE WAR AGAINST FAT: OBESITY, DIETING, AND EXERCISE

> Along with this, however, something new emerges now, namely a definite dread – namely, a fear of getting fat.
>
> L. Binswanger, The Case of Ellen West
>
> What causes the most damage is not the actual weight itself, but the fear of weight.
>
> Hillel Schwartz, *Never Satisfied*

A terror of becoming fat is typically the central driving experience in the development of anorexia or bulimia. In contemporary Western societies, in which obesity is associated with significant health problems, fatness has also taken on symbolic meanings – namely, the repository of all the traits that are considered morally despicable.[1] By the time they reach elementary school, children have already absorbed the conviction, widely disseminated in the adult culture, that fatness means stupidity, laziness, slovenliness, a lack of will power.[2] Even otherwise enlightened and educated adults have difficulty in parting with the notion that these are self-evident truths about fat people. In order to penetrate more deeply into the sociocultural origins of the contemporary wave of eating disorders, we need to come to grips with our cultural obsession with fatness and the means we have adopted to combat it – dieting and exercise. But first, some discussion of the way the struggle against fat manifests itself in the eating disorders is in order.

An Intense Fear of Obesity

For anorexics, the fear of weight gain, of ballooning up, of "becoming a whale," is the spectre of the ultimate catastrophe. Many patients say

Middle Ages; they are just rich and powerful and do nothing, and everybody works for them. Looking and feeling exhausted shows that one does a lot, and without that I feel so undeserving."[7] As Bruch suggests, the characteristic hatred of fat within the anorexic family represents an "aristocratic attitude" that values being able to do without in the midst of abundance.

A struggle against obesity is even more evident in the family histories of bulimics. The percentage of the parents with a history of obesity is unusually high, particularly relative to middle-class norms.[8] In the families of bulimics, overeating is a common phenomenon, as is the use of food as a means of reducing emotional distress and solving problems. These families "move toward" food, in contrast with the families of anorexics who evidence a more avoidant attitude.[9] The bulimic's struggle with her own very frequent tendencies towards overweight often reflects, on a psychological level, a struggle to differentiate herself from her mother, who for a variety of reasons she has come to disparage. Very often, she attempts to escape her mother's fate by identifying with her father, and as is typical of the eating-disordered patient, the struggle is expressed in the arena of body image. Fat, then, comes to stand for the rejected qualities of the mother, whereas thinness reflects the father's power and independence.[10] Bulimics often fluctuate widely between overweight and underweight, which is, on a psychic level, an enactment of the ambivalence and instability that surrounds these issues of identity.

Obesity: The Wider Cultural Context

Increasing rates of obesity appear to be endemic to the process of industrialization and are associated with a whole host of factors: relative food abundance, diets rich in fat and sugars, a more sedentary life-style.[11] In food-poor, mostly rural societies in which famine is a recent memory or perhaps even a present reality, to be fat is seen as desirable, a sign of wealth and status. This association may even hold good today, for example in India or Kenya.[12] Importantly, though, as a society becomes more affluent, the typical social-class distribution of obesity usually reverses. In the affluent societies, thinness is the symbol of status, whereas obesity becomes *déclassé*. The linkages between obesity and social class in the Western nations are not merely symbolic: study after study shows the prevalence of obesity in the industrialized nations to be higher in the lower socioeconomic strata.[13]

The intense medical interest in obesity in the Western nations is of course due to its association with a variety of health problems – hypertension, coronary heart disease, diabetes. These correlations have been documented in a number of studies, particularly the large-scale studies attempting to assess risk factors for coronary heart disease. Also, in recent years, there is a growing concern about an apparently increasing prevalence of obesity among children and adolescents, a problem which appears to be strongly correlated with the number of hours that a child watches television. Television viewing is of course an activity that includes both major life-style factors that place one at risk for obesity – sedentariness and snacking (typically on junk food rich in fat and sugars).

Undoubtedly, obesity is a serious medical problem, particularly for those who are "morbidly overweight." Nevertheless, debates have proliferated recently about whether the health effects of obesity have been overstated, and in particular whether they justify alarmist comments by the United States Surgeon General about the health risks of a small percentage of overweight. Recent data suggest that moderate degrees of overweight (say 15 percent over the statistically normal weight for one's height) may not be associated with elevated risk for health problems – in fact the reverse may be true.[14] This is especially the case for women, on whom the effects of mild overweight are different than they are for men. In females, weight accumulation is distributed subcutaneously, whereas for men it results in much more medically dangerous trunkweight.[15] It is curious, therefore, that the social bias against obese women is much greater than it is against men (see below). Some have suggested that the current medical teachings about the dangers of a small degree of overweight represent the covert penetration of aesthetic standards into what should be strictly objective judgements, and even that obesity itself is a culture-bound syndrome. In support of this notion, it has been pointed out that the weight–height standards for women in the older acturial tables were arbitrarily reduced, for reasons that were unexplained.[16]

Indeed, there is little question that obesity is a complex cultural construct that has become loaded up with an enormous amount of ideological baggage that has little to do with objective reality. A recent historical study by Hillel Schwartz traces in detail the development of the anxiety about fatness in the United States from the middle of the nineteenth century to the present.[17] According to Schwartz (in an argument too complex to be recapitulated here) our collective notions about body size reflected altered notions about the self and its appetites as we became a twentieth-century society. The new positive value placed on thinness that emerged in the early twentieth century was crucially tied to the new kinesthetic values that governed industry (efficiency experts), the arts (new dance styles that emphasized mobility), and technology (the flying machine). Concepts of efficient management were now beginning to be applied to the self and to domestic life (e.g. home economics). The ideology of obesity and dieting underwent a number of transformations and elaborations throughout the twentieth century. In the contemporary context, the concern with fatness is colored by our experience of a society which is beset by problems with overproduction, with waste, with excess world population. It reflects the increasingly difficult problem of self-management in an ever-more fragmented social world that is confronted with the question of the "limits of satisfaction." Schwartz's thesis considerably broadens our understanding of why eating disorders, which are partly an expression of the struggle against obesity, would become rampant in those modern societies in which consumerism has come to a fever pitch, but which also place a particularly strong emphasis on self-reliance and self-control (particularly the United States, but also England and contemporary Japan).

Obesity is then a mirror of our sense of not being in control of ourselves, a projection of our dysregulated appetites. Our attitudes towards fat and dieting are colored by our fantasy that in a world of excess and of undefined limits, we could eat nothing.[17] We do not simply want to be thin, nor is our wish to reduce only a positive impulse towards "health:" we *hate* our fat. The imagery of the struggle with obesity in popular culture is the imagery of warfare: "zap fat," "blast bulges," our magazine covers scream at us as we check out at the supermarket counter. Drastic (and dangerous) measures are undertaken to fight obesity: gastric balloons, gastric stapling, and most recently liposuction. These methods may have some application in life-threatening, intractable, "morbid obesity," but in our weight-obsessed culture, they are always in danger of being appropriated for purely cosmetic ends. The most recent example of this is the use of the hazardous procedure of liposuction as cosmetic surgery, which has become somewhat of a craze in the United States in the late 1980s.[18]

In contemporary Western societies, the obese have become a despised underclass, victims of discrimination in employment and social life. The moral stereotypes of obesity (which have never been confirmed by objective personality research) include attributions of laziness, self-indulgence, greed.[19] Thinness, on the other hand, has come to stand for self-control, refinement, the civilized containment of appetites. As Werner Cahman once said, in a discussion of the stigma of obesity, "one is reminded of Puritan attitudes, but even more so of the Platonic psychology, according to which the rational function of the mind is represented by the governing classes: the spirited by the military; and the appetitive by the economic. Mind and heart, that is, intelligence and courage, are then to combine to rule over the big, dull stomach."[20] Cahman's characterization, although trenchant, omits one crucial point: the Platonic ruling class was exclusively *male*. And it is the particular problem of fatness of females, so important in understanding the gender-specificity of eating disorders, to which we now turn.

Obesity in Women: Is Fat a Feminist Issue?

Despite the pervasiveness of our concern with fat, the issue of fatness is not blind to gender. In fact, the cultural stereotypes surrounding obesity have their most potent, binding effect on women. An understanding of these issues will lead us to a better understanding of the dilemmas of those who struggle most insistently and desperately against the fat woman's fate: anorexics and bulimics.

Fatness plays a critical role in female biological development. Before puberty, the percentage of body fat tissue is approximately the same in both sexes. However, during puberty the development of body fat accelerates in girls, so that ultimately, despite smaller stature when compared with adult males, women carry a greater percentage of their body mass as fat tissue. As was pointed out in chapter 4, for women the growth of fat tissue is critically connected with the emergence of the reproductive cycle. Generally speaking, the rate of obesity in adult females tends to be specifically higher than in males, a difference that may be rooted in these biological substrates.[21]

As we discussed in the previous chapter, the cultural standard for middle- and upper-class women has been one of increasing thinness. In recent decades, numerous types have been idealized by fashion – the prepubertal Twiggy in the 1960s, the less stringent but still slender models of the late 1970s and 1980s, and now the muscular woman. Despite variation, though, all of these types have one central feature in common – they are *not fat*.[22] Given the role of fatness in female biological development, the norm of thinness poses specific conflicts with inherent properties of female biology – it is virtually an instance of culture versus nature. And this conflict is exaggerated by the phenomenon noted by epidemiologists of obesity of the "socio-economic reveral of fatness in females." In childhood, middle- and upper-class girls are usually fatter than their less affluent age-mates; but at puberty the relative degree of fatness in both groups reverses (under the influence of dieting?), so that by adulthood lower-class women are considerably fatter.[23] Girls who develop eating disorders, therefore, may not only be fighting the normative biological trends of female development, but may be at double risk because of the nutritionally privileged impact of a middle or upper-class family.

In the United States, in particular, fat women are especially stigmatized. One study showed that obese high seniors were typically denied college admission much more frequently than their age-mates of comparable intelligence.[24] Informally, many college admissions counselors will readily admit that an overweight student is much more likely to "flunk an interview" than a thinner peer. Fat women have also been subjected to pervasive discrimination in employment, and only recently have the American courts formally recognized the stigmatization of obesity as a form of legal discrimination.[25] Particularly in competitive settings, fat women have difficulty with acceptance: in order to prove themselves of comparable worth with men, women must conform their bodies to a more masculine shape. Of course, at the same time, some degree of "femininity" must be maintained. It is a difficult balancing act.

Fat is therefore unquestionably a feminist issue. Susie Orbach, the author of a best-selling book so titled, makes the somewhat startling suggestion that women with problems of "compulsive overeating" (a syndrome that from a psychiatric standpoint is vaguely defined) unconsciously *want* to be fat; it is thinness that they fear.[26] For many women, she suggests, the desire to be large represents an imagined state in which appetites could be satisfied rather than restricted, in which women would be free to "take up space" in a world which still allows them only the narrow space defined by a body whose dimensions are prepubertal. From this standpoint, it is the obese woman who is the overt rebel against the patriarchal limitation of female desire; the anorexic, by contrast, dutifully complies and even caricatures societal expectations. Caricature, though, is also a form of protest, however indirect; for the anorexic, dieting becomes a tacit "hunger strike."

It is doubtful that most women desire fatness, even unconsciously.

However, Orbach confirms what has been convincingly argued by
Bruch, and elaborated by others; that underneath the extremes of
their visible size, the anorexic and obese woman share common
ground.[27] Both suffer from profound feelings of unworthiness and a
sense of external determination; and, as Orbach points out, both
tacitly accept the cultural definition of female worth in terms of her
body shape. But both, in differing ways, rebel against cultural
definitions of normative femininity, even though the rebellion takes
the form of a symptom. As usual, the bulimic lies somewhere in the
middle, both encompassing and yet not able to live with either
extreme. She is, in Bruch's phrase, a thin-fat person.[28]

Dieting: An Ideology for the Self-Absorbed

In early Christianity, individuals were exhorted to counter the threat
posed by bodily appetites through fasting. Contemporary societies
have adopted a secular counterpart; it is called dieting. Lacking a
moral vocabulary, contemporary societies have projected the notions
of good and evil onto the images of our own bodies: the idea of God
(the qualities of perfection, of cleanliness, of goodness) is now
contained in the image of thinness; while that of the Devil (i.e.
corruption by the appetite, sloth, greed) is embodied in fatness. We
are actually much closer to the Puritan tradition than we are the early
Christian, particularly in our struggle for individual self-regulation
and our dedication to the work ethic. The passion, the obsessiveness
that surrounds the topic of dieting tells us that we are dealing with an
underlying religious idea, but one which masks itself as the epitome of
secular rationalism. For what could be more reasonable than wanting
to lose weight?

It is interesting in this regard that dieting receives such strong
emphasis among fundamentalist Christians in the United States.[29]
Indeed, Christian writings on dieting have revealed the essentially
moral nature of the struggle for weight control, and the way it has
come to represent the struggle within the self for a sense of goodness.
Reports of eating disorders in the daughters of the families of
Fundamentalist Christians suggest a milieu that in many respects
magnifies the patterns described as typical in the general culture: an
emphasis on externals and appearance, a discounting of subjectivity, a
rigid, dichotomous mode of thinking about moral issues, and a gender
ideology that women subordinate themselves to male authority.[30]

The importance of dieting as a cultural institution is indicated by the economics of the highly variegated dieting industry. Americans spend billions annually on diet goods and services: bariatric physicians, weight-loss programs, weight spas, reducing pills, diet foods. Losing weight has become a component of the gross national product. Diets themselves that are promoted in popular books have become something of a designer industry, with particular methodologies going in and out of fashion like annual (or seasonal) clothing styles. A recent "Consumer Guide," by Theodore Berland, called *Rating the Diets*, offers a balanced and sensible evaluation of over 50 of the best-known plans.[31] It is interesting, though, to view the diets as if one were an anthropologist from a foreign culture. Dieting is associated with the haunts of the rich and famous (the *Beverly Hills Diet*, the *Hilton Head Metabolism Diet*, the *Palm Beach Long-life Diet*), with success and competition (*Eat to Win*), with futurism (the *Blast-off Diet*, the *21st Century Diet*), with the appeal to authority (diets entitled Dr. —'s Diet), even with hedonism (the *Wild-weekend Diet*). The dichotomous thinking of the dieter is evident in the *Fit-or-Fat Target Diet*, as is the push-button mentality in the *How to Lose 5 Lbs Fast* method. One title, *Thin Kids*, whose content is evaluated enthusiastically by Breland, would send a shudder down the spine of any therapist who works with eating disorders.

Within this milieu of weight obsession, a few still, small voices from the scientific community have begun to speak out on the great illusion promoted by the diet industry – that dieting is an effective way to lose weight. Obesity experts have now documented that while large amounts of weight can be lost on any given diet, it will almost inevitably be regained. What is more, the cycle of weight loss and weight gain of the "yo-yo dieter" is not only medically dangerous but makes each successive dieting attempt more difficult. Set-point theory, which posits that weight for an individual tends to be regulated within a certain range, is beginning to find an audience, at least in the scientific community.[32] But these skeptical voices buck the tide. However much we may think of ourselves as a scientifically enlightened society, magical thinking holds sway when it comes to our most cherished illusions. Indeed, such rational persuasion is exceedingly ineffective with eating-disordered patients, who will commonly respond to readings of *The Dieter's Dilemma* or *Diet's Don't Work* with the comment, "I hate that book."

The Disease is Dieting

Anorexic or bulimic patients tend to be particularly vulnerable to cultural messages about dieting, which offer the promise of taking control of one's life through the alteration of body shape. Many thousands (or probably millions) of efforts at dieting are undoubtedly started and stopped, with no effect whatsoever other than a small amount of mental and material expenditure. However, the anorexic or bulimic woman latches on to dieting for a different purpose – to give her life direction, to obliterate emotional pain, to solve a problem of identity. Once again we come back to the idea of the defense of an ethnic disorder, drawn from the repertoire of behaviors on which a culture places great value.

The complexity of anorexia nervosa and bulimia has led many to be wary about the possible oversimplification of the view that it all simply comes down to excessive dieting. However, an important and remarkable series of studies by C. Peter Herman and Janet Polivy has suggested that the consequences of dieting, particularly when taken to extremes, may be sufficiently pernicious to account for many of the symptoms of eating disorders.[33] Herman and Polivy invited a group of students who consistently dieted (and a group of non-dieting subjects) to their laboratory to partake in an experiment that was ostensibly a study in "taste discrimination." The subjects were initially asked to drink either one or two milkshakes, and then to fill out some rating scales on the taste of some food that was served in the laboratory. In order to complete the rating, subjects were told to "eat as much as you like." Non-dieting subjects, as expected, tended to sample less food after two milkshakes than after one. But the dieters (in Herman and Polivy's terms, "restrained eaters") surprisingly showed just the opposite trend; they ate *more* after two milkshakes than after one. Herman and Polivy suggest that non-dieters regulate their appetite according to normal cues of satiety; but the chronically deprived dieters *counterregulate* – that is, the normal control of their food intake by physiological cues of fullness is somehow disrupted by the chronic effects of dieting.[34]

The mechanism by which this dysregulation occurs was illuminated by some further studies. Dieters were divided into two groups, each of which was given an equal amount of preload, with identical caloric content; however, one group was told that the food was calorie-rich, while the other was told that it was calorie-poor. Which group consumed more in the sham taste-discrimination task? Again, contrary to what one would expect, it was the calorie-rich group who consumed more food. The authors suggest the interpretation that the dieter, having been told that she just consumed calorie-rich food, assumes that "I blew it," that most common lament of the failed dieter. Having blown it, the subject then throws all caution to the wind and gorges herself on laboratory food. The effect is a "cognitive," and not necessarily a physiological one: it is not so much what the dieter has eaten, as what she thinks about what she has eaten that triggers a counterregulatory binge.[35]

Additional research extended the findings further. In dieters, disinhibited eating is triggered by a lowering of mood, drinking alcohol, or the elevation of emotional stress.[36] All of these are common triggers of binge-eating among bulimics. And in one important study, it was found that the disinhibited eating usually exhibited by dieters is radically reduced when another subject or observer is present in the laboratory room.[37] This corresponds well with the reports of most bulimics that their binge-eating typically takes place alone, and is much less likely to do so in the presence of others.[38]

In an overview of their work, Herman and Polivy suggest that the common view in the culture is that excessive eating is what makes dieting "necessary." Their research, on the other hand, suggests that the direction of causality is the other way around. To put it concretely, it is not binging that causes dieting, but dieting that causes binging.[39] In their words, therefore, "the disease is dieting." Herman and Polivy's work is extremely important, especially in accounting for the bulimic swings from gorging to starvation. It is perhaps less useful in accounting for anorexia nervosa, except for the fact that the longer a patient remains anorexic (that is, restrained), the more likely she is to develop the chaotic dysregulation of eating typical of bulimia.

The Exercise Connection

Contemporary anorexics draw not only on the contemporary cultural obsession with dieting, but a significant percentage become caught up in compulsive patterns of exercise. Hyperactivity has been recognized as a symptom of anorexia nervosa since the earliest reports, but for years its role was little discussed.[40] It was generally considered to be a secondary phenomenon – perhaps an additional method of reducing body weight, or according to some, a restless form of activity that typically accompanies starvation. Recently, though, some writers have hypothesized a more primary role for hyperactivity in the overall symptomatology of anorexia. Laboratory research, for example, demonstrates that animals who are placed on a restricted food schedule will, if given the opportunity to run, evidence an escalating spiral of increased activity and decreased food intake – often to the point of death from starvation. These "activity anorexias" in animals suggest that a cycle of heightened activity and diminished food intake may be a characteristic psychobiological response, induced by certain environmental conditions. Extrapolating to the human situation, it may provide some insight into the process by which an escalating cycle of self-starvation and increasingly frenetic activity may become "locked in," if triggered by appropriate environmental cues. In the human situation, these cues may be interpersonal but also cultural, as in the cultural sanctions of dieting and exercise.[41]

Perhaps even more than dieting, contemporary Western cultures extol and glamorize exercise. In the United States, the fitness explosion is the contemporary expression of a long-standing national fascination with sports and physical fitness.[42] Indeed, in the 1980s, a worldwide fitness boom has spread throughout the industrialized societies.[43] Exercise machines, health clubs, and new breed of professional "trainer" have together constituted a growth industry that expresses perhaps even more intensely than the preoccupation with slimming the cult of the body in the consumer societies (with which of course it is connected). In New York City, some individuals have suggested that the trainer fills a role in their lives comparable with that of the former social function of the analyst – a kind of secular guru, who provides not only physical training but moral and spiritual guidance.[44] Television commercials in the mid-1980s touted the exercise machine as the ultimate Christmas present, and depicted as the epitome of holiday bliss an attractive and physically fit young wife comforting her perspiring husband as he groaned after yet one more repetition. A new asceticism has spread through the economically anxious and competitive 1980s, one which serves no higher moral aim but which, paradoxically, promises pleasure through self-denial.[45] The culture of fitness fits well with the anorexic's needs, particularly her quest for a sense of self-mastery through severe body discipline as well as a profound concern with body shape. Indeed, among other purposes that it serves, the pursuit of exercise in the broader culture is one more tool – and a particularly effective one at that – in the battle against fat.

The specific role of exercise in anorexia and bulimia, although familiar as a clinical phenomenon, has not been given sufficient study. In one of the few systematic enquiries, a group of Australian researchers found that exercise, not dieting, was the main behavior that precipitated severe weight loss in nine out of 26 cases of anorexia nervosa.[46] In these patients, the families had a general involvement with exercise, suggesting that the behavior in the patient was perhaps triggered through emulation of a parent. A case report in the *Lancet* depicted what may well become an increasingly common presentation, a masked case of anorexia nervosa presenting clinically as an exercise injury. The subject was a 30 year-old woman who complained of severe bilateral injuries to her knees. She revealed during interview that she also suffered from amenorrhea, and was distressed because of her inability to bear children. It turned out that she had gone on a severe weight-reducing diet in her twenties, and when she had regained most of the weight later, she initiated a punishing exercise regime, which at first consisted of running up to 120 miles a week. At the point of seeking medical help, she complained that "exercise was taking up all of her spare time seven days a week," and that a typical day included running 5 miles, swimming 96 lengths in a full-size pool, attending an aerobic dance class (or canoeing or fencing), and doing body-building exercises.[47]

The connection between exercise and anorexia is particularly evident in the high prevalence of shape and weight disorders among young athletes, a problem that has received increasing attention in the literature on sports medicine.[48] Young athletes are often expected to maintain percentages of body fat significantly below the norms for their age level, and this coupled with the intense pressures of coaches and parents as well as the demands of competition itself can lead those who are vulnerable directly into anorexia or bulimia. In fact, surveys of large numbers of elite college athletes reveal that shockingly high numbers admit to using what have been called "pathogenic weight control behaviors" – prolonged fasting, vomiting, diet pills, laxatives, and diuretics.[49] These practices appear to cut across all sports, but they are especially prevalent in those activities that demand weight and/or shape control – for example, gymnastics, figure skating, and wrestling. Wrestlers, in particular, often undergo dramatic fluctuations in caloric intake as they attempt to make a particular weight class and then return to a normal weight in the off-season. While few systematic prevalence studies have been conducted, it is evident to many clinicians who see patients with eating disorders that wrestlers constitute a population at high risk for bulimia or anorexia. And interestingly, on the high school or college level, this is a population that is exclusively male.

Running, which in a sense was the vanguard and at one time the premier activity of the fitness boom, appears to have a particular kinship with anorexia nervosa – a link which becomes evident from the attraction that it holds as a form of exercise for anorexics.[50] A highly disciplined activity that enhances feelings of self-mastery and offers a sense of transcending the limits of the body, running for some becomes an all-consuming compulsive activity that can displace one's interest in other pursuits, particularly other people. In his highly influential book, George Sheehan suggested that through running the jogger finds his identity "because in being a runner, in moving through pain and fatigue and suffering, in imposing stress upon stress, in eliminating all but the necessities of life, he is fulfilling himself and becoming the person he is."[51] As among anorexics, running evokes feelings of identification with the ideology of asceticism and martyrdom:

When I run the roads I am a saint. For that hour I am an Assisi, wearing the least and meanest of clothes. I am Ghandi, the young law student, trotting ten or twelve miles a day and then going to a cheap restaurant to eat his fill of bread. I am Thoreau, the solitary, seeking union with the world around him. On the roads, poverty, chastity and obedience come naturally.[52]

As in anorexia, running provides a sense of mastery, even of perfection through body discipline, for a person who senses the world as otherwise puzzling and uncontrollable:

Discipline in running, discipline in training comes easily. Discipline in real life is another story. The mind and the will and the imagination are not as easily controlled as the legs and the thighs, and the panting chest. Running, of course, helps. The art of running, as Eugene Herrigal wrote of the art of archery, is a profound and far-reaching contest of the runner with himself. And that contest should be to his perfection.[53]

About fat, Sheehan does not equivocate: "The struggle against the slowly advancing glacier of lard begins before we attain our maturity. It never ends. In this war against fat, you have to be a career person."

Just like anorexics, runners tend to be obsessively preoccupied with their body image, and many have an analogous habit of pinching their skin or scanning themselves to test for signs of the hated imperfections of fat. The famous "runner's high," possibly based on elevated levels of circulating endorphins, seems clearly analogous to the "faster's high" of the anorexic, which ultimately may be rooted in the same psychological and biological forces. Both seek a sense of transcendent perfection through self-denial, a narcissistic quest that is achieved through heroic asceticism. Both find the world of interpersonal relationships disappointing and unsatisfying and tend to be repelled by the comforts and excesses of affluence. In a sense, as Sours pointed out, anorexia and running may both be manifestations of the same broad changes that have taken place in middle-class culture, the seeking of a self-imposed trial of self-denial in a world in which the soul has been lost.

In a remarkable publication that stunned the clinical community, Yates, Leehey, and Shisslak described a number of patients who manifested what they called an "obligatory running syndrome," which in turn reflected, in their view, an "analogue of anorexia nervosa."[54] The authors described three men in their thirties and forties, who had began running following major life crises – in two cases the breakup of a marriage, and in a third the decline of a "polite but disappointing marriage." All three were high achievers – one a highly skilled artisan who "carved statues in exquisite detail," the second a successful architect, and the third a physicist who finished his degree because he had never been good at science and wanted to "meet the challenge." In a striking parallel with anorexics, all three had been "good boys" from achievement-oriented families in which the expression of emotion had been strongly discouraged. Each man recalled feeling overweight, "fat," and in poor health prior to beginning his running regime. All three had become totally obsessive and ritualistic about their running regimes, and had long ignored physical injuries for which they had finally sought help. One of the subjects, for example, "ran at least 10 miles a day, regardless of the weather or his state of health. He had a recurrent Achilles tendinitis and a slight limp – the result of an improperly healed stress fracture. He maintained a library of books about running and a diary of his running speed calculated in miles per hour for each hour travelled." (p. 252) Each of the obligatory runners had an obsession with thinness. The subject above felt that his running was optimal only when he reached a very low ratio of fat to lean body mass, which he had precisely specified.

The concept of obligatory running generated intense controversy, as was evident in the flood of letters to the medical journal in which the article was originally published.[55] Many respondents argued, perhaps somewhat defensively, that Yates had denigrated a liberating, health-promoting activity (running) to the status of a pathology (anorexia). But the original article only intended to draw an analogy between the psychology of compulsive running and anorexia, not to diagnose the entire running population. Not surprisingly, a number of subsequent studies have failed to find any *general* tendencies towards psychopathology among runners.[56] But in an as yet unpublished study that utilized a more aggressive and focused questionnaire, weight obsessions and other pathological eating attitudes were found to be widespread in a large sample of dedicated runners.[57] Particularly striking was the extent to which these runners admitted to severe caloric restriction and binge-eating, as well as the practice of compensating for binges by adding miles to an already rigorous training schedule. "Paying the price" for one's caloric "debts" is of course a characteristic element of bulimic psychology. Running, however, particularly in moderation, is obviously a healthier activity than purging. This fact may be of some clinical significance; prescribing exercise may be one means of interrupting the bulimic cycle.

The phenomenon of obligatory running and other forms of compulsive exercise points to some issues of more general cultural significance. In contemporary societies, given the turmoil in personal relationships and the individual's growing sense of isolation, men as well as women are prone to developing addictive, obsessive solutions to the problems of life – and particularly, in our weight-obsessed society, to an insistent focus on body weight in shape. In men, these modern issues of identity are more likely to take place in middle age, when an incipient sense of physical decline precipitates a profound threat to one's sense of competence and self-esteem. What is more, men are much more likely to emphasize activity and exercise over dieting, a choice that is more compatible with sex-role expectations. It may well be, then, that among men, problems comparable to anorexia are often masked beneath a preoccupation with exercise and sports. But the underlying issues – a weakened sense of identity and self-esteem, and obsessive quest for perfection fought out concretely in terms of health, body-image, and particularly fatness – are indeed analogous.

In the late 1980s, there is now evidence in America of a decline in interest in running, and even of a decline in the obsession with dieting. The new interest is in body building, and with an appearance that emphasizes not so much thinness, but strength. Meanwhile, the battle with fatness and obesity remains.[58] It is too early to tell what impact these changes in ideal body image will have, particularly on the prevalence of eating disorders. But the larger issues, to which eating disorders are related, remain: the problem of self-regulation in a culture of plenty, in which traditional moral ideologies have given way to the ethics of obsessionality.

7

THE TEMPLATES OF A DISEASE

"Don't go crazy, but if you do, you should behave as follows."

George Devereux, *Basic Problems in Ethnopsychiatry*

The deviant behavior patterns that become prevalent in a society tend to follow particular models or templates that are immediately and widely "recognized" by members of the culture. *Amok*, for example, represented a certain recognizable pattern of going crazy that was widely known, at least formerly, in Southeast Asia. When a person, typically a man, reached a certain point of tension or stress that was intolerable, the subsequent explosive outburst of violence was a "standardized," ready-made structure into which his homicidal rage could be discharged. Running through villages, randomly lashing out at strangers, fiercely eluding capture, the *Amok* runner followed a totally predictable (if frightening) pattern within his own culture. Everyone recognized an *Amok* and knew what to expect, not least the *Amok* runner himself. As Devereux put it, "the young Malay hopes he will never find himself in straits so desperate that only one acceptable solution remains open to him: running *amok*. He knows, however, that should such a situation arise, he *will have* to become an *amok* runner and *he will know how to* conduct himself properly."[1] Standardized patterns of psychopathology in a culture are *patterns of misconduct*, known to the actor and recognized by the observer. When it comes to enacting deviance, Devereux suggests, culture proved a directive to the effect of "Don't go crazy, but if you do, you should behave as follows."[2]

The influence of such a social model of disorder was probably involved in the spreading of the hysterical pattern in the nineteenth century. Hysteria illustrates dramatically how a pattern of deviance can be communicated by processes of social "contagion" or imitation. The hysterical patient, as Szasz once suggested, is playing the role of someone who is sick, although without being conscious of doing so.[3]

The symptoms of hysteria – paralysis, blindness, anaesthesia – are readily copied or simulated, and they also offer an opportunity for the dramatization of personal problems. "Who are you copying now?," Freud queried of his famous patient, Dora. In an era in which the dramatic gesture was fashionable in the cities of Europe, hysterical symptoms could easily become the dominant model of disorder because of their consistency with a certain cultural style.[4]

But in the case of hysteria, an additional force may also have been operative, and that is the unwitting influence of healers themselves, who came to expect that a certain pattern of behavior would manifest itself. Such iatrogenic effects were clearly in evidence in the famous lecture-demonstrations of Charcot, which were not only widely attended by physicians, but also by writers, artists, and other members of the Parisian intelligentsia. Charcot formulated in detail the symptoms of an "hysterical attack," which consisted of a precise sequence of convulsions, dramatic enactments, and the like. Unbeknownst to him, however, his assistants had secretly coached the patients on precisely how to respond to his hypnotic suggestions. The patients had also learned about convulsive symptoms from being housed on the same ward as the epileptic patients. Only later did it become evident that the "stages of an hysterial attack" discovered by Charcot could only be found in Paris, an embarrassment that ultimately cost the great neurologist his scientific reputation.[5]

Contemporary social-learning theory provides some concepts that enable a better understanding of how templates for deviant behavior are disseminated. For example, the research of Albert Bandura and his colleagues show how easily complex patterns of behavior can be acquired by the simple observation of "model." What is more, such imitation will be facilitated if the model is a figure of high prestige, or particularly if the model can demonstrate that his or her behavior leads to social power or the control over resources.[6] In the case of deviant behavior, or an ethnic disorder, spreading of the symptoms would be enhanced if they were modelled by figures of high prestige or visibility in the culture, or by peers (or other socially influential figures) who themselves are observed to receive positive reinforcement for their symptomatic behavior.

Anorexia by Proxy

In her last paper, Bruch suggested that within her own lifetime she witnessed the transformation of anorexia nervosa from an individual into a social disease. Even as recently as the 1960s, she suggested, cases of anorexia nervosa occurred in individuals who had never heard about the disorder: it was as if each created the symptoms anew out of the crucible of their own individual experience. But more recently, she suggested, as the disease has become more common and increasingly known, the clinical picture has undergone a subtle transformation. The classical anorexic was driven by a fierce quest for individual autonomy: what was remarkable was the clinical uniformity of the solution to a problem that each patient had struggled to come to grips with on her own. In contrast, many of today's patients had heard about the disease before becoming sick, and many had "tried it out" after seeing a television program about the disorder or doing a research project in a biology class. Also, Bruch suggested, today's patients have less resistance to social influence, and they often "cling to or compete with each other." In short, "the desire to be special or unique is expressed with less vigor and urgency, and I cannot suppress the suspicion that some of the symptoms are imitated or faked." Bruch even goes as far as to suggest that the numerous programs for the treatment of eating disorders may have contributed to the socialization of the disease.[7]

The fact that anorexia nervosa itself can be directly imitated and emulated, producing in some instances a simulated form of the illness, is evident in a report by a Washington, DC psychiatrist. Two patients, both of whom had serious neurological illnesses, loudly proclaimed that they had had "eating disorders," but it turned out that in neither case was the disorder authentic. The first patient, who suffered from multiple sclerosis, first manifested her symptoms – which consisted of refusing meals and vomiting – after having been exposed to a number of anorexic patients in an adolescent ward of a hospital. Her "anorexia" was both a means of protecting herself against a very real developmental depression, but also a way of denying the seriousness of her own neurological disease. The second patient is an even more blatant instance of simulation. During her hospitalization, she also was exposed to numerous anorexic patients and reported during a "rap" group that she had had a previous hospitalization for anorexia nervosa, from which she stated that she had recovered through a behavior-modification program. Given the fact that she was at this point obese, she totally terrified the anorexic patients, who concluded that obesity would indeed be their fate were they to comply with the hospital's refeeding protocol. Ultimately, though, the patient confessed that her tale of previous anorexia had been fabricated. Interestingly, both of these patients were of lower socioeconomic class, and therefore to become "anorexic" was to emulate the "status" of the apparently well-heeled anorexic patients on the ward.[8]

An even more remarkable instance of such acquired anorexia was that developed by a patient who had been blind since the age of 2.[9] This patient originally developed a severe depression in the context of a borderline personality, and had made multiple suicide attempts that resulted in her psychiatric hospitalization. She only developed anorexic symptoms after meeting several patients in the hospital who had the disorder. Initially, she had found these patients to be "very weird," but apparently found in their symptoms a suitable method for the enactment of her own self-destructive impulses. The disorder that she did develop was authentic, at least in comparison with the two patients we just discussed. The patient pinched herself to make sure that she was "not fat," and carried a computerized scale around with her whose voice synthesizer offered messages such as "You have gained one pound today." She thought incessantly about food, and lost considerable amounts of weight. Despite the validity of the diagnosis of anorexia, it seems unlikely that she would have developed her symptoms without suitable models. The development of a disorder of body image is particularly remarkable in her case, in that she could only receive the information about anorexia from hearing about it. We usually think of disorders of body image as contingent on the visualization of body shape. Apparently, in her case, acquired knowledge about the disorder was enough to trigger internal feelings of fatness. But beyond the special circumstances of this case, it is probably true that many patients with histrionic or borderline personalities are especially vulnerable to internalizing the dominant model of psychopathology of their own era. Thus, in the era of *The Exorcist* (in the late 1960s and early 1970s), many such patients may have more typically presented clinically as "possessed."[10] And even as late as the 1940s, many such patients still manifested "astasia-abasia", a nineteenth-century hysterical pattern, in hospitals in New York.[11]

The preceeding case histories were instances in which the disorder was a late "acquisition" and was superimposed on an already existing problem. However, the factors of imitation and competition play a role in many cases in which anorexia is the primary symptom. In particular, contemporary anorexics tend to be highly competitive, often vying to outdo each other in their degree of gauntness or the amount of food on which they can survive. Partly, this can be understood in the context of the intensely competitive atmosphere surrounding contemporary dieting, particularly among female adolescents.[12] In a culture in which the temptation to overeat has such threatening consequences to self-esteem, a disease in which one eats nothing and becomes scrawny represents the ultimate dieting triumph and therefore is likely to arouse mixed feelings of envy, resentment, and admiration. Even more mature women tend to be competitive about weight. As one writer pointed out, it is not uncharacteristic for many women, on entering a room, to quickly scan the scene to see if they are about to be shown up by an extremely thin woman.[13] Female nurses who care for anorexic patients are particularly vulnerable to these competitive feelings; "how does she do it?" is not an infrequent comment that follows a contentious interaction with a patient.

Hilde Bruch noted an increase in competitiveness among the anorexic patients she observed in the 1970s. She provided some examples in her posthumously published *Conversations with Anorexics*. One patient, whom Bruch named "Megen – a perfect size 1," was quite literal about how she experienced her triumph in terms of contemporary fashion. Having recently gained some weight from her low of 80 pounds, she looked back wistfully at the time when she could "turn heads" by asking for a size 1 in a clothing store: "It was like the whole store, everybody was standing around, would go, 'Golly you are thin – that must be nice.' And everybody, 'Oh, that's great – you can find these clothes, and everything is made for slender people nowadays, and how wonderful it must be to be thin.'"[14] Anorexia apparently commands respect in the contemporary boutique (or at least that of the late 1970s), in which women over size 9 have difficulty in finding a dress. Another patient, whom Bruch dubbed "Norah, the competitor," developed anorexia after going on a group trip over the summer during which another girl developed the illness. Having lost a large amount of weight, Nora thought about her eating in entirely competitive terms:

I think of all the people I am competing with at school, the ones who don't eat, and then I bet they are not eating over Thanksgiving . . . One of my friends from high school lost weight when she went to college, and when I want to eat ice cream, I think, "I bet she doesn't do it," and then I can't eat it either.[15]

Competition among peers is one essential way in which anorexic symptoms can be spread or modeled. In her autobiography, Aimee

Liu reported how one of her friends, whom she had always admired for her popularity, shocked her at one point by asking her "how she did it" (i.e. lost weight). Liu's response was non-committal – she was stunned at suddenly being in a superior role with this person, whom she herself had always envied. Several months later, she was even more shocked at the sight of her formerly full-bodied friend's gauntness.[16]

The competitive aspects of anorexia are probably particularly heightened in a country such as America, in which, as one writer points out, people compete not only for success but also about diseases, particularly if they are fashionable. The frequent (and incorrect) comment that anorexia is now an "American" disease probably stems from a perception of the competitive and *au courant* aura that currently surrounds the illness.[17]

The Role of the Mass Media

In the present era, behavioral modeling is radically enhanced by the mass media. Much discussion has been conducted about how fashion models or television characters influence the body ideals that are so important in understanding anorexia nervosa. Less has been said, however, about how the media may influence the modeling of the disorder itself. Anecdotal evidence suggests that such influences may be important in the shaping of anorexic symptoms. In a Canadian study, one subgroup of anorexic patients developed their symptoms after the airing of a documentary program about eating disorders. Like the pseudo-anorexics described in the preceeding section, these patients little resembled the classic personalities associated with eating disorders before their anorexic symptoms appeared.[18] Another report described the development of anorexia nervosa following a viewing of the television version of the popular account, *The Best Little Girl in the World*, whose protagonist was widely admired by the patient and her friends.[19] It is possible that these media accounts function similarly to fictional films about adolescent suicide, which have sometimes been followed by an elevated rate of suicide attempts.[20] Apparently, self-destructive behavior may be legitimized by the implicit glamorization of television, particularly among those who are susceptible.

While television dramas and reports have had an impact, undoubtedly the most prolific source of information about eating disorders has been the popular press – especially articles in women's magazines, but also a seemingly never-ending stream of autobiographical books. As Sours once pointed out, probably no psychiatric disorder in history has received as much publicity as anorexia nervosa. By the early 1980s, the number of articles on anorexia nervosa had mushroomed, but by the mid-1980s the focus had switched to bulimia.[21] The spectacle of an affluent young woman starving herself to death is a fertile subject for sensationalistic journalism. The glamorization of anorexia was most blatantly evident in a mid-1970s article in *Playgirl* that identified anorexics as today's "Golden Girls," but a sensational aura is also fostered by such titles as "When dieting goes wild," "Anorexia nervosa: dying of thinness," and "My sister and I tried to outdiet each other with some pretty scary results."[22] Not all of this literature sensationalizes, however; the ostensible purpose in many cases is to sound the alarm (for example, an article entitled "Danger – you can overdo dieting").[22] However, it is likely that much of it, even if unwittingly, may encourage identification and imitation.

Thus, for example, one article on anorexia began:

What sort of person gets anorexia nervosa? Most of them are female, young (under twenty), *bright, energetic and articulate. Good in school, good in sports, the anorexic rises to competition and achieves. She is slender, attractive, usually fun to be around.* But she worries . . . about grades, about her friends, about her looks. Is she getting fat? Wouldn't she look better if she lost just a few more pounds? *She is constantly dieting, becoming thinner and thinner. She talks about it all the time. She works harder and harder in gym; she is an exercise nut. Running around all day, she skips meals.*[24] (emphases mine throughout)

It is difficult to imagine that many adolescents would *not* admire most of these attributes. As a result, it seems that the disorder is implicitly glamorized. A personal account by a recovered anorexic in *Seventeen* magazine described the effect:

I came across stories of anorexics and bulimics in magazines and devoured them. "When Kitty weighted eighty-six pounds, she still perceived her body as obese. After eating one chocolate chip cookie, she stayed up all night doing jumping jacks." I wanted to know how anorexics did it – how they managed to stop eating, how they got so thin. The tragedy of their stories escaped me . . . The anorexics I read about were glamorous to me. I did not see them as pathetic; I wanted what happened to them to happen to me. It did.[25]

Autobiographical books on eating disorders have also in some instances contributed to the social modeling of the disease. Health

professionals involved in the treatment of eating disorders have expressed concern with the extraordinary emphasis in many of these tracts on the detailed descriptions of symptoms, which may unwittingly provide symptomatic strategies for those who are vulnerable. An example of this possibility is the autobiography of Cherry Boone O'Neill, who describes growing up in a well-known performing family, the development of a severe anorexic disorder during her adolescence, and her subsequent recovery through psychotherapy, medication, and involvement in a Christian community. O'Neill's story is valuable in many respects, particularly her description of how a number of seemingly normal stresses – adolescent sexual anxieties, identity confusion, an enmeshed family, a number of deaths inadequately grieved, performance pressures – can, when added together, precipitate the nightmarish descent into anorexia nervosa. Undoubtedly what makes the book so vivid is the excruciatingly detailed description of the years of starvation, the punishing exercise regimes, the bizarre and secretive eating rituals (at one point, she describes eating the remains from a dog's dish), and the consumption of frightening quantities of laxatives.[26] In a subsequent book O'Neill published a sample of the many letters she received in response to her book and lectures, along with her typically sensitive and well-informed responses. Most of the letters expressed gratitude to O'Neill for bringing the disorder out of the closet and providing numerous sufferers with hope of recovery.

However, one letter indicates the potential risks of detailed symptom description, when it comes to techniques of weight control:

When you came to Australia, I saw you on television . . . I purchased your book in order that I might learn more about my own problems. I suffer from the "slimmer's disease", as you have probably guessed. In some ways your story helped me to better understand myself but some of the techniques you used to lose weight were unknown to me and I borrowed them. In some ways your book actually made my problem worse. I wish you hadn't gone into certain details of you illness . . .[27]

O'Neill (to her credit) acknowledged her dismay at having unwittingly provided someone with methods for inducing emaciation, and admitted to having had misgivings from the very outset about providing detail. After apologizing, she suggested to the writer that "ultimately you must bear responsibility for your own decisions. This is part of growing up and getting well." In fairness, though, it should be pointed out that this is the only letter that O'Neill received reporting such imitation.

Probably the most widely known accounts of eating disorders are those of Hollywood stars. Karen Carpenter, whose death from complications associated with anorexia nervosa was widely publicized in articles and documentaries, seemed to epitomize the gap between the surface of casual friendship and "good vibes" and the underlying sense of loneliness and personal alientation that was so much a part of the culture of the 1970s.[28] But more recently, there is the instance of Jane Fonda, whose long struggle with bulimia was the subject of the first chapter in her best-selling workout book.[29] Her intent was clearly to discourage others from the use of abusive methods of weight control, and rather to adopt the fitness/health ideology of the 1980s, of which Fonda has undoubtedly been one of the most influential proponents. But the risk of sanctioning or rationalizing purging remained, particularly by a figure whose maintenance of a youthful image in her late forties was viewed with astonished admiration by a culture obsessed with the problems of appearance and aging.

Getting Skinny with the Stars: The Case of the Beverly Hills Diet

In a sense, the entire culture of diet books is a breeding ground for eating disorders. Anorexics and bulimics are typically avid readers of diet books, and often weave them directly into the fabric of their symptoms. This is an issue that has been given little systematic study, but it is an impression from clinical experience that is widely shared. In light of the research reviewed in the last chapter on restrained eating, though, this should come as no surprise. Particularly conducive to eating disorders are diets that suggest severe caloric restriction, or that implicitly or explicitly encourage binging. The rice diet, which has been a respectable history in the treatment of medical obesity, crops up frequently, in this author's experience, in the history of anorexic patients. Often, it was utilized by a parent or sibling in a struggle against obesity. A prescription for bulimia seems implicit in the Diet Workshop's Wild Weekend Diet, which recommends 800 calories per day during the week and 2,100 plus on the weekend; in the concise formulation of Theodore Berland, "sparse during the week; pig-out on the weekend." This diet is intentionally structured to follow the renunciation-to-indulgence cycle of the typical working week; it presents a tantalizing instance of how disturbed eating may be a magnification of "normal" contemporary eating patterns (see below).[30]

But undoubtedly the most notorious example of a prescription for eating disorders is that of the *Beverly Hills Diet*, a book that sold over a million copies in the early 1980s and, in this author's experience, was used as a manual by a number of patients in the early stages of their disorder.[31] This tract encourages the use of large amounts of fruit (it dictates eating nothing but fruit for the first few days), and propounds a pseudo-scientific notion of "conscious combining," which translates into consuming large amounts of food, such as fruit, that will "cancel out" the fattening effect of other foods. The overall purpose, as one critique suggested, is to make binge-eating possible through the liquefaction of foods that would otherwise produce "fat." The author of the Beverly Hills Diet expresses unabashed enthusiasm about the elimination of foods that would compromise skinniness: "If you have loose bowel movements, hooray . . . Keep in mind that pounds leave your body in two main ways – bowl movements and urination. The more time you spend on the toilet, the better."[32] She raises a hypothetical reader's rhetorical question: "Won't I be living in the bathroom after eating all that fruit?" Her answer: "Hopefully, but probably not. . ."[33]

The Beverly Hills Diet was initially heralded as the Final Solution to the problem of fat, as is evident from the cover story of an issue of *Harper's Bazaar* which proclaimed it "the diet phenomenon of the 1980s" and went on to intone: "A unique, boldly original new food program, now sweeping across the US, has already been tried and tested in Beverly Hills among the movie stars, the trend-setters and the ultra-body conscious."[34] The author herself had, with all due modesty, proclaimed it "the skinny voice of America, the diet conscience of the world." The publication of the book soon generated some devastating critiques, however. One article in the *Journal of the American Medical Association*, whose authors reported seeing a number of Beverly Hills dieters who had suffered from dizziness, headache, and fatigue, pointed out that the plan was built on a virtually grotesque misunderstanding of the physiology of digestion.[35] The most blatant example was the author's assertion that "As long as food is fully digested, fully processed through the body, you will not gain weight. It is only undigested food, food that is 'stuck' in your body for whatever reason, that accumulates and becomes fat." As the critics pointed out, precisely the opposite is true – only digested food can be absorbed and so transformed. The author gives evidence of a kind of magical thinking that is characteristic of anorexics: the "feeling" of fat (i.e. being full) is confused with a change in body shape.

Even more devastating was a critique by obesity experts Susan and

O. Wayne Wooley.[36] The Wooleys comment that the author has written a virtual handbook for anorexic behavior: "the spectre of starvation haunts the pages of the Beverly Hills Diet." With its virtual obsession with every mouthful of food (documented by complicated charts scheduling every morsel of intake), its suggestion of hyperactivity associated with reduced food intake ("three little grapes and you're ready to run a mile"), its association of hunger and an empty stomach with feelings of moral purity, the Beverly Hills diet represents "an unwitting translation of the anorexic's delusional system into the jargon of pop culture and pseudo-science."[37] Repeatedly, it equates the feeling of fullness after meals with "being fat," and it engages in typical dichotomous thinking, the morality of body shape: the world is divided up into "fatties" and "skinnies." The diet guru, with a metaphor that could beautifully articulate the panicked feelings of countless anorexic patients, describes the scale as "that little mechanical device that has more effect on us than the atom bomb," and, in another passage, as "your non-judgemental lover." And in a fantastic formula for body-image distortion, she asserts "the scale forces us to see and feel ourselves as we really are . . ." Particularly virulent, the Wooleys suggest, is the author's tacit encouragement of bingeing (with enough "conscious combining," you can eat anything you want) and purging (the praise of catharsis described above). In fact, the diet "marks the first time an eating disorder – anorexia nervosa – has been marketed as a cure for obesity. It is a case of one disease being offered as a cure for another."[38] Consistent with the premise of this chapter about the social modeling of eating disorders, the Wooleys suggest that it represents "a form of direct training in anorexic behavior," the "mass-marketing of anorexia nervosa."

The Beverly Hills Diet also represents something else: the assimilation of eating disorders to the culture of narcissism and tinsel. The author made no secret about the adoption of the diet by the rich and famous. Indeed, not only was it adopted by more and more celebrities, but "the chanteuse set was singing its glories."[39] In a sense, the philosophy of this book represents the fulfillment of the trend described by Bruch: the assimilation of a disorder that once represented a solitary quest by a few isolated individuals obsessed with self-discipline to the chaotic and impulse-ridden life-style of the self-indulgent.[40] Indeed, as the author promised, "Once you are perfect, you have your choice of *everything* . . . Now you can go to bed at night feeling good about yourself . . . Now you can keep your eyes open when you pass the mirror . . . and make love with the lights on."[41] In the words of one of the converts to the diet, "I did it and I'm totally in love with myself."[42]

By the late 1980s, it appears that enthusiasm for the Beverly Hills Diet has waned, even though the book is still on the shelves in the shopping malls. Word has gotten around about its dangers, and in any case it was bound to succumb to the fate of "last-year's diet" – oblivion. Diets, as we pointed out in the last chapter, are as ephemeral as any fashion styles. But the Beverly Hills Diet illustrates better than anything else the social sanction for a "template of deviance." Perhaps its demise reflects a turning of the tide, but it is too early to tell.

The Socialization of Bulimia

A striking fact about bulimia is that, compared with anorexia nervosa as a symptom, it is relatively easily "learned," or acquired.[43] This may partially account for the tremendous heterogeneity of bulimic patients, the difficulty of locating a characteristic "bulimic personality." As we suggested earlier, the bulimic cycle may reflect a temporary "experiment" in weight control by an otherwise psychiatrically "normal" subject, an addictive "stress" syndrome used to discharge emotional tension much in the same way as alcohol, or in the extreme a masochistic behavior that is used to hold together a tenuously organized borderline personality. The flexible assimilation of bulimia to all of these very different conditions is a function of its social "availability," its visibility as a template of deviance.[44]

Bulimic behavior has become so common on college campuses that it has the character of a fad, comparable, as Orbach suggests, to pot-smoking.[45] Binging and purging seems to sweep like a brush-fire through college dormitories, almost like one of the famous epidemics of mass hysteria. One student from a large university in the northeastern United States reported that in her dormitory, one floor had become known as the "bulimic floor:" residents of the floor were eyed suspiciously when entering a bathroom, whose odor evoked images of the Roman vomitoria. A particularly astonishing development, also, is the emergence of bulimia as a group activity. Patients sometime report "trying it with a friend;" notes are compared, particularly techniques of purging. Perhaps even more shocking are reports of the practice of collective bulimia in sororities. One student recounted that in a prestigious college in the western USA, it was common for her sorority sisters to "pig out" at a fraternity house, and then return to the sorority and vomit together in the bathroom. The sorority is a breeding ground for eating disorders, given the emphasis of most sisters towards social life, the resulting preoccupation with physical appearance, and, of course, the competition. In a systematic study of two sororities, Crandall found that binge-eating was the norm rather than the exception, and in one, greater degrees of binge-eating were associated with higher degrees of popularity. Furthermore, binge-eating tended to be concentrated among certain networks of friends, in a pattern that suggested a high degree of social influence.[46]

In speaking about such "social" bulimia, the question has been raised about whether such activity should be dignified with clinical status. One writer argued strongly that "fad bulimia" should be clearly distinguished from the authentic clinical pattern; the distinguishing features of the former are its superficiality and its transience.[47] The distinction may in some instances be difficult to make in practice, although it is unlikely that most fad bulimics will ever appear for treatment. The existence of fad bulimia is one probable reason why some reports that make claims that 20 or 50 percent of college women have an eating disorder are most likely inflated. This is not to minimize the clinical problems that do exist.

The acquisition of the bulimic pattern from social models is evident in the reports of clinical patients, most of whom report having heard about it from a friend, or reading about it in a magazine article.[48] One patient even claimed that she got the idea from an inquiry by a doctor into her weight-control practices.[49] Patients typically describe being "initiated" into the practice by a friend, a sibling, or in one case, the patient's mother. Such learning by imitation does not of course account for or explain the clinical disorder; for this, one must understand the predisposing factors (personality, mood disorder, weight history) that led the person to incorporate and finally become addicted to such self-abusive behavior. But these data do suggest that social factors provide the model or template for the particular form that the symptomatic behavior takes.

The magazine articles and books that we discussed previously for anorexia nervosa are if anything more contributive to bulimia. Purging techniques, in particular, are eagerly snapped up by those who are vulnerable. Particularly astonishing, though, has been the appearance of printed material directly advocating the adoption of bulimia. An advertisement in the *New York Times* (printed, astonishingly, on the "Health" pages) promoted a book called *Responsible Bulimia*, to be obtained by mail order.[50] The advertisement claimed that the author had safely practiced bulimia for several years, which had enabled him to eat freely, control his weight, and preserve his health through dental care and medical monitoring. Bulimia, the advertisement claimed, was an age-old health practice, sanctioned by the ancients (the latter part of the claim is questionable, as Roman physicians criticized the practice). The book, whose cover depicted the handsome and well-dressed author holding two large plates of food, included a personal communication to myself indicating that the author had now (six months after the appearance of the advertisement in the *New York Times*) totally reversed his position, that bulimia was "physically destructive" and "emotionally devastating," and that he now strongly discouraged its use.[51] The book itself makes a case for bulimia as an alternative to drastic medical options for the control of obesity, with which the author had struggled. The book includes statements that would make any therapist who works with eating disordered patients shudder:

I recently read an article which talked about some women who have been bulimic for 30 years. The therapists felt it a great tragedy that there were people who had suffered for 30 years with bulimia. I would say "congratulations" to these women. They are heroines in my eyes. They have been enjoying the hunger-free thin life for 30 years, and have managed to survive with their health intact.[52]

Completely ignoring Jane Fonda's reports of years of suffering and ultimate denunciation of bulimia, he writes "If such a health-conscious female like Jane Fonda can use bulimia for several years, then perhaps it is just further indication that bulimia is not necessarily the degrading, irresponsible practice which the eating disorder people would have us believe."[53] It is not known how many people were affected by *Responsible Bulimia* or the monthly newsletter published by the author. Unfortunately, those who saw the advertisement in the *New York Times* (which in itself was a form of implicit sanction) were not the beneficiaries of the author's subsequent retraction.

Eating Disorders are Disorders of Eating: The Anorexic–Bulimic Conflict

The social patterning of eating disorders can also be viewed in a much broader perspective, in relation to issues about food, eating styles, and weight control in the advanced industrial societies. In the food-abundant, urban cultures of the West, food has become a pervasive symbol of affluence and the contemporary ethic of pleasure-seeking. In contemporary societies, as Roland Barthes pointed out, virtually every situation has become an occasion for eating – working, driving, television watching, and of course socializing.[54] At the same time, though, contemporary eating has become radically desocialized and individualized; collective eating rituals, particularly the family meal, have undergone a radical decline.[55] In fact, in the United States, very little eating is taken at regularly scheduled "meals." We have become a culture of "grazers" or "foragers;" snacking, usually in the form of irregularly scheduled episodes with unpredictable nutritional intake, has replaced the tradition of three-meals-a-day.[56] These trends are particularly in evidence on college campuses, where eating disorders are most rampant. Students tend to eat irregularly, with meal-skipping a way of life for many.[57] Meanwhile, snack food – particularly of the high-carbohydrate, high-calorie type – is everywhere available, in the bookstore, in the student center, even in designated areas in the library. The fast-paced life of the professional has also resulted in new eating styles, under pressure of the "chronic shortage of time." A recent book on nutrition by a respected researcher devotes some space to the problem of satisfactory eating and nutrition when at professional conferences.[58] In the highly pressurized, sometimes frenetic academic or professional environment, it is therefore not surprising that disorders of alimentation have become common; to some extent, they directly reflect the desocialization of contemporary eating patterns. In this sense, eating disorders are not only reflections of cultural preoccupations with shape and weight; they also mirror the general disorganization of social eating *per se.*

But changes in eating patterns are not only qualitative, but also quantitative. In the advanced industrial societies, food is a consumer product, elaborately packaged, promoted, and marketed. Eating, even excessive eating, is therefore good for business, particularly the food business. As food has been transformed into one of the "designer" products of the affluent society, its forms have proliferated.[59] The contemporary consumer who seeks ice-cream is confronted at the supermarket with a choice between Hagen-Daz, Tofutti, Ice Milk, or just plain old Sealtest; at the ice-cream factory, between Heavenly Hash, Rocky Road, Peach Brandy, or Plain Vanilla. Food, in fact, has now become a medium of fashion, ranging from discount to upscale. Contemporary food advertising, particularly in the magazines directed at housewives, has been likened to pornography, with its glossy depiction of the untouchable, its evocation of forbidden fantasies of indulgence.[60] Food advertising is still aimed at women, who, despite the public imagery of liberation, are apparently still considered responsible for its preparation. This selectivity provides one further reason why eating disorders, and particularly the problem of "compulsive overeating," are more prevalent in females.[61] Food is a sanctioned and legal form of oral gratification, apparently safer than alcohol and certainly more acceptable than drugs. In any case, the widespread prevalence on binge-eating in the United States, particularly among college students, is symptomatic of a society in which the problem is not starvation, but rather of surplus.[62] It is not surprising that a book called *The Joy of Pigging Out* was recently displayed in the windows of local bookstores; it is in fact symptomatic of the times.[63]

But while overconsumption is encouraged by an economy whose hunger for profits seems limitless, the ultimate contradiction that leads us back to eating disorders is the simultaneous demand, also economically promoted (but by a different industry), to be thin – a requirement which, as we have seen, is critically involved in the proliferation of anorexia and bulimia. To return to the argument of Hillel Schwartz (see chapter 6), the problem of obesity (but to which we can now add those of anorexia and bulimia) must ultimately be traced to the problem of self-regulation in societies in which alienated production and consumption have run riot. To experience the pleasures of plenty while eating nothing is the fantasy of the normal contemporary dieter, but which reaches obsessional proportions for the anorectic/bulimic/obese. Ultimately, the social modeling of eating disorders must be understood in terms of this "anorexic–bulimic" conflict, which seems to be entrenched in the very fabric of contemporary life.[64]

8

THE POLITICS OF ANOREXIA

The symptoms of an ethnic disorder, according to Devereux, invariably represent a kind of social negativism, an unstated rebellion against prevailing cultural expectations. They signify, he suggests, a society's "disavowal of itself," the negation of its most cherished explicit ideals. Paradoxically, though, such antisocial behavior may be secretly admired and revered, perhaps because others within the culture secretly identify with the symptomatic person's dilemma.[1] After all, the conflicts in the person who develops the ethnic disorder are much more widespread than the actual number of individuals who manifest symptoms. The social response to the person with an ethnic disorder, therefore, is typically an ambivalent one, a mixture of admiration, fear, and hostility. Like any deviant, society attempts to bring back such individuals "into the fold" through various mechanisms of social control – with varying degrees of success.

A recent anthropological account by Littlewood and Lipsedge proposes that ethnic disorders (they use the more traditional term "culture-bound syndromes") reflect the efforts of certain individuals of inferior status – typically defined by age or sex – to protest against or otherwise escape from their oppression by the more powerful. Such protests are typically not consciously acknowledged, nor labeled as such; they reflect what Turner has called "the power of the weak" – in psychiatric terms, manipulation.[2] By taking on the identity of a deviant, the symptomatic person is able to indirectly punish or at least gain some degree of control over those who are more powerful than herself, even though her behavior is simultaneously self-destructive. Because the rebellion is indirect and unarticulated, such efforts typically do not result in a fundamental change in the status quo, and invariably result in the relegation of the deviant to a marginal status or an alternative identity. They do afford the deviant some measure of escape from what is experienced as an intolerable situation. In pre-industrial societies, such deviant behavior was not identified as illness, but was often "mystically rationalized" – for example, as "possession." An interesting example can be found in the Zar cults of Ethiopia. Certain women, who were suffering at the hands of abusive or exploitative husbands, would become members of such cults and engage in a spectrum of intolerable and outrageous behaviors – frenzied dancing, dressing as men, sometimes brandishing weapons. Since possession by Zar spirits had cultural credibility, substantial sums of money or possessions could be extracted from the errant husband by the healers of the Zar cults. Meanwhile, the woman herself could escape from a punishing marriage situation by assuming the alternative identity of the Zar, which had a certain degree of social status, and she might even ultimately attain the stature of a healer.[3] Importantly, as is typical for such mystically rationalized rebellion, the societal order of male dominance was not fundamentally altered by the adoption of a Zar identity. Within limits, though, the phenomenon of Zar possession enabled some unlabeled protest against and escape from a social situation of powerlessness.

According to Littlewood and Lipsedge, in contemporary Western societies, such manipulative and disguised protests are typically enacted through psychiatric disorders or "mental illness" – the "scientistic" equivalent of mystical rationalization.[4] And since women continue to suffer the limitations of inferior social status and a relative lack of power, it should come as no surprise that the overwhelming majority of ethnic disorders in the West occur predominantly among females. Such considerations may also partly account for the fact that females continue to constitute a disproportionate number of psychiatric patients. Ethnic disorders such as hysteria, agoraphobia, and now anorexia nervosa, whose prevalence has been and continues to be overwhelmingly female, have therefore been the characteristic expressions of female powerlessness from the late nineteenth century to the present. Hysteria, as we have seen, represented a strategy of coming to grips with the socially prescribed dependency and passivity that was central to the nineteenth-century female sex role: through becoming hysterical, a woman both rebelled against, and yet exaggerated, this stereotype. The "secondary gains," which played such a central role in hysterical symptoms, represented the "escape from obligations" with which so many women felt burdened, as well as the achievement of some degree of power through her passive tyrannization of the household and her capacity to frustrate the physician.[5] Similarly, agoraphobia, a disorder which involves a phobic avoidance of public spaces, public transportation, and crowds, can in many instances be seen as a metaphoric encapsulation of the situation of the dependent and unassertive wife (indeed, it is sometimes referred to, somewhat inaccurately, as "housewife's disease"). Studies of the family dynamics of agoraphobics, many of whom are young married women with small children, suggest that the symptom can be viewed as a strategy by which a woman could effectively dominate her husband, by commanding his presence and aid, while simultaneously conforming to role expectations of dependency.[6] In such an imbroglio, the husband continues to maintain his dominant position; social reality has not fundamentally changed.

In this context, anorexia nervosa can be understood as the most recent in a long tradition of stereotyped expressions of "female distress." In this chapter, we will explore its political dimensions.

Some Historical Forerunners: Holy Anorexics, Hunger Artists, and Hunger Strikers

The use of self-starvation as a tool of manipulation and control over self and others actually has a long history, and it is a tactic that has been especially deployed by women. J. Hubert Lacey, an English psychiatrist, has suggested that the story of St Wilgerfortis, who lived around the tenth century AD, presents some striking parallels to anorexic behavior. Wilgerfortis (literally "strong virgin"), the daughter of a Portuguese king, starved herself when confronted with the prospect of marriage to a brutal king of Sicily.[7] As a consequence of her resulting emaciation, the marriage arrangement was broken off by the suitor, upon which her father had her crucified. Apparently, Wilgerfortis's fate resonated with the experience of countless young women, as cults based on her martyrdom sprung up all over Europe. Interestingly, it was customary to make an offering of food at the shrines dedicated to her memory. In his recounting of the legend, Lacey suggests that a dark area in an English statue of Wilgerfortis (St Uncumber) represented a beard, which suggests the symptomatic lanugo (body hair) of anorexia nervosa. This notion has been disputed by other scholars, who argue that the dark area represents a veiled crucifix.[8] More problematic is Lacey's assertion that Wilgerfortis, like contemporary anorexic patients, was "fearful of the implications of sexuality" associated with her adolescence. Unlike contemporary patients, the saint's conflict was hardly an internalized one. Rather,

her self-starvation was much more literally a means of fending off sexual enslavement.

The story of Wilgerfortis is shrouded in historical uncertainty, and is probably of interest mainly for its mythic implications. More credible historically are the numerous instances of self-starvation among women in the late medieval and postmedieval period in Europe, many of whom were ultimately sanctified by the Church. These women, who have been called "holy anorexics" by Rudolph Bell in his startling work on the subject, in many ways strikingly resembled contemporary anorexics, despite the vast cultural divide between the medieval and the modern world.[9] Like contemporary patients, most began their fasting in adolescence (although some began later), typically in order to resolve an acute sense of self-doubt and unworthiness and as a solitary quest for a sense of spiritual and moral perfection. Their radical ascetic behavior, which reduced their bodies to an asexual and non-reproductive state, made them unsuitable for marriage and was typically in defiance of parental expectations for an arranged marriage or at least a conventional life. In fact, Caroline Bynum has suggested that the highly unconventional and masochistic behavior of these women served as a subtle reproach to their families, many of whom were part of a secular and materialistic mercantile class and were embarrassed by their daughter's fanatical asceticism and religiosity.[10] As Bynum points out, the fasting of these holy women went far beyond conventional religious practices of the time, which, unlike those of early Christianity, were more circumscribed by an ethos of moderation.[11]

Of particular interest is the sexual politics of these early instances of self-starvation. Most of these women were unwilling to accept the conventional limitations of the female role, and aspired to something higher. And yet the notion of spiritual autonomy or authority for women in the Church was totally unacceptable. The radical abstinence of these women aroused considerable suspicion among the male clergy, and they were typically monitored carefully by their male confessors. Despite their spiritual and moral accomplishments, and the sometimes reluctant admission of their virtue by male authority, it was impossible for these women to gain official acceptance in the Church on an equal footing with their male confessors. Rather, as Bynum suggests, they fashioned an alternative religious identity, a kind of charismatic lay priesthood, one which was elaborated in distinctly female metaphors of bodily suffering and nurturance.[12] Like many contemporary anorexics, these holy women starved themselves but gave to others, often literally in the form of feeding the poor. These women often had a following, but their their admirers were not typically drawn from the ranks of the official Church, but rather from the lay public, many of whom identified with their sense of suffering and charismatic inspiration. It is a somewhat similar situation to contemporary anorexics, who evoke a sympathetic response from their feminist interpreters (who tend to work outside the clinical establishment) as well as the lay public, while the (mostly male) clinical establishment remains skeptical of any redeeming features of their behavior.

Although there are striking parallels between medieval and modern anorexia, it is important to note the differences. A vast gulf separates the medieval and modern world, and therefore we should expect that the meaning of self-starvation would differ. Most striking is the fact that contemporary anorexics starve themselves in the pursuit of a particular external body shape, a wholly secular goal that seems at least superficially to have little in common with the moral and spiritual ideals of a Catherine of Siena.[13] Medieval fasters expressed themselves through a rich and elaborate spiritual vocabulary, which was drawn from the magico-religious world view of medieval Christianity. Todays' anorexics have no comparable language for the expression of moral or spiritual conflict, a fact that may have something to do with their widely noted inability to articulate their inner experiences while they are ill. Yet, even among modern anorexics, who speak in terms of control and thinness, there is an echo of the struggle of the medieval holy woman for a sense of purity and perfection, as well as the impulse to nurture others while depriving themselves. And one extraordinarily gifted anorexic woman – the celebrated but intellectually notorious Simone Weil – articulated an alternative Christian vision, replete with metaphors of food and eating, that is reminiscent of the nearly heretical visions and formulations of medieval fasters.[14]

Although holy anorexics may have used food refusal as a tactic of power, their protest had to be carefully cloaked in the guise of religious self-denial. A more blatantly manipulative use of self-starvation can be found in the fasting practices of ancient India. Fasting was an integral part of the Hindu tradition (as it remains today), but it was also put to more openly secular purposes. For example, it was common practice in the villages of ancient India for a man who was owed a debt to entrench himself in front of the tent of the debtor and fast until the debt was repaid.[15] It has been suggested that such "masochistic blackmail" may have prefigured the triumphant use of fasting by Ghandi, which became the ultimate symbol of passive resistance by the Indian nation against British authority. As Ghandi himself pointed out, though, such tactics cannot be effective unless the authority against which one protests is susceptible to moral blackmail. In his words, "one cannot fast against a tyranny."[16]

Hunger strikes, of course, represent the quintessentially political use of self-starvation. Historically, the hunger strike has been employed by the socially oppressed, as a means of embarrassing or humiliating those in control and ultimately extracting concessions from them. The hunger strike is a powerful symbolic tool, which typically evokes a sympathetic response in those who identify with the hunger striker's plight. And although historically the hunger striker is invariably from the ranks of the oppressed, it is interesting that throughout history the vast majority of political hunger strikers have been male (the one exception is that of the suffragettes).[17] Womens' fasting, on the other hand, has only been permissible in religious contexts. Apparently, even when they are from the downtrodden, it is more permissible for males to engage in direct aggression – even when it takes a passive form. For women, the protest must remain veiled in a mystical or symptomatic language. Anorexia nervosa, of course, falls in this latter category.

By the nineteenth century, fasting had become totally secularized in the figure of the hunger artist, whose public feats of asceticism gained considerable notoriety in Europe and the United States.[18] Unlike hunger strikers or saintly maidens, hunger artists had no moral or religious agenda. Rather, their food refusal was a sheer act of will and self-control for its own sake, a public spectacle devoid of moral content. The fascination with hunger artists coincided almost exactly with the emergence of anorexia nervosa as a recognized disease, although the latter remained obscure in the public consciousness until about a hundred years later. Nevertheless, as Kafka's story suggests, the inner psychology of the hunger artist and the anorexic were virtually identical – the narcissistic pursuit of perfection through the mastery of appetite.[19] And, as Hillel Schwartz points out, the public interest in hunger artists, which parallels in many ways the contemporary fascination with anorexia nervosa, grew out of an increasing unease with the problem of self-control in a society in which greed, accumulation, and consumption were already running rampant.

In the early twentieth century, the suffragettes became the first women to utilize self-starvation as a direct form of political protest. It is probably overextending a metaphor to argue, as Showalter has, that the suffragettes "brilliantly put the symptoms of anorexia to work in the service of a feminist cause."[20] The suffragettes' hunger strikes were hardly motivated by a sense of personal or interpersonal conflict. Nevertheless, it may not be totally accidental that the intrafamilial protest of the anorexic seemed to anticipate the hunger strikes of the suffragettes, in a period in which debates about the rights of women had moved to the forefront of public consciousness. Perhaps, as Showalter suggests, it is possible to view nineteenth-century anorexia as well as hysteria as a kind of proto-feminist revolt, but one which for the individuals involved could not be articulated in anything other than a symptomatic vocabulary. In view of the central role that female identity conflicts play in contemporary eating disorders, it is possible that similar parallels may hold in the late twentieth century. This makes it understandable why contemporary feminists have seen the problems of the anorexic or bulimic woman as uniquely symbolic of the contemporary female dilemma.[21] Of course, most anorexics are not feminists, nor can the women's movement be held responsible for their situation.[22] In fact, it could be argued that the process of recovery from an eating disorder, which requires a more tolerant acceptance of the body as well as the development of a "self-respecting identity" (Bruch's phrase), itself involves the emergence of an implicitly feminist consciousness.

Addiction to Control

Fasting, as generations of mystical seekers and health faddists have known, yields an enormous sense of exhilaration, purity, and spiritual power. Feelings of lightness, of enhanced sensory clarity, of transcending the ordinary compulsions of the body can drive the faster into escalating the heroic efforts at self-denial. Fasting became popular in the 1970s not fundamentally as a technique of dieting (although medical fasts for the obese came into vogue during the period), but as a technique of getting high, one of many popularized alternatives to psychedelic drugs. Health cultists are familiar with the potentially addictive lure of fasting, and typically prescribe strict time limits for the duration of a fast, knowing that without such an external structure, the faster may push the process beyond the boundary of physical and psychological safety.[23]

The sense of enthrallment yielded by fasting is ultimately rooted in physiological processes. But for the person predisposed to developing anorexia nervosa, fasting has an especially powerful psychological appeal, even though it is initially hit upon virtually by accident. Before an anorexic begins dieting, she feels secretly enslaved, dependent, and manipulated. As dieting turns into fasting, it begins to yield an exhilarating sense of power and independence. One of Bruch's patients, Betty, explained that "losing weight was giving her power, that each pound lost was like a treasure that gave her power. This accumulation of power was giving her another kind of 'weight,' the right to be recognized as an individual." It is only later, when starvation becomes chronic or bulimia supervenes, or when it dawns on her that thinness and food refusal bring no real power, that the euphoria gives way to depression. And although the fasting may be perpetuated by endogenous, physiological factors, the sense of empowerment that derives from food refusal is extremely critical to understanding why an anorexic patient will defend her starvation so radically, as if her life depended on it.

The anorexic stance has been likened to the classic posture of asceticism, in which the total subjugation of appetite yields a transcendent sense of perfection and purity.[24] For most patients, though, it is an asceticism that is not embedded in an explicit philosophical, moral, or religious context. It is more a purely psychological defense mechanism, common and to some extent adaptive among adolescents, but exaggerated in anorexics to the point of obsession. Anorexics deny themselves in order to become unencumbered of the uncertainties and vulnerability that are unavoidable accompaniments of relationships with others. They are driven to the behavior almost wholly from a sense of intolerable dependence and enmeshment. Some writers have noted an explicit preoccupation among many anorexics with religious themes; most, however, can only articulate their quest in terms of a secular goal, that of attaining a particular external body shape. But as one observer noted, "the asceticism of anorexia nervosa may appear perverse rather than good, debased rather than noble, foolish rather than heroic, but even in its most misguided forms it may contain within itself an ineradicable element of the numinous."[25]

The Politics of the Family

The fierce struggle for self-control and a sense of power in anorexia is actually rooted in a profound sense of powerlessness. And this core feeling is rooted in the experience of the eating disordered patient in the family. It is the imbalance of power in the family, and the resulting profound deficiency in the child's capacity for independent self-assertion, that leads to such radical measures of self-control in adolescence or later. Probably no symptom has a greater capacity to drive family members to distraction than a determined effort on a child's part to starve herself. But the noisy battles and vituperative clashes that take place over the issue of food once the anorexic patient becomes ill are often a symptomatic expression of a power struggle that had been latent, although suppressed, from early on.

Family therapists have done much to illuminate the dynamics of power in the families of anorexics. Salvadore Minuchin, for example, suggests that the family dynamics of anorexia are typical of those that more generally give rise to "psychosomatic" symptoms, such as diabetes or gastrointestinal disorders.[26] Such families tend to be excessively "enmeshed," fearful of the implications of individuality, unable to openly express conflicts and differences. In the families of anorexics, the child who develops symptoms becomes "triangulated" into the parents' relationship, which is loaded with unresolved conflict. Conflict between the parents is typically denied and "detoured" through the anorexic, who is therefore unable to achieve individuation. The dynamics of enmeshment are compounded by the fact that these families typically find the world beyond the family a fearful place. In many instances, only a dramatic ritual will have the power to free the anorexic from the grip of this powerful centripetal dynamic. The most notorious and dramatic example is the "family lunch session," in which the therapeutic team engenders a "therapeutic crisis" by joining the family and patient for a common meal. Such an encounter may take some of the charge out of the battles over food, by defining the meeting as "just having lunch" and by diverting the discussion along pathways other than the patient's eating. But, conversely, it may confront the issue head on by prescribing the parents to get the patient to eat. The almost inevitable failure of the parents to force the anorexic to eat exposes the absurdity and futility of the struggle. The anorexic's refusal to eat casts a certain spell over the family, and deflects attention from more fundamental issues and conflicts. This is a major reason why, in addition to its obviously life-threatening nature, the parents and siblings become totally focused on and preoccupied with the symptom. Such a dramatic intervention can in some instances trigger a startling improvement in the identified patient's eating behavior.

The issue of power is also central in the work of the Italian psychiatrist, Mara Selvini Palazolli, who has treated large numbers of anorexic families in Milan, Italy. In a paper addressing cultural factors, Palazolli noted a steady increase in the number of anorexics since the Second World War, which she attributes to the emergence of a consumer-oriented, affluent society, an increasing degree of child-centeredness among middle-class families, and the contradictory situation of women under the increased pressure from emancipation. However, in order to understand any particular case, these broader social pressures must be understood within the specific context of the individual family. According to Palazolli, it is typical in the families of anorexics for the parents' relationship to be characterized by rancor, bitterness, and deep resentments of each partner by the other. These conflicts have never been admitted to, but rather covered over by a façade of harmony and deflected through an excessive solicitousness towards the children. Such minute attention to every single aspect of a child's needs may be appropriate or at least tenable prior to adolescence but it is completely inappropriate for adolescents. Adolescents' developmental needs are to become relatively autonomous of parental control and to reformulate values that are inevitably critical of those of the prior generation. It is this reorganization of the structure of the family at adolescence that the families of anorexics are particularly unable to negotiate. Palazolli suggests that one important reason why anorexia is so much more common in girls is that, despite contemporary social rhetoric of emancipation, girls continue to be subjected to a much greater degree of parental control than boys. When an anorexic begins dieting, and as her weight loss begins to be noticed and commented upon by her parents, she quickly finds that starving herself is a way of "bringing her parents to their knees," even though inwardly she feels more out of control than ever. This is the point at which hospitalization and eventually psychotherapy typically begins.[27]

In her more recent work, Palazolli has adopted the metaphor of the "game" to describe these familial dynamics.[28] Game implies a situation that is rule-governed, but yet also implies the dynamic unfolding of interaction patterns in time. Anorexics and bulimics conduct power struggles over the issues of food and eating; and it is only in the affluent societies, in which food is readily available and offered, that such "games with food" can occur.[29] In one typical case, which she characterizes as a "psychotic family game," the anorexic perceives her father as weak and submissive to her mother's demands and manipulations. This is actually a misperception on her part, since the father's helplessness is only surface: he "passively controls," while the mother "actively controls." The "dieting ploy" or "silent hunger strike" is a way of showing the father how to "get at" or retaliate against the mother. In effect, the symptom states, in an enactive language, "look, this is how you can get to her, this is the way to drive her crazy." This is of course not only a game built on a false premise, but one with potentially deadly consequences.[30]

Therapy in such families must involve a deft and expert deployment of counterpower by the therapist, a set of tactical maneuvers that could match the dramatic ploys of any primitive shaman. Family-therapy techniques have the aura of ritual drama, of shamanistic countermagic. The "problem" may be radically redefined or "reframed," "prescriptions" or "injunctions" may be delivered by the therapist, or the symptom itself may be paradoxically mandated. The latter technique, initially formulated by Palazolli and her colleagues, was dramatically illustrated in a case report by Peggy Papp, an American family therapist. Papp works with a "consultation group," which issues oracular injunctions from behind a one-way mirror. In this particular case, that of a 21-year old anorexic girl, it was suggested to the family that the therapists are reluctant to prescribe change, particularly for the anorexic to gain weight too rapidly, for fear that if she gains curves and begins to menstruate, then her father will feel "increasingly isolated in a family of women" and the parents' estrangement will be intensified. The purpose of this seemingly out-rageous prescription, which stands conventional therapeutic wisdom on its head, is to expose the intimate connection of the symptom with the family system and thereby dramatically reveal its function. And while cautioning an anorexic against gaining weight may seem virtually unethical, the therapist is only telling the patient and the family to do what it is already doing, in effect mirroring to the family its secret truth: the instruction comes at first as a shock, a joke. But, at least in this particular case, the anorexic began to eat and appears soon after with a significant weight gain.[31] In her more recent work, Palazolli has suggested the use of what she calls the "invariant pre-scription:" the parents are directed to go out together as a couple, to refrain from discussing their evening together with the children, and to take careful notes on their children's reactions.[32] The results achieved by these measures are reported to have been dramatic; and of course, what has happened is that the problem of the excessive overinvolvement of the parents with the children has been directly dealt with, by prescribing behavior on the part of the parents that demands disengagement. Through enacting the prescription, the deadlock in which the anorexic symptom has become entrenched is broken.

Power issues are also critical in the family dynamics of bulimia nervosa. In these families, conflict and strife are typically much more out in the open than in the families of restricting anorexics. In this often explosive atmosphere, problems with alcohol and drug abuse or compulsive overeating and obesity are commonplace. Despite the presence of overt conflict, the open communication of feelings is often difficult. In these families, separation is as difficult as is being together; it is as if a knot of ambivalence holds the family together. Bulimia-nervosa patients internalize this powerful ambivalence about relationships, which is typically evident in their own pattern of intense involvement and withdrawal. For bulimics, a critical or sometimes overtly abusive father typically plays a particularly important role in their development: they often perceive their mothers as weak and ineffectual, or otherwise unable to cope with the father. Root, Fallon, and Friedrich, in an important work on the family therapy of bulimia,[32] propose a feminist understanding of the experience of victimization and sense of powerlessness that is so common among bulimics. The inability to leave home, so critical in the emergence of bulimic symptoms, typically is the culmination of generations of female difficulties with achieving independence.

Bulimic symptoms themselves are often a covert means of striking back, a symptomatic expression of rage. In some cases, the bulimic's devouring of a family's food supply is a barely masked retaliation for her sense of victimization. In one instance, a 17 year old, who was the recipient of sexual harassment and physical punishment from her alcoholic father as well as a lack of support from her mother, struck back by binging all of the food in the kitchen late at night. When her young brother and sister awoke in the morning before school, they had no food to eat. In this case, the manipulative tactic hardly seems subtle, but the patient felt that her eating episodes were "out of her control." The mother was enraged with the daughter's provocative behavior, but felt helpless in the face of her "illness." In other instances, vomiting, in addition to whatever psychological purposes it serves, becomes a violent form of retaliation for what is experienced as abusive parental intrusion. One 15 year old, for example, felt abused, harassed, and embarrassed by her father's unruly dog, who served as a surrogate for her father's own anger and sexual frustration towards his wife. The daughter, who maintained a carefully cultivated façade of physical attractiveness and goodness, fought back by vomiting into garbage bags that she kept hidden in her room. This was an unacknowledged expression of feelings of rage, disgust, and powerlessness. In this case, a parental divorce led to a marked lessening of the bulimic symptoms.

As in anorexia, the bulimic's quest for power is ultimately self-destructive. But unlike anorexia, the symptom often remains hidden beneath a façade of normality. Unlike the emaciated anorexic, whose appearance shocks others into responding, the bulimic's abusive food habits are often only known to herself. The ultimate "power" that resides in her symptom is in the rewards of the compliments that she receives for her thinness; and unfortunately, it is this feedback that unwittingly reinforces the symptom and contributes to its chronicity.

The Cultural Politics of a Disease: Illness as Metaphor

The symptoms of an ethnic disorder exaggerate cultural values to the point of caricature; they are thus both an affirmation and a disavowal of a society's esteemed ideals. Because of this dual function, the response to those with ethnic disorders is typically an ambivalent one. On the one hand, they are seen as pariahs, rebels, or deviants; but on the other, they evoke responses of admiration, envy, even awe. In Devereux's characterization, ethnic symptoms are typically "antisocial social behaviors." Like any deviant behavior with a negative sign, the patient tends to evoke controlling and punitive responses from others. But precisely because these rebellious behaviors represent antisocial tendencies that are latent within everyone, they may be secretly admired and even imitated:

Cultural materials that represent society's basic disavowal of itself are also precisely the ones that troubled individuals synthesize and give expression to by their behavior – and do this in a manner that can earn them society's approval or its disapproval. These antisocial social values . . . permit the individual to be antisocial in a socially approved and sometimes even prestigious manner.[34]

The fact that anorexics sometimes evoke admiration was evident in a query into the responses of the friends and relatives of a number of anorexic patients.[35] Most showed concern or alarm regarding the patient's low weight. Surprisingly, though, more positive than negative comments were voiced about the patient's condition. Typical remarks were "she is fashionable," "slender," or "in control." One respondent (a boyfriend of the patient) went so far as to say that "she is triumphant." Terms such as "gaunt" and "haggard" were much less frequently utilized. The authors of this study were dismayed by the implications. Such barely masked glorification of the patient's thin appearance and "control" could easily by reinforcing and thus serve to reduce her already tenuous will to recover. In the literature, in fact, there have been a number of reports in which a patient's recovery has been covertly resisted or sabotaged by a parent, who fears that weight gain will make the patient "fat."[36] Some parents may even carry a secret, perverse pride that their child has an "élite" affliction.

The glamorization of anorexia nervosa is not surprising in that the disorder "embodies" cultural ideals such as slenderness, self-control, and competition. This enmeshment of anorexia with positive values makes it more understandable why it has become a widely imitated template of deviance in societies which hold these values dear. In an environment in which many fashion models border on anorexia, it is not surprising that the disorder itself has become "fashionable." Many anorexics themselves have testified from the secret gratifications afforded by a condition to which people respond with such admiration and envy. Thus, Aimee Liu commented to a friend who also was anorexic, "They're in awe of us. It sounds insane, but maybe it's something like [being a] celebrity. Everybody wants to be thin, after all. Right? Including the doctors, our mothers, and our friends. We've achieved what they can't. They're jealous. They want to take it away from us." The romanticization of anorexia also makes it understandable why for some patients, the disorder becomes such a central part of their identity. As one of Bruch's patients remarked, she could never give up her illness because without it she would be "nothing."[38] Such an overidentification with the illness has unfortunately become common among eating disordered patients, and represents a further stage in the socialization of the disease. And while it is understandable that a person with such painfully low self-esteem might feel strengthened by identifying with a glamorous affliction, the elevated status of eating disorders can obviously place significant obstacles in the way of the process of recovery.

THE POLITICS OF ANOREXIA

Bruch once commented that anorexics command respect because of the universality of the human fear of famine. Individuals who starve themselves voluntarily evoke both awe and terror; in this sense the power of the anorexic and the hunger artist become identical. Perhaps this response is particularly potent in periods of relative affluence, and particularly in those societies in which food abundance is one of its central symbols. Many anorexics in fact identify explicitly with the "wretched of the earth," and their food refusal becomes a token of rebellion against the values and attitudes of middle-class affluence. For the vast majority, though, these ideas are typically not translated into political action; rather, they remain as justifications for an exclusively personal rebellion.

The unfortunate projection of a heroic mythology onto anorexia is reminiscent of Sontag's discussion of the status of tuberculosis in nineteenth-century Europe. In *Illness as Metaphor*, Sontag pointed out that tuberculosis was a quintessentially romantic symbol, carrying such meanings as refinement, sensitivity, a higher nature.[39] In comparison, one thinks of one group of psychiatrists who characterized their anorexic patients as "pale, angel-faced gamins."[40] Interestingly, tuberculosis also was a disease of the young, which often resulted in death. In the nineteenth century, the symbolism of death was centrally linked with romantic ideology of estheticism and sensitivity. In addition, like anorexia nervosa, tuberculosis was also a disease of thinness (albeit involuntary, in the case of tuberculosis), with the wan appearance of the consumptive carrying the significance of aristocratic sensitivity and refinement.[41] The consumptive body "burned itself up" or "wasted away with passion;" and yet, this imagery was one of essentially passive vulnerability. Similar meanings may have been attached to the thinness sought by nineteenth-century anorexics.[42] Over the course of the twentieth century, however, the connotations of thinness seem to have changed. As noted above, contemporary anorexics are noted for their heroic exercise, their self-discipline, their "control." Such imagery seems more appropriate to competitive societies, in which a changing female role has placed a new emphasis on female activity and achievement. In the late 1980s, however, the glorification of extreme thinness seems to be undergoing somewhat of a decline. In an era haunted by the horrors of AIDS, wasting diseases of any type may have lost a great deal of their lustre.

Although anorexia may be glamorized and romanticized, particularly in its earlier stages, the disorder eventually evokes reactions of horror, shock, and revulsion. Indeed, what is initially a hyperaffirmation of cultural demands ultimately turns into a hateful parody (the "social antisocial behavior" described by Devereux). Not only is it frightening, but there is something distinctly hostile and intimidating about the emaciation of the anorexic, as if she were somehow saying to the world "You want me to be thin, I'll show you what thin is." It has been pointed out that many anorexics are involved in caricature, in mockery, in impersonation, typically directed at members of the immediate family.[43] But the anorexic's grotesquely reduced body can also be seen as an implicit critique of the absurdity of the cultural obsession with body shape. Just as the hysteric's bodily gyrations and patomines were a kind of parody of nineteenth-century images of female sexuality (Charcot called them "les attitudes passionelles,"), so the anorexic's emaciation serves as a kind of caricature of modern culture's unrealistic demands for thinness. From this standpoint, it could be said that one of the cultural functions of anorexia has been the provocation of a discourse about the hazards of dieting, just as hysteria in a sense provoked a critique of sexual repression.[44]

Ethnic disorders, as Devereux suggested, always involve social negativism, rebellion. The negative reactions provoked by an anorexic patient can partly be seen by her refusal to cooperate and conform with normative social expectations. By starving herself, the anorexic totally rejects the ultimate tokens of affluence and success – plentiful food. Nothing could be a greater affront to a middle-class family's pride in the fruits of its efforts, particularly given the role that food typically plays in these families. Also, anorexics typically are accused of "refusing to grow up" or "refusing to be a woman," the latter being the classic formulation of the earlier psychoanalytic literature. But, as feminist writers have pointed out, such a formulation, while perhaps literally true, is implicitly judgmental, in that it accepts normal femininity as unproblematic.[45]

Nevertheless, there is no question that anorexics can be the most provocative and even intimidating patients. The resulting anxiety, frustration, and anger have often provoked extreme countermeasures in treatment, a response that can have disastrous consequences. The imagery of battle and power struggle that surrounds the history of the treatment of anorexic patients is reflected in the following call to arms by a noted English psychiatrist:

When encountered in its extreme form, these patients are formidable adversaries, giving and expecting no mercy. The doctor may well falter and quail, compromising with them, and in effect allowing them to dominate their treatment and continue their downward path unchecked. To succeed with these patients a doctor must be as ruthless as they are, confine them to bed and force them to obey.[46]

The game that anorexic patients play with death is the ultimate stimulus for drastic medical intervention. Doctors find themselves in the position in which the ultimate responsibility of the physician – that of preserving life – is challenged by a patient who typically stubbornly refuses intervention and claims that she is "just fine." The situation is inevitably complicated by the perplexing question about the extent to which the patient's starvation is voluntary.[47] Anorexics are notorious among hospital staffs for their deceitful and manipulative behavior, which includes finding all sorts of ingenious ways of disposing of food, of filling their pockets with weights or drinking large amounts of water prior to weighing, of secretly doing pushups in their rooms, despite admonitions to the contrary. Perhaps it is this combination of intractability and deceitfulness that accounts for the nightmarish list of psychiatric austerities in the earlier history of the treatment of anorexia: forced tube feeding, electroshock, even leucotomy. Even the more recent (and more benign) techniques of behavior modification, which have reported a high success rate in promoting short-term weight gain, have come under fire by writers such as Bruch, who argues that any technique that deprives a patient of her sense of autonomy undermines progress in the long run.[48]

The power struggles and contentiousness that characterize the treatment relationships between the anorexic patient and her doctors are somewhat reminiscent of the rancorous relationship between the hysterical patient and her Victorian physician.[49] In the case of anorexia, as in hysteria, there may often be a subtext, an undertone, of sexual politics, a struggle between the authoritative male physician and the rebellious (although ultimately powerless) female patient. This is not to say that only female therapists should treat anorexics, since they too can easily become enmeshed in control issues.[50] The point is that as long as the treatment situation is defined in terms of a power struggle and an effort by the doctor to overwhelm and subdue the disease, it is bound to fail. "Getting the anorexic to eat," whether by forced feeding or by the more subtle tactics of behavior-modification programs, is never a sufficient treatment in and of itself. What is critical is a full appreciation of the anorexic's ambivalent feelings about control, what Lawrence has called the "control paradox." As Lawrence points out, the anorexic is typically viewed as overemphasizing control; but what is typically unappreciated by such a view is that she also feels profoundly out of control, powerless.[51] It is of course the ultimate irony that a disease that grows out of a sense of personal weakness and external domination in the family ultimately replicates the struggle for control on the stage of the treatment situation.

In the present climate, the politics of treatment may also lead the therapist to err in the opposite direction. Therapists who approach the treatment of anorexia nervosa through a strong feminist framework may perceive (and perhaps identify with) the patient as a victim of societal oppression. This may in turn lead to a dogged "hands-off" attitude towards the patient's eating and weight-related behavior. Such an approach, presumably justified by the ethics of non-interference, can sometimes lead to a dangerous neglect of the hazardous consequences of low body weight. In addition, all therapists, whether male or female, must examine their own attitudes towards shape and weight, which are inevitably culturally influenced. There may be a tacit sanction of a weight that is lower than what is healthy for the patient, or (and this can particularly be a problem for female therapists) competitive feelings about the patient's body weight.

In an enlightening discussion of the dynamics of power in the therapeutic relationship, Angelique Sallas suggests that the most important first step in treatment is to communicate clearly to the patient that the therapist is to change the symptom.[52] It is critical for the therapist to convey to the patient the idea that her search for control is valid; it is only the means that she has chosen that are ineffective, and self-defeating. No effective treatment of the eating disorders can ignore the symptom, which has such destructive and potentially life-threatening consequences. If an anorexic patient is about to starve to death, there is little point in attempting psycho-therapy. In fact drastic medical intervention, for example in the form of intravenous hyperalimentation, may be the only viable alternative. However, without an appreciation of the patient's sense of powerlessness and search for self-esteem, treatment is doomed to failure from the outset.

The Politics of Bulimia

A curious fact is that while bulimia is probably far more prevalent than anorexia nervosa, it has received much less popular attention that anorexia, and when the subject does come up, it is often an object of fun. The behavior was satirized in an episode of Saturday Night Live, and stand-up comics have derided the existence of bulimia in a world in which people are starving. Bulimia is viewed as self-indulgent behavior (not to mention disgusting), and it is implicitly assumed that binge-eating or vomiting are completely under voluntary control. What is more, given the general competitiveness surrounding the issue of weight control, the bulimic's practice of "eating her cake and heaving in too" is viewed as a form of cheating. In contrast with the perception of incredible self-discipline, for which the anorexic is admired, bulimics therefore tend to be disdained and misunderstood. Negative attitudes towards bulimics are unfortunately shared by some clinicians. Among these was the otherwise impeccably objective Hilde Bruch, who lamented the passing of classical anorexia nervosa and the ascendancy of bulimia:

They make an exhibitionistic display of their lack of control or discipline, in contrast to the adherence to discipline of the true anorexics . . . The modern bulimic is impressive by what looks like a deficit in the sense of responsibility. Bulimics blame their symptoms on others; they may name the person from whom they "learned" to binge, in particular those who introduced them to vomiting . . . from then on, they behave as completely helpless victims. Though relatively uninvolved, they expect to share in the prestige of anorexia nervosa. Some complain about the expense of their consumption and will take food without paying for it. They explain this as due to "kleptomania," which indicates, like "bulimia," an irresistible compulsion that determines their behavior.[53]

Of course, it is true that the bulimic is much more impulsive than the ascetic, restricting anorexic. But this too is attributable to cultural changes, in that contemporary society encourages consumption and overeating, and also more supportive of an undisciplined, impulsive life-style. Bulimic behavior has much more in common with the addictions than it does with the obsessional conscientiousness characteristic of anorexia nervosa. The shift in the wider culture to a more narcissistic and impulsive ethos may have a great deal to do with the ascendancy of bulimia, and the decline of what Bruch calls "true" primary anorexia nervosa.

Because bulimic behavior is viewed either as self-indulgent or as under voluntary control, the seriousness of the problem has tended to be disregarded. In New York State, for example, it is still difficult to obtain insurance coverage for the hospital treatment of bulimia, whereas treatment for anorexia nervosa tends to be more readily funded. In a way, the status of bulimia resembles the mostly discarded (but still persistent) stereotypes of alcoholism, which asserted that the behavior is under voluntary control; as such it is interpreted as a moral defect. People often say to the bulimic, "why don't you just stop?," completely neglecting the possibility that those who have a problem with bulimia have no such ability to quickly reliquish their symptoms with a simple exertion of "will power".

Unlike anorexia, therefore, bulimic behavior is not praised or seen as "special;" quite the contrary. Nevertheless, the bulimic also obtains unwitting reinforcement of her behavior, but by a somewhat different pathway than the anorexic. The bulimic who manages to maintain a low weight is invariably complimented for her thinness. One patient remarked that men began to notice her and respond to her whenever her weight dropped below a certain point. Of course, such a response tends to reinforce not only binging and purging activity, but also the secrecy with which the behavior is maintained. Aside from the few that proudly announce their problem, most bulimics feel profound shame and embarrassment about their behavior. The positive social reinforcement for her low weight often places profound practical obstacles that oppose progress in treatment.

When compared with anorexia nervosa, the politics of bulimia represent something of a treat. Through her extreme thinness, the anorexic makes a public statement, one which is perceived as a protest, a rebellion. The power struggles between the anorexic and those around her testify to the political character of the anorexic symptom. In contrast, the bulimic woman, even after her symptoms have developed, tends to be outwardly compliant and conforming. Her protest has gone underground, so to speak, her anger at her situation secretly discharged through the violence of binging and purging rituals. Feminist writers seem to have much more readily identified with the anorexic than the bulimic woman: the anorexic presents a posture of defiance, the bulimic one of capitulation.[54] However, more attention needs to be paid to the much more pervasive problem of bulimia, which, while perhaps not as immediately life-threatening as anorexia nervosa, carries the potential for serious long-term health problems.

From the standpoint of gender, it can be argued that bulimia represents in an especially critical way the difficulty that many women have in achieving the satisfaction of their emotional needs. Food and nourishment are especially linked for women with the idea of caring.[55]

For the bulimic women, the ambivalence about one's own emotional needs that affects women in the wider culture is felt in a particularly poignant way.[56] The "solution" to the problem of identity fashioned by the bulimic is to develop a split between her external façade of self-control and pleasing femaleness, on the one hand, and the neediness, anger, and "messiness" of her kitchen and bathroom rituals, on the other. The delicate balance between the controlled external self and the out-of-control secret self is tenaciously maintained. One of the primary functions of psychotherapy for the bulimic is to provide a relationship in which she can allow herself to be nurtured. Her difficulty in allowing this to happen is precisely why the psychotherapy of bulimics is often characterized by "stops and starts." Group therapies (or less formal support groups) are particularly helpful for bulimics. The sharing of experiences in groups does much to overcome the painful isolation and secrecy in which the bulimic is entrapped. And the identification with other women who have had highly similar social experiences, even though individually diverse, is inherently empowering.[57]

+ relates to feminism

Eating Disorders and Female Empowerment

Perhaps the ultimate irony is that, to quote Minuchin, "in a society in which the new woman's consciousness promises a change in the relationship of the sexes, we are seeing more and more anorexics." Ironic, indeed. According to Kim Chernin, the contradiction is not accidental, but rather represents a situation in which the female role is indeed changing, but, perhaps in response, the patriarchal ideals of body size are imposed ever more insistently. Indeed, as Chernin points out, contemporary female consciousness itself is polarized into two camps. The first, that of feminism, utilizes such metaphors as the "expansion" of consciousness, the "enlargement" of female possibilities, the "widening" of female horizons; while the second, the culture of dieting, speaks of "reduction," of "narrowing," of becoming "smaller." Chernin suggests that the marketing of the thinness ideal reflects a conspiratorial effort to keep women in their place, in a period in which female assertiveness threatens the perpetuation of male control. But, as she herself points out, women can also be seen as colluding in their own oppression, as most (and especially anorexics or bulimics) have internalized the mysoginistic hatred of female fatness.[58]

The politics of eating disorders ultimately revolve around the politics of gender. The contemporary epidemic of these conditions is a reflection of the ambiguities of female identity in a period of change and confusion. Perhaps as women are able to achieve real power in the world, and the size and shape of their bodies are no longer taken to be the true measure of their worth, eating disorders will sharply decline in incidence. Already, at the end of the 1980s, there is speculation that the crest of the wave of eating disorders has passed. But as a popular magazine of the new woman proclaims "nine bodies for the 1990s," it is difficult to foresee a future in which symptoms that revolve around the control of the female body will disappear.[59] Undoubtedly, a century from now, our current preoccupation with eating disorders will appear as quaint as nineteenth-century hysteria appears to us now. But who knows what other vocabulary of discomfort will take their place?

LIST OF ABBREVIATED REFERENCES

ANMDA: Garfinkel, P. E. and Garner, D. M. *Anorexia Nervosa: A Multidimensional Approach*. New York: Brunner Mazel, 1982.

CA: Bruch, H., *Conversations with Anorexics*. New York: Basic Books, 1988.

ED: Bruch, H. *Eating Disorders: Obesity, Anorexia and the Person Within*, New York: Basic Books, 1973.

ETBN: Johnson, C. L. and Conners, M. E. *The Etiology and Treatment of Bulimia Nervosa*. New York: Basic Books, 1987.

GC: Bruch, H. *The Golden Cage*. New York: Vintage, 1978.

HPANB: Garner, D. M. and Garfinkel, P. E. (eds) *Handbook for the Psychotherapy of Anorexia Nervosa and Bulimia*, New York: Guilford Press, 1985.

LMB: Crisp, A. H. *Anorexia Nervosa: Let Me Be*. London: Academic Press, 1980.

SDSO: Sours, J. A., *Starving to Death in a Sea of Objects*. New York: Jason Aronson, 1979.

International Journal of Eating Disorders has been reduced to the acronym *IJED*.

NOTES

Notes to Chapter 1

1. Erikson, *Life History and the Historical Moment*. New York: W. W. Norton, 1975, p. 22.
2. For a discussion of the role of hysteria in nineteenth-century psychiatry, see Drinka, G. *The Birth of Neurosis*. New York: Simon and Schuster, 1984, ch. 4; Veith, I. *Hysteria: History of a Disease*, University of Chicago Press, 1965; and Ellenberger, H. *The Discovery of the Unconscious*. New York: Basic Books, 1970.
3. Veith, op. cit. (see note 2), chapters 1 and 2.
4. Goldstein, J. The hysteria diagnosis and the politics of anticlericalism in late nineteenth century France. *Journal of Modern History*, *54* (1982), 209–39.
5. Breuer, J. and Freud, S. *Studies in Hysteria*. (First published, 1896) New York: Pelican Books, 1974.
6. Szasz, T. *The Second Sin*. New York: Anchor Books, 1974, p. 105.
7. See Gull, W. W. Anorexia nervosa. *Transactions of the Clinical Society (London)*, *7* (1874), 22–8. Reprinted in R. M. Kaufman and M. Heiman (eds), *Evolution of Psychosomatic Concepts. Anorexia Nervosa: A Paradigm*. New York: International Universities Press, 1964; Lasegue, C. De L'Anorexie Hysterique. *Archives Generale de Medicine. 385* (1873). Reprinted in Kaufman and Heiman, op. cit.
8. Recent historical discussions of a pattern of self-starvation in medieval women in many ways similar to anorexia are contained in Bell, R. *Holy Anorexia*. Chicago: University of Chicago Press, 1985; Bynum, C. *Holy Feast and Holy Fast*. Berkeley: University of California Press, 1987. The "fasting girls" that appeared in the seventeenth through nineteenth centuries, who also may have been the antecedents of modern anorexics, are discussed in Brumberg, J. J. *Fasting Girls: The Emergence of Anorexia Nervosa as a Modern Disease*. Cambridge: Harvard University Press, 1988.
9. A point made by Bruch in an excellent review of the pre-1970 literature. See Bruch, H., *ED*, chapter 9.
10. The first American paper on normal-weight bulimia was that of Boskind-Lodahl, M. Cinderella's stepsisters: a feminist perspective on anorexia nervosa and bulimia. *Signs: A Journal of Women in Culture and Society*, *2* (1976), 342–6. It was followed by a seminal English publication by Russell, G. F. M. Bulimia nervosa: an ominous variant of anorexia nervosa. *Psychological Medicine*, *9* (1979), 429–48.

11. Eating binges. *Time, 116* (1980), 94; Eating their cake and heaving it too. *McCleans, 83* (1980), 51–2; *New York Times*, Jan. 25, 1981, C1.
12. Bruch, H. *ED.*
13. Russell, G. F. M. The changing nature of anorexia nervosa: an introduction to the conference. *Journal of Psychiatric Research, 19* (1985), 101–9.
14. The Renfrew Center. See Eating disorders: new treatments. *New York Times* (Sep. 2, 1985), p. 22.
15. The problem of eating disorders on campus is now recognized as one of the most significant health issues for contemporary students and has been the target of prevention studies funded by insurance companies. Support groups for students with eating disorders have become ubiquitous. See, for example, Greene, E. Support groups for students with eating disorders. *Chronicle of Higher Education* (March 5, 1986), 1, 30. Also, see Whitaker, L. C. and Davis, W. M. (eds) *The Bulimic College Student: Evaluation, Treatment, and Prevention.* New York: The Hayworth Press, 1989.
16. See Garner, D. M. and Garfinkel, P. E. *HPANB* for in-depth coverage of the major treatment modalities.
17. Bart, P. Social structure and vocabularies of discomfort: what happened to female hysteria? *Journal of Health and Social Behavior, 9* (1968), 189–93.
18. Among Devereux's more important works were *Mohave Psychiatry and Suicide: The Psychiatric Disturbances of an Indian Tribe.* Washington: Smithsonian Institution Press, 1961; *From Anxiety to Method in the Behavioral Sciences.* Paris and the Hague: Mouton, 1967; *Ethnopsychoanalysis: Psycho-analysis and Anthropology Complementary Frames of Reference.* Berkeley: University of California Press, 1978.
19. Devereux, G. (1955) Normal and abnormal. In Devereux, G. *Basic Problems of Ethnopsychiatry.* Chicago: University of Chicago Press, 1980; Devereux, G. Schizophrenia: an ethnic psychosis, or schizophrenia without tears. In Devereux, op. cit.
20. Simons, R. C. and Hughes, C. C. (eds) *The Culture-bound Syndromes: Folk Illnesses of Psychiatric and Anthropological Interest.* Dordecht, Holland: D. Reidel Publishing Company, 1985.
21. For a general discussion of the *Amok* syndrome, see the essays in Simons and Hughes, ibid., pp. 197–264.
22. Teoh, J. The changing psychopathology of *Amok. Psychiatry, 35* (1972), 345–51.
23. Carr, J. E. Ethno-behaviorism and the culture-bound syndromes: the case of Amok. *Culture, Medicine, and Psychiatry, 2* (1978), 269–93.
24. Carr, J. E. in Simons and Hughes, op. cit. (see note 20, this chapter), p. 202.
25. Tan, E. Amok: its worldwide occurrence. Summarized in *Transcultural Psychiatric Research Review, 26* (1989), 137–40.
26. Koro is discussed in Simons and Hughes, ibid., pp. 151–96.
27. Smith-Rosenberg, C. The hysterical woman: sex roles in 19th Century America. *Social Research, 39* (1972), 552–75.
28. Freud, S. "Civilized" sexual morality and modern nervousness. In Reiff, P. (ed.) *Sexuality and the Psychology of Love.* New York: Macmillan, 1963.

29. Ellenberger, H. *The Discovery of the Unconscious*. New York: Basic Books, 1970.
30. An argument formulated by Showalter, E. *The Female Malady: Women, Madness, and English Culture, 1830–1980*. New York: Pantheon Books, 1985. The idea of hysteria as proto-feminism originated in the work of Hunter, D. Hysteria, psychoanalysis, and feminism: The case of Anna O. *Feminist Studies*, 9 (1983), 465–88.
31. Torrey, E. F. *Schizophrenia and Civilization*. New York: Brunner Mazel, 1979.
32. Laing, R. D. *The Politics of Experience*. New York: Random House, 1967.

Notes to Chapter 2

1. Morton, T. *Phthisiologica: or a Treatise on Consumptions*. London, 1689.
2. The debate over fasting girls is discussed at length in Brumberg, J. J., *Fasting Girls: The History of Anorexia Nervosa as a Modern Disease*. Cambridge: Harvard University Press, 1988, chapter 3. Brumberg sees this controversy in terms of the struggle for credibility between the religious and scientific interpretations of the seemingly "miraculous" behavior of surviving without food.
3. See note 7, chapter 1.
4. A classic statement of the psychoanalytic view of anorexia is Waller, J. V., Kaufman, R. M., and Deutsch, F. Anorexia nervosa: a psychosomatic entity. *Psychosomatic Medicine*, 20 (1940), 3–16.
5. Bruch, *ED*.
6. Bruch, H. *The Importance of Overweight*. New York: W. W. Norton, 1957.
7. The trend of contemporary thinking is to question the entire notion of thinking about obesity as a primary psychiatric disorder, the latter having reached the height of its popularity in the 1950s. The strongest critique of the "obesity-as-a-neurosis" argument has been put forth by Susan C. Wooley and O. Wayne Wooley. See, for example, Wooley, S. C. and Wooley, O. W. Should obesity be treated at all? In Stunkard, A. J. and Stellar, E. (eds) *Eating and Its Disorders*. New York: Raven Press, 1984, pp. 185–93.
8. American Psychiatric Association, *Diagnostic and Statistical Manual of Mental Disorders (DSM III-R)*. Washington, DC American Psychiatric Association, 1987.
9. Hypothalamic dysfunction in anorexia nervosa has been particularly strongly emphasized by English writers. See, for example, Russell, G. F. M. The present status of anorexia nervosa. *Psychological Medicine*, 7 (1977), 363–7. For an interesting discussion of the possible relationships between hypothalamic dysfunction and clinical symptoms, see Casper, R. C. Hypothalamic dysfunction and the symptoms of anorexia nervosa. *Psychiatric Clinics of North America*, 7 (1984), 201–13. Casper argues that hypothalamic involvement is probably implicated in the fact that symptoms such as hyperactivity, body image distortion, euphoria, and a fear of fatness

gradually intensify as weight loss progresses. If these symptoms were purely psychological, they would probably preceed the disorder, rather than intensify with starvation.

10. See, for example, Bemis, K. Current approaches to the etiology and treatment of anorexia nervosa. *Psychological Bulletin, 65* (1978), 593–617; Garfinkel, P. E. and Garner, D. M. *ANMDA*, pp. 103–4.

11. Halmi, K. A., Casper, R. C., Eckert, E. D., Goldberg, S. C., and Davis, J. M. Unique features associated with the age of onset of anorexia nervosa. *Psychiatric Research, 1* (1979), 209–15.

12. Garfinkel, P. E. and Garner, D. M. *ANMDA*, p. 103.

13. Garfinkel, P. and Kaplan, A. S. Starvation-based perpetuating mechanisms in anorexia nervosa. *IJED, 4A* (1985), 651–67.

14. The analogies between anorexia and addictions have been made by Szmuckler, G. I. and Tantam, D. Anorexia nervosa: starvation dependence. *British Journal of Medical Psychology*, 57 (1984), 303–10. See also Bachmann, M. and Rohr, H. A speculative illness model of over-eating and anorexia nervosa. *Psychological Reports, 53* (1983), 831–8. Addiction models for eating disorders are not without their critics, however. For a discussion of some of the problems, see Bemis, K. "Abstinence" and "non-abstinence" models for the treatment of bulimia. *IJED, 4* (1985), 407–38.

15. Keys, A. Brozek, J. Henschel, A., Mickelson, O., and Taylor, H. L. *The Biology of Human Starvation*, Minneapolis: The University of Minnesota Press, 1950.

16. Garfinkel and Garner, *ANMDA*, pp. 341–2.

17. A review of outcome studies, with a discussion of the problems in recovery criteria, is given in Hsu, F. The outcome of anorexia nervosa: a review of the literature (1954 to 1978). *Archives of General Psychiatry, 37* (1980), 1041–6.

18. A number of vivid personal accounts of the devastating impact of anorexia nervosa on a family can be found in Kinoy, B. P. *When Will We Laugh Again?* New York: Columbia University Press, 1984. This volume is based on personal experiences of families and patients who have had contact with the American Anorexia/Bulimia Association of Teaneck, New Jersey, one of the largest lay support organizations in the United States.

19. For an extensive review, see Garfinkel and Garner, *ANMDA*, chapter 4 (Hypothalamic and Pituary Function); also, an excellent collection of contemporary papers is contained in Pirke, K. M. and Ploog, D. *The Psychobiology of Anorexia Nervosa*. New York: Springer-Verlag, 1984.

20. Garfinkel and Garner, *ANMDA*, chapter 4.

21. Beaumont, P. J. V. Endocrine function in magersucht disorders. In Pirke and Ploog, op. cit. (see note 19), p. 121.

22. Garfinkel and Garner, *ANMDA*, pp. 42–4, 51.

23. Keys, et al., op. cit. (see note 15, this chapter).

24. These characteristics have been documented in at least two separate formal studies. See Garfinkel, P. E., Moldofsky, H., and Garner, D. M. The heterogeneity of anorexia nervosa: bulimia as a distinct subgroup. *Archives of General Psychiatry, 37* (1980), 1036–40; and Casper, R. C., Eckert, E. D.,

Halmi, K. A., Goldberg, S. C., and Davis, J. M. Bulimia. Its incidence and clinical importance in patients with anorexia nervosa. *Archives of General Psychiatry*, *37* (1980), 1030–4.

25. Garfinkel and Garner, *ANMDA*, p. 46. For a study of the characteristically distressed patterns of interaction in the families of bulimic anorexics, see Humphrey, L. L. Structural analysis of parent–child relationships in eating disorders. *Journal of Abnormal Psychology*, *95* (1986), 395–402.

26. See, for example, Brisman, J. and Siegel, M. Bulimia and alcoholism: two sides of the same coin? *Journal of Substance Abuse Treatment*, *1* (1984), 113–18. Also Pyle, R. L., Mitchell, J. E., and Eckert, E. D. Bulimia: a report of 34 cases. *Journal of Clinical Psychiatry*, *42* (1981) 60–4; Bulik, C. Drug and alcohol abuse by bulimic women and their families. *American Journal of Psychiatry*, *144* (1987), 1604–6.

27. Johnson, C. and Larson, R. Bulimia: an analysis of moods and behavior. *Psychosomatic Medicine*, *44* (1982), 341–51.

28. Pope, H. G. and Hudson, J. I., and Mialet, J. Bulimia in the late nineteenth century: the observations of Pierre Janet. *Psychological Medicine*, *15* (1985), 139–44.

29. Bruch, H. Four decades of eating disorders. In Garner and Garfinkel (eds), *HPANB*.

30. Russell, G. F. M. The changing nature of anorexia nervosa: an introduction to the conference. *Journal of Psychiatric Research*, *19* (1985), 101–9.

31. Boskind-Lodahl, M. Cinderella's stepsisters: a feminist interpretation of anorexia nervosa and bulimia. *Signs: A Journal of Women in Culture and Society*, *2* (1976), 341–56.

32. Russell, G. F. M. Bulimia nervosa: an ominous variant of anorexia nervosa. *Psychological Medicine*, *9* (1979), 429–48).

33. Halmi, W. A., Falk, J. R., and Schwartz, E. Binge-eating and vomiting: a survey of a college population. *Psychological Medicine*, *11* (1981), 697–700.

34. American Psychiatric Association. *Diagnostic and Statistical Manual of Mental Disorders (DSM-III)*. Washington: American Psychiatric Association, 1980.

35. American Psychiatric Association. *Diagnostic and Statistical Manual of Mental Disorders (DSM-IIIR)*. Washington: American Psychiatric Association, 1987. The arguments for revision of the diagnostic criteria for bulimia in the DSM-III were presented in Fairburn, C. G. and Garner, D. M. The diagnosis of bulimia nervosa. *IJED*, *5* (1986), 403–20.

36. Pope, H. G. and Hudson, J. I. *New Hope for Binge Eaters*. New York: Harper and Row, 1984, pp. 12–13.

37. Herzog, D. Bulimia: the secretive syndrome. *Psychosomatics*, *23* (1982), 481–7.

38. Pope, and Hudson, op. cit. (note 36), pp. 33–6.

39. Garner, D. E. and Olmstead, M. The significance of self-induced vomiting as a weight-control method among non-clinical samples. *IJED*, *5* (1986), 683–700.

40. Some interesting case histories of professional women with bulimia are described in Squires, S., *The Slender Balance*. New York: Pinnacle Books,

1983. Inquiries published in women's magazines in both the United States and Germany elicited large numbers of such apparently well-functioning bulimics. See Johnson, C. L., Stuckey, M., Lewis, L. and Schwartz, D., Bulimia: A descriptive survey of 316 cases. *IJED*, *1* (1982), 1–16.

41. See, for example, Sours, J. A. *SDSO*, pp. 349–50; and Root, M. P. P., Fallon, P., and Friederich, W. N. *Bulimia: A Systems Approach to Treatment*. New York: Norton, 1986, pp. 72–5.
42. See Johnson, C. L. and Conners, M. E. *ETBN*, pp. 120–22.
43. Johnson and Conners, *ETBN*, chapter 5.
44. Wooley, S. C. and Wooley, O. W., Intensive outpatient and residential treatment for bulimia. In Garner and Garfinkel, *HPANB*, pp. 395–6.
45. Fairburn, C. G. Cognitive-behavioral treatment for bulimia. In Garner and Garfinkel (eds) *HPANB*, chapter 8 (pp. 160–92).
46. Rosen, J. C. and Leitenberg, H. Exposure plus response prevention treatment of bulimia. In Garner and Garfinkel (eds) *HPANB*, chapter 9 (pp. 193–212).
47. Pope and Hudson, op. cit. (see note 36).
48. See, for example, Strober, M. and Katz, J. L. Do eating disorders and affective disorders share a common etiology? A dissenting opinion. *IJED*, *6* (1987), 171–80.
49. For an interesting study of this hypothesis, see Geracioti, T. D. and Liddle, R. A. Impaired cholecystokinin secretion in bulimia nervosa. *New England Journal of Medicine*, *319* (1988), 683–8.
50. For discussions of some of the experimental evidence for set-point theory, see Keesey, R. E. A set-point analysis of the regulation of body weight, in Stundard, A. J. (ed.) *Obesity*, Philadelphia: W. B. Sauders, 1980, pp. 144–165, and Keesey, R. E. and Corbett, S. W. Metabolic defense of the body weight set-point, in Stunkard, A. J. and Stellar, E. (eds) *Eating and Its Disorders*, New York: Raven Press, 1984, pp. 87–96. An extremely accessible and yet thorough discussion of the basis and implications of set-point theory is contained in Bennett, W. and Gurin, J. *The Dieter's Dilemma*, New York: Harper and Row, 1982.
51. Garner, D., Rockert, W., Olmsted, M. P., Johnson, C. G., and Coscina, D. V. Psychoeducational principles in the treatment of bulimia and anorexia nervosa. In Garner, D. M. and Garfinkel, P. E., *HPANB*, pp. 536–537.
52. For example, the precise physiological mechanism of the set-point, or "appestat," has yet to be determined. The entire concept is an inference from various behavioral findings in animals and humans.

Notes to Chapter 3

1. See Bemis, K. M. Current approaches to the etiology and treatment of anorexia nervosa. *Psychological Bulletin*, *85* (1978), 593–617 for a review.
2. See Al-Issa, I. *The Psychopathology of Women*. Englewood Cliffs (New Jersey): Prentice-Hall, 1980 for a review of the sex prevalence of various disorders.

3. See, for example, Bruch, H. *ED*, chapter 15; Scott, D. W. Anorexia nervosa in the male: a review of clinical epidemiological and biological findings. *IJED*, *5* (1986), 799–820.
4. See, for example, the study by Jones et al. (note 10, below) that shows that the proportion of female anorexic patients actually rose in the 1970s over the previous decade. A selective increase in the percentage of female patients has also been reported by Garfinkel, P. E. and Garner, D. M. See *ANMDA*, pp. 103–4.
5. Hill, O. W. Epidemiologic aspects of anorexia nervosa. *Advances in Psychosomatic Medicine*, *9* (1977), 48–62.
6. The quotation is from Palazolli, M. P. Anorexia nervosa: a syndrome of the affluent society. *Transcultural Psychiatric Research Review*, *22* (1985), 199–204. The book by Palazolli is *Self-Starvation*, first published in English in London in 1974, and then in the USA in 1978 (see note 17).
7. Von Baeyer, W. The meaning of sociopathological factors in the anorexia nervosa syndrome. In Meyer, J. E. and H. Feldmann (eds) *Anorexia Nervosa*. Stuttgart: Verlag, 1965 Also Ishikawa, K. Ueber die Eltern von anorexia-nervosa-Kranken, same volume.
8. Theander, S. Anorexia nervosa: a psychiatric investigation of 94 female patients. *Acta Psychiatrica Scandinavica* (Suppl.), *214* (1970), 1–194.
9. Kendall, R. E., Hall, D. J., Hailey, A., and Babigan, H. M. The epidemiology of anorexia nervosa. *Psychosomatic Medicine*, *3* (1973), 200–3.
10. Jones, D. J., Fox, M. M., Babigan, H. M., and Hutton, H. E. Epidemiology of anorexia nervosa in Monroe County, New York: 1960–1976. *Psychosomatic Medicine*, *42* (1980), 551–8.
11. Szmuckler, G., McCance, C., McCrone, L., and Hunter, D. Anorexia nervosa: a psychiatric case register study from Aberdeen. *Psychological Medicine*, *16* (1986), 49–58.
12. Willi, A. and Grossman, S. Epidemiology of anorexia nervosa in a defined region of Switzerland. *American Journal of Psychiatry*, *140* (1982), 564–68.
13. Faltus, F. Anorexia nervosa in Czechoslovakia, *IJED*, *5* (1986), 581–5.
14. An increase in the number of anorexia nervosa patients in Japan since the Second World War was first noted by Ishakawa (see note 7), who attributed the increase to changes in the traditional family structure. More recently, see Suematsu, H. et al. Statistical studies on anorexia nervosa in Japan: detailed clinical data on 1,011 patients. *Psychotherapy and Psychosomatics*, *43* (1985), 96–103.
15. French writings on anorexia nervosa have been prolific, and have made particularly strong contributions along phenomenological lines. A selected list of titles from the contemporary period includes Kestemberg, E., Kestemberg K. J. and Decubert, S. *Le Faim et Le Corps*. Paris: P.U.F. Edition, 1972 (psychoanalytic treatise); Jeammet, P. Psychogenic thinness and mental anorexia. *Revue Pratique*, *92* (1982), 257–72; Lang, F. and Rousset, H. Anorexia nervosa: disease with a future. *Lyon Medicale*, *3* (1984), 357–63; Laxenaire, M. and Marchand, P. Anorexia nervosa: has it changed? *Annales Medico-Psychologiques*, *140* (1982), 448–53; Consoli, S.

and Jeammet, P. Epidemiology of mental anorexia. *Semaine de Hospitaux*, 60 (1985), 2141–3. The latter is a review of mostly American and British studies.

16. The German literature on anorexia nervosa is extensive. A short list of some representative recent titles include Gerlinghoff, M. Anorexia nervosa. *Munchener Medizinische Woschenschrift*, *129* (1987), 89–90; Fichter, M. *Magersucht and Bulimia*. Berlin: Springer-Verlag, 1985; Bonenberger, R. and Klosinski, G. Parent personality, family status and family dynamics in anorexia nervosa patients with special relations to father daughter relations (a retrospective study). *Z. Kinder Jugenpsychiatr.*, *16* (1988), 186–95; Gerlinghoff, M. Disorders of the maturation process and psychosexual development of anorexic patients. *Schweiz. Arch. Neurol. Psychiatr.*, *139* (1988), 61–73; and Engel, K. and Hohne, D. Prevalence of anorectic behavior in a normal population. An epidemiologic study with conclusions and treatment in anorexia nervosa. *Z. Psychosom. Med. Psychoanal.*, *35* (1989), 117–29. In the last named study, the authors found anorexic symptoms to be relatively common in a non-clinical population, with significant cases occuring at the rate of 1 to 2 per cent. A somewhat earlier German literature on anorexia nervosa stressed social and anthropological factors in the disease, as well as its broader human implications. For example, an early article by E. Bilz (Anorexia nervosa: a psychosomatic syndrome from a paleoanthropological viewpoint, *Bibliotheca Psychiatrica*, *14* (1971), 219–44) compared the feeding behavior of anorexics with that of the solitary honey bear, in contrast with the more organized behavior of baboon troops; that is, as a regression to snacking or foraging behavior, which is more primitive and asocial than communal feeding organized around meals seen in the apes. See also Massing, V. A. and Beckers, W, A discussion of the origins and increase in pubertal anorexia. *Z. Psychosom. Med. Psychoanal.*, *1* (1974), 53–9, for a discussion of sex-role conflicts in anorexic patients.

17. In Italy, M. Selvini Palazolli has been working with anorexia nervosa since the Second World War, since which time she has noted a steady increase in the number of cases. An overview of her work, with commentary on the rising prevalence, is given in *Self-Starvation*, New York: Jason Aronson, 1978.

18. In Belgium, extensive work with anorexia nervosa patients has been reported in a series of publications by Walter Vanderycken and his colleagues. See, for example, Vandereycken, W. and Pierloot, R. Long-term outcome research in anorexia nervosa. *IJED*, *2* (1983), 237–42; Vandereycken, W., Vandereycken, W., Kog, E., and Vanderlinden, J. *The Family Approach to Eating Disorders*. New York: Spectrum Books, 1987.

19. See, for example, Kasperlik-Zaluska, A., Migdalska, B., Kazubska, M., and Wisniewska-Wozniak, T. Clinical, psychiatric, and endrocrinological correlations in 42 cases of anorexia nervosa. *Psychiatria Polska* (Warsaw), *15* (1981), 574–83; Sutovec, J. and Frank. V. Body image in patients with mental anorexia. *Ceskosloveriska Psychiatrie* (Prague), *78* (1982), 180–4; Lopicic-Perisic, Z. et al. Therapy of mental anorexia. *Psihijatrija Danas* (Belgrade), *13* (1981), 91–5.

20. An early Soviet paper on anorexia, with clinical descriptions virtually identical to those described in the US, the UK, and Western Europe, was Ushakov, G. Anorexia nervosa. In Howells, J. G. (ed.) *Modern Perspectives in Adolescent Psychiatry*. New York: Brunner Mazel, 1971. A review of the world literature, with passing reference to native cases and the current "intense interest" in the problem (presumably in the Soviet Union) was Korkina, M. V. and Marilov, V. V. The contemporary state of the problem of anorexia nervosa. *Zhurnal Nevropathologii I Psyikhiatrii, 74* (1974), 1574–83. More recently a series of papers has been published by M. Korkina, V. V. Marilov and others, whose work is at Patrice Lumumba University, Moscow. See, for example, Korkina, M. V., Marilov, V. V., Tsivilko, M. A., and Kareva, M. A. Anorexia nervosa in males. *Zhurnal Nevropathologii I Psyikhiatrii, 79* (1979), 1562–8; Korkina, M. B. et al. Distorted self-perception and eating behavior of patients with anorexia nervosa. *Zhurnal Nevropathologii I Psyikhiatriic, 86* (1986), 1813–19; On the special case of the pathology of drive in schizophrenic patients with anorexia nervosa. *Zhurnal Nevropathologii I Psyikhiatrii, 86* (1986), 1689–94. Epidemiological data are not given, but samples of over 100 patients at this one center have been studied.

21. Ballot, N. Anorexia nervosa – a prevalence study. *South African Medical Journal, 27* (1981), 992–3.

22. Pumarino, H. and Vivanco, N. Anorexia nervosa: medical and psychiatric characteristics of 30 patients. *Revista Medica de Chile, 110* (1982), 1081–92.

23. Mennell, T. *All Manners of Food: Eating and Taste in England and France from the Middle Ages to Present*. Oxford: Basil Blackwell, 1985.

24. Shrihar Sharma, personal communication.

25. Burton Bradley, personal communication.

26. Cited in Wilson, C. P. *Fear of Being Fat*. New York: Jason Aronson, 1983.

27. Buchrich, N. Frequency of presentation of anorexia nervosa in Malaysia. *Australian and New Zealand Journal of Psychiatry, 15* (1981), 153–5.

28. Crisp, A. H. *LMB*, pp. 7–10.

29. Theander, op. cit. (see note 8, this chapter).

30. Jones et al., op. cit. (see note 10, this chapter).

31. Crisp, A. H., Palmer, R. L., and Kalucy, R. S. How common is anorexia nervosa? A prevalence study. *British Journal of Psychiatry, 128* (1976), 549–54.

32. Slade, R. *Anorexia Nervosa Reference Book*. New York: Harper and Row, 1984, p. 129.

33. Nylander, I. The feeling of being fat and dieting in a school population. *Acta Sociomedica Scandinavica, 1* (1971), 17–26.

34. For English college students, see Button, E. J. and Whitehouse, A. Subclinical anorexia nervosa. *Psychological Medicine, 11* (1981), 509–16; comparable findings for American students in Thompson, M. G. and Schwartz, A. M. Life adjustment of women with anorexia nervosa and anorexic-like bheavior. *IJED, 1* (1982), 47–60.

35. Bruch, *ED*.

36. Crisp, *LMB*, p. 62.

37. Garfinkel, and Garner, *AMNDA*, p. 103.
38. Silber, T. Anorexia nervosa in blacks and hispanics. *IJED, 5* (1986), 121–8; Hsu, L. K. G. Are the eating disorders becoming more common in Blacks? *IJED, 6* (1987), 113–24.
39. Huenemann, R. L., Shapiro, L. R., Hampton, M. C., and Mitchell, B. W. A longitudinal study of gross body composition and body conformation and their association with food and activity in a teen-age population. *Journal of Clinical Nutrition, 18* (1966), 325–38.
40. Thomas, J. P. and Szmuckler, G. I. Anorexia nervosa in patients of Afro-Caribbean extraction. *British Journal of Psychiatry, 146* (1985), 653–6.
41. Buchan, T. and Gregory, L. D. Anorexia nervosa in a black Zimbabwean. *British Journal of Psychiatry, 145* (1984), 326–30. A report on a Nigerian patient was contained in Nwaefuna, A. Anorexia nervosa in developing countries. *British Journal of Psychiatry, 138* (1981), 270–1.
42. Nasser, M. Comparative study of the prevalence of abnormal eating attitudes among Arab female students of both London and Cairo. *Psychological Medicine, 16* (1986), 621–5.
43. Hooper, M. S. H. and Garner, D. M. Application of the eating disorder inventory to a sample of black, white and mixed race schoolgirls in Zimbabwe. *IJED, 5* (1986), 161–9.
44. Halmi, K. A., Falk, J. R., and Schwartz, E. Binge-eating and vomiting: a survey of a college population. *Psychological Medicine, 11* (1981), 697–706.
45. Pope, H. G., Hudson, J. I., and Yurgelun-Todd, D. Anorexia nervosa and bulimia among 300 suburban shoppers. *American Journal of Psychiatry, 141* (1984), 292–4.
46. Pope, H. J. and Hudson, J. I. *New Hope for Binge Eaters*. New York: Harper and Row, 1984; Drenowski, A., Yee, D. K., and Krahn, D. D. Bulimia in college women: incidence and recovery rates. *American Journal of Psychiatry, 145* (1988), 753–5.
47. Halmi, et al. op. cit.
48. American Psychiatric Association. *DSM-III: Diagnostic and Statistical Manual of Mental Disorders*, 3rd Edn. Washington, DC: American Psychiatric Association, 1980.
49. Pyle, R. L., Mitchell, J. E., Eckert, E. D., Halvorson, P. A., Neuman, P. A., and Goff, G. M. The incidence of bulimia in freshman college students. *IJED, 2* (1983), 75–85.
50. Pyle, R., Halvorson, P., Neuman, P., and Mitchell, J. The increasing prevalence of bulimia in freshman college students. *IJED, 5* (1986), 631–41.
51. Johnson, C., Lewis, C., Love, S., and Stuckey, M. The incidence and correlates of bulimic behavior among a high school population. *Journal of Youth and Adolescence, 13* (1984), 15–25.
52. Rosenzweig, M. and Spruill, J. Twenty years after Twiggy. *IJED, 6* (1987), 59–66.
53. Zinkland, H., Cadoret, R., and Widmer, R. Incidence and detection of bulimia in a family practice population. *Journal of Family Practice, 18* (1984), 555–60.

54. Cooper, P. J. and Fairburn, C. G. Binge-eating and self-induced vomiting in the community: a preliminary study. *British Journal of Psychiatry, 142* (1983), 139-44.
55. Kutcher, S., Whitehouse, A. M., and Freeman, C. P. L. "Hidden" eating disorders in Scottish psychiatric inpatients. *American Journal of Psychiatry, 142* (1985), 1475-8.
56. Fairburn, C. and Cooper, P. J. The epidemiology of bulimia nervosa. *IJED, 2* (1983), 61-8; Fairburn, C. G. and Cooper, P. J. Self-induced vomiting and bulimia nervosa: an undetected problem. *British Medical Journal, 284* (1982), 1153-55.
57. Aimez, P. Une affection meconnue, la boulimie. *Gazette Medicale, 91* (1984), 87-93. Also, see Aimez, P. Epidemiological inquiry into the DSM-III criteria of bulimia. *Annales Medico-Psychologique, 146* (1988), 677-87. A questionnaire in a magazine with the heading "Are you bulimic?" drew over 1700 responses, about 450 of which met DSM-III criteria for bulimia.
58. Pudel, V. and Paul, V. H. Bulimia nervosa: epidemiology, pathogenesis, and therapy. *Munchener Medizinische Wochenschrift, 128* (1986), 119-22.
59. Nogami, Y. and Yabana, F. On Kibarashi-gui (Binge-eating). *Folia Psychiatrica et Neurological Japonica, 31* (1977), 159-66. Also, Kiriike, N., Nagata, T., Tanaka, M., Nishiwaki, S., Takeuchi, N. and Kawakita, Y. Prevalence of binge-eating and bulimia among adolescent women in Japan. *Psychiatry Research, 26* (1987), 163-9. The authors found prevalence rates comparable to those in US studies, varying from 2 to 8 per cent.
60. Schwartz, H. *Never Satisfied: A Cultural History of Diets, Fantasies, and Fat,* New York: Free Press, 1986.
61. Bruch, *ED,* p. 81.
62. Theander, op. cit. (see note 8, this chapter).
63. Dally, P. *Anorexia Nervosa.* London: William Heinemann Books, 1969.
64. Askevold, F. Social class and psychosomatic illness. *Psychotherapy and Psychosomatics, 38* (1982), 256-9.
65. Garfinkel, P. E. and Garner, D. M. *ANMDA,* p. 167. Also, Santonastoaso, P., Favaretto, G., and Canton, G. Anorexia nervosa in Italy: clinical features and outcome in a long-term followup study. *Psychopathology, 20* (1987), 8-17.
66. Herzog, D. B., Norman, D. K., Rigotti, N. A., and Peopose, M. Frequency of bulimic behaviors and associated social maladjustment in female graduate students. *Journal of Psychiatric Research, 20* (1986), 355-61.
67. This is a phenomenon well known to clinicians, but poorly documented. For some case histories, see Squire, S. *The Slender Balance.* New York: Putnam, 1983.
68. Larson, R. and Johnson, C. Bulimia: disturbed patterns of solitude. *Addictive Behaviors, 10* (1985), 281-90.
69. For an excellent recent collection of papers on the problem of bulimia in college students, see Whitaker, L. C. and Davis, W. N. *The Bulimic College Student: Evaluation, Research and Prevention.* New York: Hayworth Press, 1989. In this volume, two essays particularly worthy of note regarding the college environment are Dickstein, L. Current college environments: do

these communities facilitate and foster bulimia in vulnerable students? (chapter 8, pp. 107–34), and Bowen-Woodward, K. and Levitz, L. S. Impact of the college environment in bulimic women (chapter 12, pp. 191–204).

70. Smith, S. and Smith, C. *The College Student's Health Guide*. Los Altos, Calif.: Westchester, 1988, pp. 317–28.
71. Sher, B. R. The National Directory of College and University Mental Health Services for Eating Disorders. In Whittaker and Davis, op. cit. (see note 69), pp. 299–338. This appendix contains a listing of those Universities providing services.
72. I am grateful to Christopher Athas, Vice-President of the National Association of Anorexia Nervosa and Associated Disorders, for providing me with this information.
73. Orford, J. *Excessive Appetites: A Psychological View of Addictions*. New York: Wiley, 1985.

Notes to Chapter 4

1. Bruch, H. Four decades of eating disorders. In Garner, D. M. and Garfinkel, P. E. *HPANB*, p. 9.
2. See Appendix B: Sex differences in death, disease, and diet. In Hoyenga, K. B. and Hoyenga, K. T. *The Question of Sex Differences: Psychological, Cultural and Biological Issues*. Boston: Little Brown, 1979. The greater female tolerance for starvation was known as early as the twelfth century, where Heloise argued that "nature herself has protected our sex with a greater power of sobriety. It is indeed known that women can be sustained with less nourishment, and at much less expense, than men" (cited in Bynum, C. *Holy Feast and Holy Fast: The Religious Significance of Food to Medieval Women*. Berkeley: University of California Press, 1987, p. 387).
3. Beller, A. *Fat and Thin: A Natural History of Obesity*. New York: McGraw-Hill, 1977. This book contains a great deal of information about fatness, prticularly from an evolutionary and anthropological perspective.
4. Katherine Halmi, personal communication.
5. Pope, H. G. and Hudson, J. I. *New Hope for Binge Eaters*. New York: Harper and Row, 1984.
6. Erikson, E. H. *Identity, Youth and Crisis*. New York: W. W. Norton, 1964; Erikson, E. H. *Life History and the Historical Moment*. New York: W. W. Norton, 1975.
7. Malzberg, B. Are immigrants psychologically disturbed? In Plog, S. and Edgarton, R. B. *Changing Perspectives in Mental Illness*. New York: Holt, Rhinehart, and Winston, 1969, pp. 395–421.
8. Murphy, H. B. M. Culture and schizophrenia. In Al-Issha, I. *Culture and Psychopathology*. Baltimore: University Park Press, 1982.
9. See, for example, Komarovsky, L. *Women in College*. New York: Basic Books, 1985; also Bardwick, J. L. *In Transition*. New York: Holt, Rhinehart, and Winston, 1979.

10. Smith-Rosenberg, C. The hysterical woman. *Social Research, 39* (1972), pp. 652–75.
11. For example, Schwartz, D. M., Thompson, M. G., and Johnson, C. L. Eating disorders and the culture. In Darby, P. L., Garfinkel, P. E., Garner, D., and Coscina, D. *Anorexia Nervosa: Recent Developments in Research.* New York: Alan R. Liss, 1983, pp. 83–95.
12. Bruch, H., *ED*, pp. 254–5. This is one of the three core deficiencies in anorexia nervosa cited by Bruch, the others being a disturbance body image of delusional proportions and an inability to accurately perceive internal need states.
13. Bruch, H. *GC*, chapter 4 ("How It Starts").
14. Block, J. *Sex Roles and Ego Development.* San Francisco: Jossey Bass, 1985.
15. Block, ibid.
16. Miller, J. Baker *Towards a New Psychology of Women.* Boston: Beacon Press, 1976.
17. Bruch, *GC*, p. 25.
18. Slade, R. *The Anorexia Nervosa Reference Book.* New York: Harper and Row, 1984, chapter 8.
19. Miller, J. B. op. cit. (note 16).
20. Bruch, *GC*, Preface, p. ix (original emphasis).
21. Bruch, *ED*, p. 98.
22. Casky, N. Interpreting anorexia nervosa. In Suleiman, S. (ed.) *The Female Body in Western Culture.* Cambridge, Harvard University Press, 1986.
23. Bruch, H. *CA*, p. 108.
24. Bruch, *CA*, p. 126.
25. Bruch, *GC*, p. 27.
26. Waller, J. V., Kaufman, R., and Deutsch, F. Anorexia nervosa: a psychosomatic entity. *Journal of Psychosomatic Medicine, 11* (1940), 3–16.
27. Beaumont, P. J. V., Abraham, S. F., and Simson, K. The psychosexual histories of adolescent girls and young women with anorexia nervosa. *Psychological Medicine, 11* (1981), 131–40.
28. Liu, A. *Solitaire.* New York: Harper and Row, 1979.
29. Crisp, A. H. *LMB*; also Crisp, A. H. The psychopathology of anorexia nervosa: getting the "heat" out of the system. In Stunkard, A. J. and Stellar, E. (eds) *Eating and its Disorders.* New York: Raven Press, 1984, pp. 209–34.
30. Frisch, R. E. and MacArthur, J. Menstrual cycles: fatness as a determinant of minimum weight for height necessary for their maintenance and onset. *Science, 185* (1974), 949–51.
31. Curran, J. P. Convergence toward a single sexual standard? In Byrne, D. and Byrne, L. A. (eds) *Exploring Human Sexuality*, New York: Harper and Row, 1977.
32. Brumberg, J. J. *Fasting Girls: The Emergence of Anorexia Nervosa as a Modern Disease*, Cambridge: Harvard University Press, 1988, pp. 270–1.
33. Boskind-Lodahl, M. Cinderella's stepsisters: a feminist analysis of anorexia nervosa and bulimia, *Signs: A Journal of Women, Culture, and Society, 2* (1976), 342–56.

34. See, for example Swift, W. J. and Letven, R. Bulimia and the basic fault: a psychoanalytic interpretation of the binging-vomiting syndrome. *Journal of the American Academy of Child Psychiatry*, 23 (1984), 489–97; Johnson, C. L. and Conners, M. E. *ETBN*, chapter 6.

35. See Johnson, and Conners, ibid. These authors characterize the family environment of bulimics as typically "disengaged, chaotic, highly conflicted and neglectful. Family members use indirect and contradictory patterns of communication, are deficient in problem-solving skills, are non-supportive of independent behavior, and are less intellectually and recreationally oriented than the families of normal controls, despite their higher achievement orientations. These family characteristics generally result in children feeling disorganized, disconnected, insecure, and anxious" (p. 137). In line with the theme I am elaborating in this chapter, Johnson and Conners remark that "Despite the high risk loading of both biological and familial factors, if the child were able to lean on a consistent and stable structure within the sociocultural milieu she might be able to compensate for the lack of structure within her immediate family. Unfortunately, particularly for young women, the broader sociocultural context simultaneously exacerbates feelings of instability and, ultimately, suggests a pathological adaptation to that instability" (p. 138).

36. Boskind-White, M. and White, W. *Bulimarexia*. New York: W. W. Norton, 1983; Steiger, H., VanderFeen, J., Goldstein, C., and Leicher, P. Defense styles and parental bonding in eating-disordered women. *IJED*, 8 (1989), 131–41. The latter found the father–daughter bond to be disturbed for all types of eating-disordered women.

37 Wooley, S. and Wooley, O. W. Ambitious bulimics: thinness mania. *American Health*, Oct. (1986), 60–74.

38. For an interesting discussion of the particular vulnerabilities to bulimia created by campus life, see Dickstein, L. J. Current college environments: do these communities facilitate and foster bulimia in vulnerable students? *Journal of College Student Psychotherapy* (Special Edition: The Bulimic College Student: Evaluation, Treatment, and Prevention), 3 (nos 2, 3, 4) (1988–9) 107–34.

39. Komarovsky, L. *Women in College*. New York: Basic Books, 1985.

40. See, for example, Deutsch, C. H., The dark side of success. *New York Times*, Sep. 10 (1986), p. C1 for a discussion of the after-hours addictions of a number of high-flying corporate women. Interesting anecdotal descriptions of bulimic professionals are contained in Squire, S. *The Slender Balance*. New York: Pinnacle Books, 1983. The prevalence of bulimic syndromes among medical students in documented in Herzog, D., Pepose, M., Norman, D. K., and Rigotti, N. A., Eating disorders and maladjustment in female medical students, *Journal of Nervous and Mental Disease*, 173 (1985), 734–7. For an interesting discussion of the issues and a case history, see Barnett, L. R. Bulimia as a symptom of sex-role strain in professional women. *Psychotherapy*, 23 (1986), 311–15. Barnett suggests that "bulimarexia may represent the ambivalence toward filling the sociocultural stereotype of femininity and

asserting her personal power in a world that rewards hypermasculinity." As she points out, the most devastating insult that male colleagues or teachers can deliver to a female medical student is that she is "behaving like a nurse."

41. The notion of the "superwoman" was introduced by the journalist Ellen Goodman. See *Closer to Home*. New YOrk, 1979. A "manifesto" of this ideology is contained in a book by Cosmopolitan editor, Helen Gurley Brown, *Having It All*, New York, Pocket Books, 1982.

42. Brown, ibid.

43. Steiner-Adair, C. The body politic: normal female adolescent development and the development of eating disorders. *Journal of the American Academy of Psychoanalysis, 14* (1986), 95-114.

44. Timko, C., Striegel-Moore, R. H., Silberstein, L. R., and Rodin, J. Femininity/masculinity and disordered eating in women: how are they related? *IJED, 6* (1987), 701-12.

45. Rost, W., Neuhaus, M. and Florin, I. Bulimia nervosa: sex role attitude, sex role behavior and sex role related locus of control in bulimarexic women. *Journal of Psychosomatic Research, 26* (1982), 403-408.

46. Kanter, R. M. *Men and Women of the Corporation*. New York: Basic Books, 1977.

47. Lawrence, M. Women, education and identity: thoughts on the social origins of anorexia. *Women's Studies International Forum, 7*, 201-9.

48. The conception of anorexia as a problem in nurturance has been sensitively discussed by Levenkron, S. Structuring a nurturant/authoritative psycho-therapeutic relationship with the anorexic patient. In Emmet, S. W. *Theory and Treatment of Anorexia Nervosa and Bulimia: Biomedical, Sociocultural and Biological Perspectives*. New York: Brunner Mazel, 1985. See also Lehman, A. and Rodin, J. Styles of self-nurturance and disordered eating. *Journal of Consulting and Clinical Psychology, 57* (1989), 117-22.

49. It is, however, likely that some male anorexics and bulimics go unrecognized, both because health professionals are reluctant to diagnose eating disorders and because eating disordered males may be reluctant to come forth with "female" problems. See Andersen, A. and Mickalide, A. D. Anorexia nervosa in the male: an underdiagnosed disorder, *Psychosomatics, 24* (1983), 1066-75.

50. See Jones, D. J., Fox, M. M., Babigan, H. M., and Hutton, H. E. Epidemiology of anorexia nervosa in Monroe County, New York: 1960-1976. *Psychological Medicine, 42* (1980), 551-8.

51. Herzog, D. B., Norman, D. K., Gordon, C., and Pepose, M. Sexual conflict and eating disorders in 27 males. *American Journal of Psychiatry, 141* (1984), 989-90. It should be pointed out, though, that some observers who specialize in the treatment of males with eating disorders have expressed skepticism about the generality of homosexual conflicts in this population. See, for example, Andersen, A. E. Anorexia nervosa and bulimia nervosa in males. In Garner, D. M. and Garfinkel, P. E. *Diagnostic Issues in Anorexia Nervosa and Bulimia Nervosa*. New York: Brunner Mazel, 1988, pp. 166-208.

52. Yager, J., Kurtzman, F., Landsverk, J., and Wiesmeier, E. Behaviors and

attitudes related to eating disorders in homosexual male college students. *American Journal of Psychiatry, 145* (1988), 495–7. In this study, which surveyed students attending homosexual rap groups at UCLA, gay students scored much higher than comparable heterosexual males on the Eating Disorder Inventory, a measure of self-reported attitudes and behaviors characteristic of eating disordered patients. However, the actual presence of an eating disorder through direct interview was not determined.

53. Silberstein, L. R., Mishkind, M. E., Striegel-Moore, R. H., Timko, C., and Rodin, J. Men and their bodies: a comparison of homosexual and heterosexual men. *Psychosomatic Medicine, 51* (1989), 337–46.

54. Some tendency of male college students to be preoccupied with losing weight was found in Drewnowski, A. and Yee, D. Men and body image: are males satisfied with their body weight? *Psychosomatic Medicine, 49* (1987), 626–34. However, in contrast with females, the men in this sample were equally divided into those who wanted to lose weight and those who wanted to gain it. See also Mishkind, M. E., Rodin, J., Silberstein, L. R., and Striegel-Moore, The embodiment of masculinity: cultural, psychological and behavioral dimensions. *American Behavioral Scientist, 29,* (1986), 545–562.

Notes to Chapter 5

1. Roland Barthes, *Roland Barthes*. New York: Hill and Wang, 1977.

2. The experience of starvation in anorexics is beautifully described by Bruch, H., *GC*, chapter 1.

3. Russell, G. F. M. The changing nature of anorexia nervosa: an introduction to the conference. In Szuckler, G. I., Slade, P. D., Harris, P., Benton, D., and Russell, G. F. M. (eds) *Anorexia Nervosa and Bulimic Disorders: Current Perspectives*. Oxford: Pergamon Press, 1986.

4. See Poovey, M. Scenes of an indelicate character: the medical treatment of Victorian women. *Representations, 14* (Spring, 1986), 137–68. Poovey's discussion is mostly directed towards the atmosphere of anxious silence surrounding the obstetrical examination, but it could well apply to the sensitive topic of body weight. Some evidence for the hidden preoccupations and some nineteenth-century anorexics with body weight and the lack of attention of physicians to same is presented in Brumberg, J. J. *Fasting Girls*, Cambridge: Harvard University Press, 1988, p. 159.

5. The literature on body-image distortion is extensive. For examples from clinical cases, see Bruch, *ED*, chapter 6; for an overview of the research literature through 1982, already prolific, see Garfinkel, P. E. and Garner, D. M., *ANMDA*, chapter 6.

6. For a complex study of body-image distortion using both methods of measurement, see Huon, G. F. and Brown, L. B. Body images in anorexia nervosa and bulimia nervosa, *IJED, 5* (1986), 421–39. These researchers raised some of the complex distinctions between perceiving the body as fat versus "feeling" that it is fat. One study found that the degree of size

overestimation is even greater in normal-weight bulimics than anorexics. See Touyz, S. W., Beumont, P. J. V., Collins, J. K., and Cowie, I. Body shape perception in bulimia and anorexia nervosa, *IJED*, 4 (1985), 259–65.

7. Bruch, *ED*, p. 90.

8. Ibid.

9. Wooley, S. C. and Wooley, O. W. Intensive outpatient and residential treatment for bulimia. In Garner, D. M. and Garfinkel, P. E., *HPANB*, p. 398.

10. Gardner, R. M. and Moncrieff, C. Body image distortion in anorexics as a non-sensory phenomenon: a signal-detection approach. *Journal of Clinical Psychology, 44* (1988), 101–7.

11. Pierloot, R. A. and Houbon, M. E. Estimation of body dimensions in anorexia nervosa, *Psychological Medicine, 8* (1978), pp. 317–24. These researchers confronted patients with their mirror image and urged them to give more accurate estimations than the initial tests. See also Crisp, A. H. and Kalucy, R. S. Aspects of the perceptual disorder in anorexia nervosa. *British Journal of Medical Psychology, 47* (1974), 349–61, who urged the patient to "drop your guard for a moment and tell me again how wide you really judge yourself to be." For a therapeutic use of body-image confrontation using videotape, see Gotheil, E., Backup, C. E., and Cornelison, F. S. Denial and self-image confrontation in a case of anorexia nervosa. *Journal of Nervous and Mental Disease, 148* (1969), 238–50.

12. Halmi, K., Goldberg, S., and Cunningham, S. Perceptual distortion of body image in adolescent girls: distortion of body image in adolescence. *Psychological Medicine, 7* (1977), 253–7; Davies, E. and Furnham, A. Body satisfaction in adolescent girls, *British Journal of Medical Psychology, 59* (1986), 279–87.

13. Lawrence, M., Anorexia nervosa: the control paradox, *Women's Studies International Quarterly, 2* (1979), 93–101 (p. 94).

14. Bruch, *CA*, p. 125.

15. This connection was first pointed out by Hilde Bruch. Also, T. Habermas, On the meaning of thinness in the body experience of anorexics – illustrated with the sculptures of A. Giacommetti. *Psychther. med. Psychologie, 36* (1986), 69–74.

16. Bruch, H. *CA*, p. 157.

17. An extraordinarily rich and amusing history of weight preoccupation in the United States, which deals extensively with turn of the century material, is Hillel Schwartz, *Never Satisfied: A History of Fat, Diets and Fantasies*. New York: Macmillan, 1986. An excellent historical discussion of the evolution of the thin-body ideal is contained in William Bennett and Joel Gurin, *The Dieter's Dilemma*. New York: Harper and Row, 1982, chapter 7. The already intense preoccupation with dieting in the 1950s is discussed in Gerald Walker, The great American dieting neurosis. *The New York Times Magazine*, Aug. 23 (1959).

18. For an overview, see Rita Freedman, *Beauty Bound*, Lexington Mass.: D.C. Heath and Company, 1986; also Cash, T. and Janda, L. The eye of the beholder, *Psychology Today*, Dec. (1984), 46–52.

19. Garner, D., Garfinkel, P. E., Schwartz, D., and Thompson, M. Cultural expectations of thinness in women. *Psychological Reports, 47* (1980), 483–91.
20. Fallon, R. and Rozin, P. Sex differences in perception of desirable body shape, *Journal of Abnormal Psychology, 94* (1985), 102–5.
21. Feeling fat in a thin society, *Glamour Magazine*, Feb. (1984), 198–201, 251–2.
22. Huenemann, R. L., Shapiro, L. R., Hampton, M. C., and Mitchell, B. W. A longitudinal study of gross body composition and body conformation and their association with food and activity in a teenage population. *American Journal of Clinical Nutrition, 18* (1966), 325–38.
23. Nylander, I. The feeling of being fat and dieting in a school population. *Acta Sociomedica Scandinavica, I* (1971), 17–26.
24. Dornbusch, S. M., Carlsmith, J. M., Duncan, P. D., Gross, R. T., Martin, J. A., Ritter, P. L., and Siegel-Gorelick, B. Sexual maturation, social class, and the desire to be thin among adolescent females. *Developmental and Behavioral Pediatrics, 5* (1984), 308–14.
25. Girls, at 7, think thin, study finds. *New York Times Health Section*, Feb. 11, 1988. The emerging concern with pre-adolescent anorexia was discussed at a forum on "Evaluation and management of the child and pre-adolescent with anorexia nervosa" at the Third International Conference on Eating Disorders, held in New York City, April, 1988.
26. Garfinkel, P. E. and Garner, D. M. *ANMDA*, chapter 5, pp. 112–17.
27. De Mille, A. *And Promenade Home*, quoted in Vincent, I. M. *Competing with the Sylph*, New York: Berkeley Books, 1979.
28. Kirkland, G. *Dancing on My Grave*, New York: Doubleday, 1986, pp. 55–6.
29. Vincent, L. M., *Competing with the Sylph*, New York: Berkeley Books, 1979.
30. Ibid., p. 78.
31. Ibid., p. 79.
32. Ibid., p. 79.
33. Hamilton, L. H., Brooks-Gunn, J., and Warren, M. P. Sociocultural influences on eating disorders in professional female ballet dancers. *IJED, 4* (1985), 465–78.
34. King, M. B. and Mezey, G. Eating behavior of male racing jockeys. *Psychological Medicine, 17* (1987), 249–53.
35. Lasch, C. *The Culture of Narcissism*. New York: Warner Books, 1979.
36. See, for example Schwartz, D. M., Thompson, M. G., and Johnson, C. L. Anorexia nervosa and bulimia: the sociocultural context. *IJED, 1* (1982), 23–35. Garfinkel and Garner, *ANMDA*, chapter 6.
37. The one major exception to this statement is the writing of Arthur H. Crisp. See, for example, Crisp, *LMB*, chapter 5.
38. Ford, C. S. and Beach, F. A. *Patterns of Sexual Behavior*. New York: Ace Books, 1951.
39. Schwartz, op. cit. (see note 17, this chapter), p. 338; Shack, W. Hunger, anxiety, and ritual: deprivation and spirit possession among the Gurage of Ethiopia. *Man, 6* (1971), 30–43.
40. Powdermaker, H. An anthropological approach to the problem of obesity. *Bulletin of the New York Academy of Medicine, 36* (1960), 286–95.

41. Mazrui, A. *The Africans: A Triple Heritage*, Boston: Little Brown, 1986, pp. 127–8.
42. Crispin, P. The essence of fattening. *Democratic Weekly* (Lagos), July 29, 1984.
43. These issues were portrayed novelistically in Buchi Emecheta, *Double Yoke*, London: Ogwugwu Afor, 1982.
44. Beller, A. S. *Fat and Thin: A Natural History of Obesity*. New York: McGraw-Hill, 1977, chapter 3.
45. Bennett and Gurin, op. cit. (see note 17), chapter 7. The Steel-engraving Lady is discussed in Banner, L. *American Beauty*, New York: Basic Books, 1983. A fascinating and provocative discussion of the corset, one that runs against contemporary feminist interpretations, is Kunzle, D. *Fashion and Fetishism: A Social History of the Corset, Tight-Lacing and Other Forms of body Sculpture in the West*, Totowa, New Jersey: Roman and Littlefield, 1982. The author suggests that some women who wore corsets were also anorexic; like some contemporary patients (and perhaps even some beauty pageant contestants), self-starvation may have been a "practical strategy" to conform to stringent clothing dimensions.
46. Veblen, T. *The Theory of the Leisure Class*, New York: MacMillan, 1899, pp. 148–9.
47. Quoted in Steele, V. *Fashion and Eroticism*, New York: Oxford University Press, 1985, p. 227.
48. On growing fat, *Atlantic Monthly* March, 1907, 430–1 (quoted in Brumberg, J. J. *Fasting Girls: The Emergence of Anorexia Nervosa as a Modern Disease.* Cambridge: Harvard University Press, 1988, p. 340).
49. Bennett and Gurin, op. cit. (see note 17, this chapter), p. 208.
50. Ewen, S. and Ewen, E. *Channels of Desire: Mass Images and the Shaping of the American Consciousness.* New York: McGraw-Hill, 1982.
51. Walker, op. cit. (see note 17, this chapter).
52. Excerpted from Harris, J. *Manhattan as a Second Language*, New York: Harper and Row, 1982, pp. 61–2.
53. See, for example, Curves from an earlier era, *New York Times*, Dec. 6, 1987, p. 98; New York feminine flourishes, *New York Times Magazine*, Oct. 25, 1987, pp. 70ff.
54. I am grateful to Patricia Fallon for this observation.
55. Coward, R. *Female Desires: How They are Sought, Bought, and Packaged.* New York: Grove Press, 1985.
56. I am grateful to Christopher Athas, Vice-President of the National Association of Anorexia Nervosa and Associated Disorders, for this information regarding the Hershey advertisement.
57. *Today* show (NBC), June 13, 1989.
58. David Garner, Presentation on "Challenging the Overvaluation of Thinness," Sixth Annual Conference on Eating Disorders, sponsored by the National Anorexic Aid Society in Columbus, Ohio, October 1987.
59. Silverstein, B., Peterson, B., and Perdue, L. Some correlates of the thin standard of bodily attractiveness for women. IJED, 5 (1986), 895–905;

Silverstein, B., Perdue, L., Peterson, B., Vogel, L., and Fantini, D. Possible causes of the thin standard of bodily attractiveness for women. IJED, *5* (1986), 907–16.

60. Silverstein, B. and Perdue, L. The relationship between role concerns, preferences for slimness, and symptoms of eating problems among college women. *Sex Roles, 18* (1988), 101–6; Silverstein, B., Perdue, L., Wolf, C. and Pizzolo, C. Binging, purging, and estimates of parental attitudes regarding female achievement. *Sex Roles, 19* (1988), 723–33.

61. Dyrenforth, S. R., Wooley, O. W., and Wooley, S. C. A woman's body in a man's world: a review of findings on body image and weight control. In Kaplan, J. R. *A Woman's Conflict: The Special Relationship Between Women and Food.* Englewood Cliffs: Prentice-Hall, 1980.

62. Obeyeseykere, G. *Medusa's Hair.* Chicago: University of Chicago Press, 1981.

Notes to Chapter 6

1. Brown, P. J. and Konner, M. An anthropological perspective on obesity. In Wurtman, R. J. and Wurtman, J. (eds) *Human Obesity.* New York: The New York Academy of Sciences, 1987.

2. Staffieri, J. R. A study of social stereotype of body image in children. *Journal of Personality and Social Psychology, 7* (1967), 101–4.

3. A profession of vegetarianism is common among anorexics. See Kadambari, R., Gowers, S., and Crisp, A. Some correlates of vegetarianism in anorexia nervosa. *IJED,* 5 (1986), 539–44. However, it is probably in most instances a secondary rationalization of caloric avoidance, not a primary philosophical commitment. A case of pre-adolescent anorexia nervosa that was triggered by an attempt to reduce cholesterol level was reported at a panel discussion on Preadolescent Anorexia Nervosa at the Third International Conference on Eating Disorders, New York, April, 1988.

4. Meat avoidance was also common among nineteenth-century anorexics. See Brumberg, J. J., *Fasting Girls: The Emergence of Anorexia Nervosa as a Modern Disease.* Cambridge: Harvard University Press, 1988. The magical and instantaneous transformation of food into body substance (fat into fat) is one of the bases of the infamous *Beverly Hills Diet* (see chapter 7).

5. The phrase is that of the English psychiatrist, John Dally. On the weight and fitness preoccupations of the families of anorexics, see Kalucy, R. S., Crisp, A. H., and Harding, B. A study of 56 families with anorexia nervosa. *British Journal of Medical Psychology, 50* (1977), 381–95.

6. Sours, J. A. *SDSO,* p. 325.

7. Bruch, H., *ED,* p. 95.

8. Herzog, D. B. Bulimia: the secretive syndrome. *Psychosomatics, 23* (1982), 481–3; Pyle, R. L., Mitchell, J. E., and Eckert, E. D. Bulimia: a report of 32 cases. *Journal of Clinical Psychiatry,* 42 (1981), 60–4.

9. The families of bulimics in general are given more to oral pleasures and addictive behaviors; alcohol abuse is also commonly a problem (although not

always) in the family. Bulik, C. M. Drug and alcohol abuse by bulimic women and their families, *American Journal of Psychiatry, 144* (1987), 1604–6.

10. These issues have been discussed by Wooley, S. and Wooley, O. W. Intensive outpatient and residential treatment for bulimia. In Garner, D. M. and Garfinkel, P. E. (eds), *HPANB*, chapter 17.

11. See Brown and Konner, op. cit. (see note 1). Also, Raymond, C. R. Biology, culture, dietary changes conspire to increase incidence of obesity. *Journal of the American Medical Association, 256* (October 24, 1986), 2157–8.

12. Furnham, A. and Alibhai, N. Cross-cultural differences in the perception of female body shapes. *Psychological Medicine, 13* (1983), 829–37.

13. See Stunkard, A. From explanation to action in psychosomatic medicine: the case of obesity. *Psychosomatic Medicine, 37* (1975), 195–236; Stunkard, A., d'Aquili, E., Fox, S., and Filion, R. Influence of social class on obesity and thinness in children. *Journal of the American Medical Association, 221* (1972), 579–84.

14. This controversy is discussed by Garner, D. M., Rockert, W., Olmsted, M. P., Johnson, C., and Coscina, D. Psychoeducational principles in the treatment of bulimia and anorexia nervosa. In Garner and Garfinkel (eds), *HPANB*, pp. 513–72.

15. Brown and Konner, op. cit. (see note 1).

16. Ritenbaugh, C. Obesity as a culture bound syndrome. *Culture, Medicine and Psychiatry, 6* (1982), 347–61.

17. Schwartz, H. *Never Satisfied: A Cultural History of Diets, Fantasies, and Fat.* New York: Macmillan, 1986. See esp. pp. 77–84, 305–7.

18. For a critical discussion of the dangers and possible abuses of liposuction, see Henig, R. M. The high cost of thinness. *New York Times Magazine*, Feb. 28, 1988.

19. See Wooley, S. and Wooley, O. W. Should obesity be treated at all? In Stunkard, A. and Stellar, E. (eds) *Eating and Its Disorders.* New York: Raven Press, 1984. Particularly provocative is the negative evidence for the common belief that the obese overeat. On the stigmatization of the obese, see Millman, S. *Such a Pretty Face: on Being Fat in America.* New York: W. W. Norton, 1980.

20. Cahnman, W. J. The stigma of obesity. *Sociological Quarterly, 9* (1968), 283–95.

21. Brown and Konner, op. cit. (see note 1).

22. Coward, R. *Female Desires.* New York: Grove Press, 1985.

23. Brown and Konner, op. cit. (see note 1).

24. Canning, H. and Meyer, J. Obesity – its possible effect on college acceptance. *New England Journal of Medicine, 275* (1966), 1172–4.

25. See, for example, Reskin, L. R. Employers must give job applicants a chance. *Journal of the American Bar Association, 71* (1985), 104.

26. Orbach, S. *Fat is a Feminist Issue.* New York: Berkeley Books, 1979.

27. On this point, see Guidano, V. F. and Liotti, G. *Cognitive Processes and Emotional Disorders,* New York: Guilford Press, 1983, chapter 12.

28. Bruch, *ED*, chapter 11.

29. The popular Christian literature linking dieting to salvation includes

Deborah Pierce, *I Prayed Myself Thin*. New York, 1960, Ann Thomas, *God's Answer to Overeating*, Washington, 1975; and Wise, K. *God Knows I Won't be Fat Again*. Nashville, 1978. These and other references are cited in Schwartz, op. cit. (see note 17), p. 439.

30. Lampson-Reiff, K. The fundamental flaw: Christianity and eating disorders. Presentation at Sixth National Conference on Anorexia Nervosa and Bulimia Nervosa, National Anorexic Aid Society, Columbus, Ohio, October, 1987.

31. Berland, T. *Rating the Diets*, Publications International Ltd, 1986.

32. Bennett, W. and Gurin, J. *The Dieter's Dilemma*. New York, Harper and Row, 1982. Schwartz, B. *Diets Don't Work*. Oakland, California: Breakthru Publishing, 1984. On yo-yo dieting, see Ups and downs of weight can be dangerous, Letter from Paul Ernsberger to the *New York Times*, May 2, 1985.

33. An overview of this work is contained in Polivy, J. and Herman, C. P. Diagnosis and treatment of normal eating. *Journal of Clinical and Consulting Psychology*, *55* (1987), 635–44.

34. Herman, C. P. and Polivy, J. Restrained eating. In Stunkard, A. J. *Obesity*, Philadelphia: W. B. Saunders, 1980, pp. 208–25.

35. Polivy, J. Perception of calories and regulation of intake in restrained and unrestrained subjects. *Addictive Behaviors*, *1* (1976), 237–43.

36. Polivy, J. and Herman, C. P. The effects of alcohol on eating behavior: influences of mood and perceived intoxication. *Journal of Abnormal Psychology*, *85* (1976), 601–6.

37. Herman, C. P. and Polivy, J. Effects of an observer on eating behavior: the induction of "sensible eating," *Journal of Personality*, *47* (1979), 85–9.

38. Larson, R. and Johnson, C. G. Bulimia: disturbed patterns of solitude. *Addictive Behaviors*, *10* (1985), 201–90.

39. Polivy, J. and Herman, C. P. Dieting and binging: a causal analysis. *American Psychologist*, *40* (1985), 193–201.

40. One of the few clinical studies that focused on hyperactivity is that of Kron, L., Katz, J. L., Gorzynski, G., and Weiner, H. Hyperactivity in anorexia nervosa: a fundamental clinical feature. *Comprehensive Psychiatry*, *19* (1978), 443–40.

41. Epling, W. F., Pierce, W. D., and Stefan, L. A theory of activity-based anorexia. *IJED*, *3* (1983), 27–46.

42. Green, H. *Fit for America, Health, Fitness and Sport in American Society*. New York: Pantheon, 1986.

43. Shaping up: the worldwide fitness boom. *Newsweek* (International Edition), Sep. 10, 1984.

44. See Klemesrud, J. Now, personal trainers push clients to new highs of fitness. *New York Times*, Style Section, Dec. 14, 1984, p. B18. See also Coach, confessor confidante: is the personal trainer the therapist of our times. *Self*, Mar. 1989, pp. 95–9.

45. MacKenzie, M. The distrust of pleasure in affluent societies: anthropology and the concept of culture in eating disorders. Presented at Third

International Conference on Anorexia Nervosa and Related Disorders, Swansea, Wales, September, 1984.

46. Beaumont, P. J. V., Touyz, S. W., and Hook, S. Exercise and anorexia nervosa. Presented at 3rd International Conference on Anorexia Nervosa and Related Disorders, Swansea, Wales, September, 1984.

47. Chalmers, J., Catalan, J., Day, A., and Fairburn, C. Anorexia nervosa presenting as morbid exercising. *Lancet*, Feb. 2, 1985, 286–7.

48. See, for example, Smith, N. J. Excessive weight loss and food aversion in athletes simulating anorexia nervosa. Pediatrics, *66* (1980), 139–142; Zucker, P., Avener, J. and Bayder, S. Eating disorders in young athletes. *Physician and Sportsmedicine, 13* (1985), 88–106; Borgun, J. S. and Corbin, C. B. Eating disorders among female athletes. *Physician and Sportsmedicine, 15* (1987), 89–95; Brooks-Gunn, J., Burrow, C. and Warren, M. P. Attitudes toward eating and body weight in different groups of female adolescent athletes. *IJED, 7* (1988), 749–757.

49. Rosen, L. W., McKeag, D. B., Hough, D. O., et al. Pathogenic weight-control behavior in female athletes. *Physician and Sportsmedicine,* 14 (1986), 79–86. Also Dummer, G., Rosen, L., Heusner, W., Roberts, P. and Counsilman, J. E. Pathogenic weight-control behaviors of young competitive swimmers. *Physician and Sportsmedicine, 15* (1987), 75–84. In the latter study, the authors were surprised to find that even in swimming, in which the demands for weight and shape control are not as rigorous as in other sports, the level of pathogenic weight-control behaviors was quite high.

50. A good discussion of the kinship between running and anorexia is given in Sours, *SDSO*, pp. 259–60, 283–6.

51. Sheehan, G. *Running and being: the total experience.* New York: Warner Books, 1978.

52. Ibid., p. 36.

53. Ibid., p. 38.

54. Yates, A., Leehey, K., and Shisslak, C. Running: an analogue of anorexia? *New England Journal of Medicine, 308* (1983), 251–5. For a subsequent analysis with useful additional commentaries, see Yates, A. Eating disorders and long-distance running: the ascetic condition. *Integrative Psychiatry, 5* (1987), 201–11.

55. Letters, *New England Journal of Medicine, 308* (1983), 47–8.

56. See, for example, Blumenthal, J. A. O'Toole, L. C., and Chang, J. L. Is running an analogue of anorexia nervosa? An empirical study of obligatory running and anorexia nervosa. *Journal of the American Medical Association, 252* (1984), 520–3; and Weight, L. M. and Noakes, T. D. Is running an analogue of anorexia?: a survey of the incidence of eating disorders in female distance runners. *Medicine and Science in Sports and Exercise, 19* (1987), 213–17.

57. This research, conducted by Dr Rebecca Prussin and Dr Phillip Harvey, was reported on in *New York Running News*, Aug.–Sep. 1989, pp. 34–6. I am grateful to Dr Prussin for sharing some of her preliminary findings with me and her permission to discuss this research here.

58. See, for example, Jane Brody. For women who haven't gotten the message

yet: thin isn't necessarily in. *New York Times*, Health Column, March 18, 1987; Trish Hall, Self-denial fades as Americans return to the sweet life. *New York Times*, The Living Section, March 11, 1987. Britton, A. J. Thin is out, fit is in. *American Health*, July, 1988, pp. 65ff. But also, Kleinfield, N. R. The ever-fatter business of thinness. *New York Times*, Sep. 7, 1986. Business Section, p. 1.

Notes to Chapter 7

1. Devereux, G. Normal and abnormal: the key problem of psychiatric anthropology. In his *Basic Problems of Ethnopsychiatry*, Chicago: University of Chicago Press, 1980, p. 42.
2. Ibid., p. 34.
3. Szasz, T. *The Second Sin*. New York: Anchor Books, 1974, p. 105.
4. Ellenberger, H. *The Discovery of the Unconscious*, New York: Basic Books, 1970, p. 256.
5. Charcot's work is discussed at length in ibid.; see also Drinka, G. *The Birth of Neurosis*. New York: Basic Books, 1984, chapter 4. For some possible healer-induced effects in the diagnosis and treatment of eating disorders, see Garner, D. M. Iatrogenesis in anorexia nervosa and bulimia nervosa. *IJED*, *4* (1985), 701–26.
6. Bandura, A. *Social Learning Theory*. New Jersey: General Learning Press, 1971.
7. Bruch, H. Four decades of eating disorders. In Garner, D. M. and Garfinkel, P. E. (eds) *HPANB*, chapter 2.
8. Silber, A. Acquired pseudo eating disorder: an imitation or fabrication of anorexia nervosa. *Journal of Adolescent Health Care*, *8* (1987), 157–5.
9. Yager, J. and Hatton, C. A. Anorexia nervosa in a woman totally blind since the age of two. *British Journal of Psychiatry*, *149* (1986), 506–9.
10. A comparison suggested to me by Craig Johnson.
11. I am grateful to Dr Paul Kaunitz for sharing this observation from the days of his psychiatric training.
12. Dwyer, J., Feldman, J. J., and Mayer, J. The social psychology of dieting. *Journal of Health and Social Behavior*, *11*, (1970), 269–87.
13. Rodin, J., Silberstein, J., and Streigel-Moore, R. Women and weight: a normative discontent. In Sonderegger, T. *Nebraska Symposium on Motivation, 1984*. Lincoln, Nebraska: The University of Nebraska Press, 1985, p. 290.
14. Bruch, *CA*, p. 149.
15. Ibid., p. 150.
16. Liu, A. *Solitaire*. New York: Harper and Row, 1979, pp. 106ff.
17. Brumberg, J. J. *Fasting Girls*. Cambridge: Harvard University Press, 1988, p. 19.
18. Martin, F. Subgroups in anorexia nervosa: a family systems study. In Darby, P. L., Garfinkel, P. E., Garner, D. J., and Coscina, D. V. (eds) *Anorexia Nervosa: Recent Developments in Research*. New York: Alan R. Liss, 1983, pp. 57–65.

19. Squire, S. *The Slender Balance.* New York: Pinnacle Books, 1983, pp. 22ff.
20. See, for example, Gould, M. S. and Shaffer, D. The impact of suicide in television movies: evidence on imitation. *The New England Journal of Medicine, 315* (Sep. 11, 1986), 690–4; and Phillips, D. and Carstensen, L. L. Clustering of teenage suicides after television news stories about suicide. *New England Journal of Medicine, 315* (Sep. 11, 1986), 685–9.
21. The number of popular articles per year on anorexia nervosa listed in the Reader Guide to Periodical Literature grew steadily from two in 1972 to 14 in 1983. The total number of articles during this period was over 50. Some representative titles include Lynch, K. Danger! You can overdo dieting. *Seventeen, 34* (1975), 106–7; Ramsey, J. Anorexia nervosa: dying of thinness. *Ms, 5* (August 1976) 103–6; When dieting goes wild, *US News and World Report, 85* (1978), 62; Conley, B. My sister and I tried to outdiet each other with some pretty scary rsults. *Glamour, 77* (1979), 38ff; My daughter was starving herself to death. *Good Housekeeping,* May 1982, 73ff. On bulimia, see Stein, B. Dangerous eat-and-purge disorder strikes young women. *People, 16* (1981), 47–8; Schildkraut, M. L. Bulimia: the secret dieter's disease. *Good Housekeeping, 194* (May, 1982), 239ff; Bernstein, F.A. Bulimia: a woman's terror. *People Weekly, 26* (Nov. 17, 1986), 30–41.
22. *Playgirl,* June, 1975.
23. For references to these, see note 21.
24. Lynch, op. cit. (see note 21).
25. Johnson, I. Starving for perfection: one girl's battle with anorexia. *Seventeen,* September, 1986, 79–80, 82, 194–6.
26. O'Neill, C. B. *Starving for Attention,* New York: Dell, 1983.
27. O'Neill, C. B. *Dear Cherry: Questions and Answers on Eating Disorders.* New York: Continuum, 1985, p. 75.
28. Levin, E. A. sweet surface hid a troubled soul in the late Karen Carpenter, a victim of anorexia nervosa. *People, 19* (Feb. 21, 1983), 52–4.
29. Fonda, J. *Jane Fonda's Workout Book.* New York: Simon and Schuster, 1981, especially chapter entitled "A body abused."
30. A popular book on the Rice Diet, which is a reputable method for the treatment of obesity, is Moscovitz, J. *The Rice Diet Report.* New York: Avon, 1986; The Diet Workshop Wild Weekend Diet is presented in Lindauer, L. *The Diet Workshop Wild Weekend Diet,* New York: Delacorte Press, 1985; for evaluations, see Berland, T. *Rating the Diets,* Skokie, Illinois: Publications International, 1986.
31. Mazel, J. *The Beverly Hills Diet,* New York: Berkley Books, 1982.
32. Ibid., p. 114.
33. Ibid., p. 217.
34. The Beverly Hills Diet. *Harper's Bazaar,* May, 1981, 72ff.
35. Mirkin, G. B. and Shore, R. N. The Beverly Hills diet: dangers of the newest weight loss fad. *Journal of the American Medical Association, 246* (1981), 2235–7.
36. Wooley, S. C. and Wooley, O. W. The Beverly Hills eating disorder: the mass marketing of anorexia nervosa. *IJED, 1* (1982), 57–68.

37. Ibid., p. 57.
38. Ibid.
39. Mazel, J. *The Beverly Hills Lifetime Plan*, New York: Bantam Books, 1983, p. 13.
40. Bruch, op. cit. (see note 7).
41. Mazel, op. cit. (see note 31), pp. 132, 134.
42. Ibid., p. 2.
43. Halmi, K. Comment at Symposium at Third International Conference on Eating Disorders, New York, April, 1988.
44. Johnson, C. Presentation at Second Annual Conference on Eating Disorders, Center for the Study of Anorexia Nervosa and Bulimia, New York, November, 1983.
45. Orbach, S. *Hunger Strike*. New York: Norton, 1986, p. 15.
46. Crandall, C. S. Social contagion of binge eating. *Journal of Personality and Social Psychology*, *55* (1988), 588–98. For an informative discussion of the problem of bulimia in sororities, see Squire, S., op. cit., pp. 73–7.
47. Cesari, J. P. Fad bulimia: a serious and separate counseling issue. *Journal of College Student Personnel*, *27* (1986), 255–9.
48. Chiodo, J. and Latimer, P. R. Vomiting as a learned weight-control technique in bulimia. *Journal of Behavior Therapy and Experimental Psychiatry*, *14* (1983), 131–5.
49. Russell, G. Bulimia nervosa: an ominous variant of anorexia nervosa. *Psychological Medicine*, *9* (1979), 429–48.
50. Advertisement in *New York Times*, Aug. 26, 1987, p. C4.
51. Tillotson, G. *Responsible Bulimia: Is It Possible?* Privately printed, August, 1987.
52. Tillotson, G. personal communication, Jan., 1988.
53. Tillotson, G., op. cit. (see note 51), p. 28.
54. Barthes, R. Towards a psychosociology of contemporary food consumption. In Forster, E. and Forster, R. *European Diet from Preindustrial to Modern Times*. New York: Harper and Row, 1975, pp. 47–59.
55. Much of this discussion draws on the ideas of Sidney Mintz. See Mintz, S. *Sweetness and Power: The Place of Sugar in Modern History*, New York: Viking, 1985, especially chapter 5. On solo eating in public in the 1980s, see Bryan Miller, Solo dining: new options in privacy vs. company. *New York Times*, March 5, 1986, pp. C1, C6.
56. An excellent discussion of the "empire of snacks" is contained in Fischler, C. Food habits, social change and the nature/culture dilemma. *Social Science Information*, *19* (1980), 937–53.
57. See, for example, Hawkins, R. C. Meal/snack frequencies in college students: a normative study. *Behavioural Psychotherapy*, *7* (1979), 85–90.
58. Wurtman, J. *Managing Your Mind and Mood Through food*. New York: Harper and Row, 1988. Also see Nancy Jenkins, For many young professionals, the way to eat is on the run. *New York Times*, Jan. 30, 1985, p. C1ff.
59. I follow here the lead of Brumberg, (see note 17), pp. 259–60.
60. Coward, R. *Female Desires: How They are Sought, Bought and Packaged*. New York: Grove Press, 1985, pp. 99–107.

61. A popular self-help approach to the problem of compulsive overeating is presented by Geneen Roth in *Feeding the Hungry Heart: The Experience of Compulsive Eating* and *Breaking Free from Compulsive Eating*. New York: Signet Books, 1984. Roth herself experienced both obesity and anorexia, and her approach is specifically directed towards females with eating problems.

62. Studies document that about 80 percent of female and 50 percent of male college students engage in eating binges. See Hawkins, R. C. and Clement, P. F. Development and construct validation of a measure of binge eating tendencies. *Addictive Behaviors, 5* (1980), 219–26. This does not mean, of course, that all these students are bulimic, but it does suggest that binge-eating is part of the American student "life-style."

63. Hoffman, D. *The Joy of Pigging Out*. New York: Warner Books, 1983.

64. This term was proposed by Holmgren, S., Humble, K., Norring, C., Roos, Bjorn-Erik, Rosmark, B., and Sohlberg, S. The anorectic–bulimic conflict: an alternative diagnostic approach to anorexia nervosa and bulimia. *IJED, 2* (1983), 3–13.

Notes to Chapter 8

1. These ideas about the social response to ethnic disorders were articulated in Devereux, G. Normal and abnormal. In Devereux, G. *Basic Problems in Ethnopsychiatry*. Chicago: University of Chicago Press, 1980, pp. 28ff.

2. I follow here a discussion by Roland Littlewood and Maurice Lipsedge, The culture bound syndromes of the dominant culture: culture, psychopathology and biomedicine. In Cox, J. L. (ed.) *Transcultural Psychiatry*. London: Croom Helm, 1986, pp. 253–73. The reference to Turner's concept of "power of the weak" is theirs, but was originally discussed by Turner in *The Ritual Process*. London: Routledge and Kegan Paul, 1969.

3. Discussed in Littlewood and Lipsedge, ibid. The phenomenon of the Zar cult is discussed further in Lewis, I. M. *Ecstatic Religion: An Anthropological Study of Spirit Possession and Shamanism*. New York: Penguin Books, 1971.

4. Littlewood and Lipsedge, ibid.

5. Smith-Rosenberg, C. The hysterical woman: sex roles in 19th century America. *Social Research, 39* (1972), 652–75.

6. For an interesting discussion of the cultural significance of agoraphobic, see DeSwaan, A. The politics of agoraphobia. *Theory and Society, 10* (1981), 359–82. DeSwaan sees the "fear of the marketplace" as an individual residue of the threats to a woman's status who ventured out alone in the city in the eighteenth century. The family dynamics of agoraphobia are discussed in Hafner, R. J. The husbands of agoraphobic women and their influence on treatment outcome. *British Journal of Psychiatry, 131* (1977), 289–304.

7. Lacey, J. H. Anorexia nervosa in a bearded female saint. *British Medical Journal, 285* (1982), 1816–17.

8. See Bynum, C. *Holy Feast and Holy Fast*. Berkeley: University of California Press, 1987, p. 194.

9. Bell, R. *Holy Anorexia*, Chicago: University of Chicago Press, 1985.

10. Bynum, op. cit. (see note 8), pp. 220–4.
11. Ibid., pp. 46–7.
12. Ibid., p. 233.
13. On this point, see the illuminating afterword to Bell's book by William Davis.
14. On Simone Weil, see Petrement, J. *Simone Weil: A Life.* Trans. Raymond Rosenthal. New York: Random House, 1976. Caroline Bynum (*supra*) rejects the notion of identifying Simone Weil as anorexic, as if this somehow detracted from her spiritual and literary accomplishments. However, the parallels between her life and her thinking and some of the central psychological themes characteristic of anorexia are too striking to ignore. For an illuminating discussion, see Herik, J. V. Looking, eating and waiting in Simone Weil. In Idinopolous, T. A. and Knopp, J. Z. *Mysticism, Nihilism, and Feminism. New Critical Essays on the Anti-Theology of Simone Weil.* Johnson City, Tenn.: Institute of Social Sciences and the Arts, 1984, pp. 57–90.
15. This material is drawn from Rogers, E. N. *Fasting: The Phenomenon of Self-Denial.* Nashville: Nelson, 1976.
16. Ibid.
17. Bynum, op. cit. (see note 8), p. 192.
18. Schwartz, H. *Never Satisfied: A Cultural History of Diets, Fantasies, and Fat.* New York: Macmillan, 1986, pp. 132–4.
19. Kafka, F. A hunger artist. In *Kafka: The complete Stories.* New York: Shocken Books, 1976.
20. Showalter, E. *The Female Malady: Women, Madness, and English Culture, 1830–1980.* New York: Pantheon Books, 1985, p. 162.
21. See, for example, Orbach, S., *Hunger Strike: Anorexia as a Metaphor for our Time,* New York: W. W. Norton, 1986; and Accepting the symptom: a feminist psychoanalytic treatment of anorexia nervosa, in Garner, D. M. and Garfinkel, P. E. (eds), *HPANB,* 83–104; Boskind-Lodahl, M. Cinderella's stepsisters: a feminist interpretation of anorexia nervosa and bulimia. *Signs: A Journal of Women, Culture, and Society,* 2 (1976), 342–56; Chernin, K. *The Hungry Self,* New York: Times Books, 1986; and Lawrence, M. (ed.) *Fed Up and Hungry.* New York: Peter Bedrick Books, 1987. For a critical view of the feminist interpretations of eating disorders, see Swartz, L. Is thin a feminist issue? *Women's Studies International Forum,* 8 (1985), 429–37.
22. Srikameswaran, S., Leichner, P., and Harper, D. Sex role ideology among women with anorexia nervosa and bulimia. *IJED, 3* (1984), 39–44.
23. See Ross, S. *Fasting.* New York: Pan Books, 1978. On the notion of anorexia nervosa as addiction to starvation, see Szmuckler, G. and Tantum, D. Anorexia nervosa: starvation dependence. *British Journal of Medical Psychology, 57* (1984), 303–10.
24. The links between anorexia and asceticism have been noted by Bruch, *ED,* pp. 11–13 and Crisp, A. H., *LMB,* pp. 5, 10. More extended discussions are contained in Mogul, S. L. Asceticism in adolescence and anorexia nervosa. *The Psychoanalytic Study of the Child, 35* (1980), 155–78; and Rampling, D.

Ascetic ideals and anorexia nervosa. *Journal of Psychiatric Research, 2/3* (1985), 89–94. Mogul cites one case in which a patient saw a parallel between her food restriction and the fast of atonement on Yom Kippur. Rampling, anticipating the later work of Bell, suggests direct parallels between the writings of Catherine of Siena and contemporary autobiographies, such as that of Cherry Boone O'Neill.

25. Rampling, ibid., p. 94. Rampling suggests that the infrequency with which these parallels are discussed has to do with the difficulty that clinicians have in going beyond their own paradigms, a point with which I am in agreement.

26. Minuchin, S., Rosman, B., and Baker, L. *Psychosomatic Families: Anorexia Nervosa in Context*. Cambridge, Mass.: Harvard University Press, 1978.

27. Palazolli, M. S. Anorexia nervosa: a syndrome of the affluent society. *Transcultural Psychiatric Research Review, 22* (1985), 199–204.

28. Palazolli, M. S. Cirillo, S., Selvini, M., and Sorrentino, A. M. *Family Games*. New York: Norton, 1989.

29. Palazolli, op. cit. (see note 27).

30. Palazolli, M. S. Towards a general model of psychotic family games. *Journal of Marital and Family Therapy, 12* (1986), 339–50. See also Palazolli, M. S. The anorexic process in the family, *Family Process, 27* (1986), 129–48.

31. This case is discussed in detail in Papp, P. *The Process of Change*. New York: Guilford Press, 1986, chapter 6.

32. Palazolli, op. cit. (see note 30).

33. Root, P., Fallon, P., and Friedrich, M. *Bulimia: A Systems Approach to Treatment*. New York: W. W. Norton, 1986.

34. Devereux, op. cit. (see note 1), p. 31.

35. Branch, C. H. H. and Eurman, L. J. Social attitudes towards patients with anorexia nervosa. *American Journal of Psychiatry, 137* (1980), 631–2.

36. See, for example, Crisp, A. H. and Kalucy, R. S. Aspects of the perceptual disorder in anorexia nervosa. *British Journal of Medical Psychology, 47* (1974), p. 358.

37. Liu, A. *Solitaire*. New York: Harper and Row, 1979, p. 188.

38. For example, see the discussion of the patient Annette in Bruch, H., *CA*, p. 62.

39. Sontag, S. *Illness as Metaphor*. New York: Farrar, Strauss, and Giroux, 1978.

40. Meyer, B. C. and Weinroth, L. A. Observations on psychological aspects of anorexia nervosa: report of a case. *Psychosomatic Medicine, 19* (1957), 389–98.

41. Sontag, op. cit. (see note 39).

42. Little is known about the specific meanings of thinness to Victorian anorexics. For a discussion of the nineteenth-century imagery of thinness, see Brumberg, J. J., *Fasting Girls: The Emergence of Anorexia Nervosa as a Modern Disease*. Cambridge: Harvard University Press, 1988, esp. chapter 6 ("The Appetite as Voice"), in which she argues that the romanticization of thinness was tied to notions of frailty, gentility, and passivity.

43. Story, I. Caricature and impersonating the other: Observations from the psychotherapy of anorexia nervosa. *Psychiatry, 39* (1976), 176–88.

44. Such an argument has been made by Swartz, L. Is thin a feminist issue?

Women's Studies International Forum, 8 (1985), 429–37. Swartz argues that anorexia nervosa has led to a "medicalization" of the problem of thinness, thereby deflecting attention from the more general cultural problem. However, it could easily be argued that the reverse is true – that is, that the public awareness about anorexia nervosa has led to a more general awareness in the public consciousness of the dangers of severe dieting.

45. See, for example, Boskind-Lodahl, op. cit. (see note 21, this chapter) and Orbach, op. cit. (note 21, this chapter).

46. Dally, J. and Gomez, J. *Anorexia Nervosa*. London: William Heinemann Medical Books, 1979. In fairness, Dally, a psychiatrist with long experience in the treatment of anorexics, advocated a far more sympathetic and sophisticated approach than is indicated in this statement, which can be taken more as a characterization of the feelings evoked in the doctor rather than the advocacy of coercive treatment. For example, in his chapter on treatment, he suggests, like most contemporary therapists, that forced tube feeding is rarely necessary. Virtually all contemporary authorities agree. See, for example, Garfinkel, P. E. and Garner, D. M. *ANMDI*, chapter 9; Crisp, *LMB*; Andersen A. E., Morse, C. L., and Santmyer, K. S. Inpatient treatment for anorexia nervosa. In Garner and Garfinkel (eds), *HPANB*, chapter 14, A. 322.

47. For a discussion of the complexities surrounding enforced treatment such as coercive feeding, see Dresser, R. Feeding the hunger artists: legal issues in treating anorexia nervosa. *Wisconsin Law Review, 2* (1984), 297–384. In a searching review of the relevant legal and moral issues, Dresser suggests that coercive treatment nof anorexics is only permissible if the patient's life is immediately threatened. She concludes that:

We live in a society that reflects inconsistency and ambivalence about the extremely thin feminine form. Sometimes the shape is revered, but if it represents severe anorexia nervosa, it is viewed with horror. Our culture is highly competitive, expecting certain of its young women to achieve not only the ideal appearance, but to perform well at work and at home. Some individuals intimidated by these demands of modern womanhood develop symptoms of anorexia. The specter of anorexia nervosa evokes uneasiness in its observers . . . Because available evidence indicates that unrestricted forcible treatment confers little or no long term benefits upon anorexics, but instead can reduce their chances for full recovery, anorexics quite possibly would be better off if their audience were forced more frequently to confront their disturbing appearance. Perhaps their presence among us would constitute a compelling challenge to the social forces shaping the strange phenomenon of anorexia nervosa (p. 374).

48. Bruch, H. Perils of behavior modification in the treatment of anorexia nervosa. *Journal of the American Medical Association, 230* (1974), 1419–22.

49. Smith-Rosenberg, op. cit. (see note 5); Showalter, op. cit. (see note 20).

50. The issue of the gender of the therapist has been raised frequently in

discussions of the treatment of anorexia nervosa. For an enlightening discussion, particularly of the advantages and pitfalls for female therapists, see Frankenburg, F. R. Female therapists in the management of anorexia nervosa. *IJED, 3* (1984), 25–33. A case can be made for the notion that females may have some advantage over males, given their own inevitably experiential understanding of the cultural pressures on women to achieve, to please men, and to control body size. But there may be disadvantages as well. For example, the competitive mind-set of anorexic patients may pose problems for both the patient and her female therapist. These may be compounded for those anorexics who have a hostile and competitive relationship with their mothers, which may in turn be projected onto the female therapist. There seems to be little question that in order to become effective, male therapists need to develop sensitivity to the particular stresses of female development. But the psychological issues confronting anorexic patients, such as those of low self-esteem, autonomy, or the need to please others, are not bound by gender. To argue otherwise is to revert to nineteenth-century definitions of sex roles, in which each gender is characterized by an exclusive set of attributes.

51. Lawrence, M. Anorexia nervosa: the control paradox. *Women's Studies International Quarterly, 2* (1979), 93–101.
52. Sallas, A. A. Treatment of eating disorders: winning the war without having to do battle. *Journal of Psychiatric Research, 19 (2–3)* (1985), 83–8.
53. Bruch, H. Four decades of eating disorders. In Garner, and Garfinkel, (eds), *HPANB*, chapter 2, p. 12.
54. Cooper, T. Anorexia and bulimia: the political and the personal. In Lawrence, (ed), op. cit. (see note 21), pp. 175–92.
55. Kaplan, J. *A Woman's Conflict*. Englewood Cliffs: Prentice-Hall, 1980.
56. Dana, M. and Lawrence, M. "Poison is the nourishment that makes one ill": the metaphor of bulimia. In Lawrence, (ed.), op. cit. (see note 21), pp. 193–206.
57. It has been increasingly recognized that the use of groups is highly relevant for the treatment of bulimia. See, for example, Jones, D. Bulimia: a false self identity, *Clinical Social Work Journal, 13* (1985), 305–16; Johnson, C., Conners, M., and Stuckey, M. Short term group treatment of bulimia. *IJED, 2* (1983), 299–308; Boskind-White, M. and White, W. C. An experiential behavioral approach to the treatment of bulimarexia. *Psychotherapy: Theory, Research and Practice, 4* (1981), 501–7; and Lazerson, J. S. Voices of bulimia: experiences in integrated psychotherapy. *Psychotherapy: Theory, Research and Practice, 21* (1984), 500–9. The approaches of Boskind-White and White and Lazerson specifically incorporate feminist concerns in their group workshops. Boskind-White and White, for example, have periods where the female therapist meets with the group alone, with the male joining the group and serving as a target for various role-playing exercises.
58. Chernin, K. *The Obsession: Reflections on the Tyranny of Slenderness*. New York: Harper and Row, 1981, p. 100.
59. 9 bodies for the 90s. *SELF*, March, 1989 (10th anniversary issue), 125–32.

INDEX

achievement: in anorexia nervosa 53, 55–6; in bulimia nervosa 62; in the wider culture 63–4; in women 51–2

activity anorexia 96

addiction: anorexia nervosa as 20; in bulimia nervosa 25, 27, 28; in bulimic anorexia 22; as symptom style 48–9, 100

affective disorder *see* depression

African patient 40

Afro-Caribbean patients 40

agoraphobia 118–19

AIDS epidemic 45, 131

amenorrhea 18

Amok 8, 101

anorexia nervosa: adolescent issues in 16; age range of patients 16; in athletes 97–8; attitudes towards 129–34; body image, 67–8; Bruch's diagnostic criteria 15; clinical course of 17–19; control in 17; deception in 17; denial in 18; as developmental disorder 16; diagnostic criteria 14–16; dynamics of 16; exercise in 17; families of 18, 86, 125–9; family therapy 125–8; fasting in 124; fear of obesity in 85–7; female identity in 53–9; historical rarity 2; history of 12–14; hyperactivity 95–6; increased incidence of 34–7; long-term outcome of 19; mortality rates 18; physical symptoms of 18; prevalence of 37–9; resemblance to addiction 18; sex ratio 16, 32–3; sexuality 58–9; somatic etiology for 19–21; somatic symptoms of 20; starvation symptoms 18; treatment of 19, 132–4

antidepressants 28–9

asceticism 37, 120–1

athletes, eating disorders in 97–100

autobiographical accounts 107–8

autonomy 53–5

ballet dancers 72–5

Bandura, A. 102

Belgium 35

Bell, R. 128

Bennett, W. 77, 78

Berland, T. 93, 109

Beumont, P. J. V. 20

the Beverly Hills Diet 109–12

binge–purge syndrome 3, 23; *see also* bulimia nervosa

biological predispositions: in anorexia nervosa 19–20; in bulimia nervosa 28–9; and female vulnerabilities to eating disorders 50–1

black population 40

body image distortion: in anorexia nervosa 67–8; commercial influences on 80–2; in normal males and females 69–70

borderline personality 27

Boskind-Lodahl, M. 23, 60

Boston 41

Bruch, H. 4, 14–16, 22, 23, 53–4, 56, 57, 58, 87, 92, 102–3, 105, 123, 124, 134, 135

Brumberg, J. J. 59

bulimarexia *see* bulimia nervosa 3, 23, 60

bulimia (in anorexia nervosa): differences from restricting anorexia 21–2; drug and alcohol abuse in 22; increasing prominence of 22; self-destructive behavior in 21–2

bulimia nervosa: affective disorder in 28; age of onset 26; alcohol use in 112; antidepressant treatment 28; attitudes toward 134–6; chronicity 27; college campus epidemic 3; description of episode 24; diagnostic criteria 24; in dormitories 112; expression of rage 128–9; as fad 112; false self in 27; family therapy of 128–9; fear of obesity in 87; female identity in 60–2; as group activity 112; identity confusion 61; imitation of 113; personalities of 26–7; politics of 134–6; prevalence of 41–6; prevalence, as compared with anorexia 25–6; in professional women 46, 62; relationships with males 62; resemblance to addiction 27–8; in Romans 23, 112; sex roles in 60–1;

Kirkland, G. 72
Koro 9

Lacey, J. H. 19
Lasegue, C. 13, 32
Lawrence, M. 133
liberation 56, 57–8, 137
Lipsedge, M. 117, 118
Littlewood, R. 117, 118
Liu, A. 58, 105–6, 130

Malaysia 8, 36, 101
males with eating disorders 32–3, 65
mass media 80–2, 106–7, 113–15
Maudsley Hospital 40
medical students with eating disorders 45
Milan school of family therapy 126
Miller, J. B. 54, 56
Minuchin, S. 125
modeling of eating disorders 102–15
Morton, T. 12

Norway 45
nurturance 64
Nylander, I. 71

obesity: in bulimia nervosa 87; in children and
    adolescents 88; discrimination against 89,
    91; fear of, in anorexia nervosa 85–7;
    kinship with anorexia 92; in males 88, 91;
    meanings of 88–90; medical significance of
    88; and set-point theory 30; and social class
    87; stereotypes of 85, 89–90
O'Neill, C. B. 108
Orbach, S. 91
Oxford 44

Palazolli, M. S. 34, 126
Papp, P. 127
Paris 77
patterns of misconduct 101
Poland 35
politics: of anorexia nervosa 129–34; of
    bulimia nervosa 134–6; of the family
    127–9; of gender 137; of self-starvation
    119–24; of treatment 132–4
Polivy, J. 94
Pope, H. G. 28
power: in anorexia nervosa 125–8; in bulimia
    nervosa 128–9
power struggles, in treatment of anorexia
    132–4
pregnancy 50
prevalence: of anorexia nervosa 37–9; of
    bulimia nervosa 41–4; of subclinical
    anorexia nervosa 38–9

psychoanalytic views of anorexia nervosa 14
puberty 51, 58–9

religious affiliation, in anorexia nervosa 39
restrained eating 94–5
running: as analogue of anorexia 99–100;
    psychology of 98–9
Russell, G. 22, 24, 66

Sallas, A. 133
Saudi Arabia 48
Schwartz, H. 88, 89, 116, 122
Scotland 34–5, 44
self-help organizations 5, 48
Seneca 12, 23
set-point theory 29
sex roles 52, 54, 56, 57; in bulimia nervosa
    60–4; in males with eating disorders 65
sexual abuse 58
sexual identity 65
sexual politics 10, 133, 136–7
sexuality: in anorexia nervosa 58–9; in the
    wider culture 59
Sheehan, G. 98
Showalter, E. 123
Silverstein, B. 82–3
Simmond's Disease 13
social class: in anorexia 44–5; in bulimia
    45–6
Sontag, S. 131
sororities 113
Sours, J. A. 107
South Africa 36
Soviet Union, eating disorders in 35–6
starvation: associated feelings 66; symptoms
    of 18; tolerance for, among women 50
Steiner-Adair, C. 65
suffragettes 122–3
suicide 106
superwoman 63–4
Sweden 34, 38, 44
Switzerland 35
Szasz, T. 101

teenage pregnancy 59
templates of deviance 100, 102, 112
Theander, S. 34, 44
thin fat person 23
thinness: cultural standards of 68–9; in
    dancers 72–5; and female identity 82–4;
    history of 76–80; meanings of, in anorexia
    nervosa 67–9; pursuit of 17
treatment 19, 20, 28–9, 82, 125–9, 133–4,
    136
Turner, V. 117
Twiggy 78, 90